HOW THINGS WORK

p

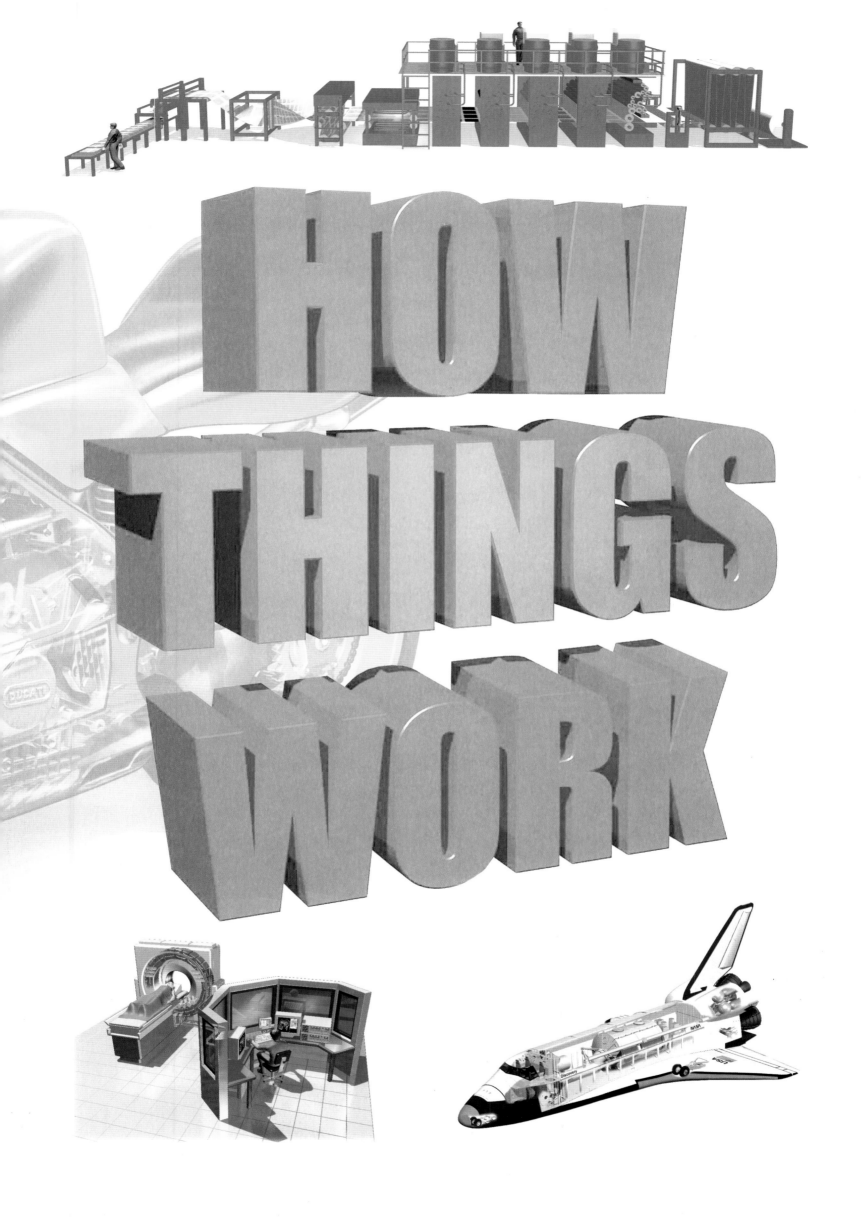

HOW THINGS WORK

This is a Parragon Book
First published in 2000

Parragon
Queen Street House
4 Queen Street
Bath BA1 1HE, UK

Copyright © Parragon 2000

Produced by
Monkey Puzzle Media Ltd
Gissing's Farm
Fressingfield
Suffolk IP21 5SH
UK

ISBN 0-75254-078-5

Printed in Dubai, U.A.E.

AUTHORS
Steve Parker, Peter Lafferty and
Steve Setford

ILLUSTRATORS
Studio Liddell, Alex Pang, Adrian Wright and Cara Kong

DESIGNER
Tim Mayer

COVER DESIGN
Victoria Webb

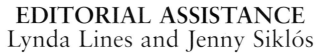

EDITOR
Linda Sonntag

EDITORIAL ASSISTANCE
Lynda Lines and Jenny Siklós

INDEXER
Caroline Hamilton

PROJECT MANAGER
Katie Orchard

CONTENTS

Wicked Wheels	6
Astonishing Aircraft	66
Groovy Gadgets	126
Monster Machines	186
Glossary	246
Index	252

WICKED
WHEELS

Getting Around 8

Mountain Bike 10

Speed Bike 12

Touring Bike 14

Superbike 16

Family Car 18

F1 Racing Car 20

Stretch Limousine 22

4WD – Four Wheel Drive 24

Pick-up Truck 26

Combine Harvester 28

Digger 30

Bulldozer 32

Transporter 34

Monster Truck 36

Luxury Coach 38

Steam Locomotive 40

Mountain Railway 42

Subway Train 44

TGV 46

Monorail 48

Jetski 50

Offshore Powerboat 52

Racing Yacht 54

Cruise Liner 56

Hydrofoil 58

Hovercraft 60

Supertanker 62

Future Vehicles 64

GETTING AROUND

EARLY WHEELS

Our modern world runs on wheels. But wheels have not always been with us. The first wheels turned around yet lay flat. Potters made bowls and vases on them in the Middle East more than 5,000 years ago. Then some bright spark in Ancient Sumeria had the idea of turning a wheel on its edge and fixing it to a cart. With another three similar wheels at the other three corners, the cart could roll along. This was a great advance on dragging heavy loads. Soon wheels were turning on war chariots, farm wagons and royal coaches.

POWER TO THE PEOPLE

For the next 49 centuries or so wheeled vehicles moved by people or animal power, especially horses and oxen. In the 1800s a human-powered vehicle was developed with two wheels and pedals, which we still use today as the bicycle. Then just over one century ago, in the 1880s, early self-propelled road vehicles appeared. They were powered by new types of engines using liquid fuels. They were developed by German engineers Gottlieb Daimler, Karl Benz and in the 1890s, Rudolf Diesel. These strange. noisy, slow, rattling vehicles were called 'horseless carriages' – a term since shortened to 'car'.

VEHICLES GALORE

Many other road vehicles were soon developed, such as lorries, trucks, public buses, coaches and off-road vehicles, such as jeeps and tractors. Now there are at least 30 main kinds of vehicles on our roads, from bikes and motorcycles to monster trucks and transporters. This book shows many of them, the parts they are made of, how they work and what they and their drivers do.

Speed Bike
With no brakes or gear changers, this bike would be very dangerous on the roads. However, its frame shape and the light–but–strong carbon fibre construction may find their way into the designs of popular mass–produced cycles.

Traffic jam
Perhaps everyone would like to travel in the lap of luxury in their own personal limousine. But traffic jams would be ten times worse than they already are.

ON THE RIGHT TRACKS

The car was not the first engine-driven vehicle. In the early 1800s stationary steam engines were used in mines to pump out water. Wagons with metal wheels that ran on metal rails were also used in mines, pulled by people or ponies to haul coal and rocks. In 1804 Cornish mine engineer, Richard Trevithick, put the two together and made the first mine steam locomotive. In the 1820s George Stephenson made better locomotives to pull a row or 'train' of wagons carrying people, and the railways were born. We still have some steam trains but there are now many other kinds. Some run deep in the subways under cities, others flash through the countryside faster than a racing car.

TAKING TO THE WATER

As steam engines were developed in the 1800s they found their way into ships. No longer did sailors depend on wind. Then petrol, diesel and gas turbine engines were also fitted to ships. Now we have a huge range of ships, boats and other water craft, from racing yachts and powerboats to supertankers.

Intercity to the future?
Super-fast trains whisk people from one city to another at speeds of more than 200 kph (125 mph). The electric locomotives are reliable and cause little pollution. But transport between small villages or hamlets needs more personal and adaptable vehicles than those which carry crowds between the big towns.

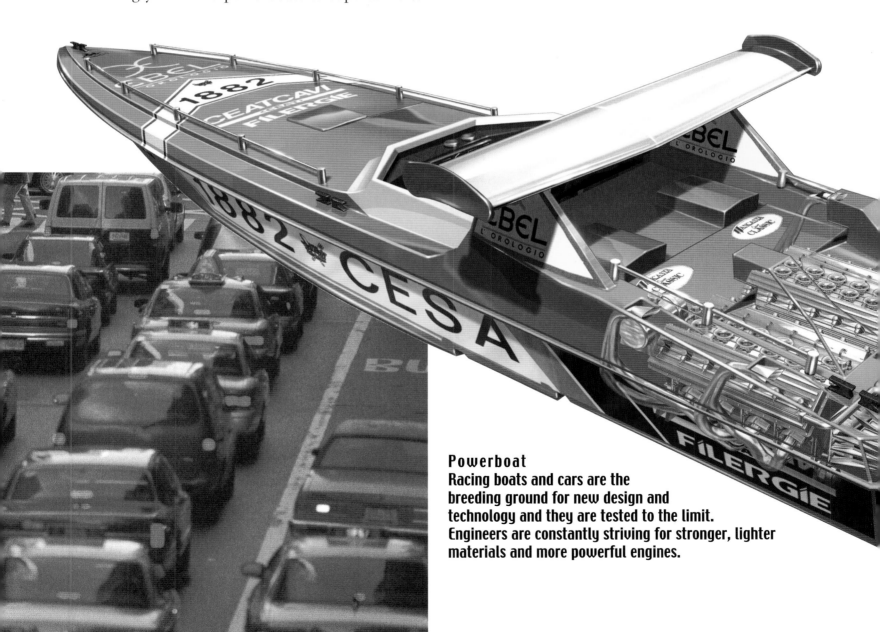

Powerboat
Racing boats and cars are the breeding ground for new design and technology and they are tested to the limit. Engineers are constantly striving for stronger, lighter materials and more powerful engines.

MOUNTAIN BIKE

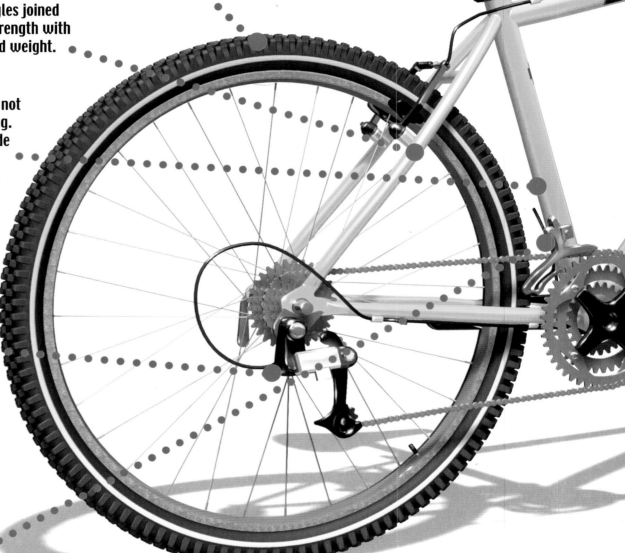

Tread tyres
The tyres have a tread of small, pyramid-shaped blocks. These give good grip on soft ground but they also allow soil or mud to slip off so it does not get stuck and harden in the tread.

Saddle height
The saddle stem tube that holds up the saddle can slide up and down inside the frame's down tube below, so the saddle height can be adjusted.

Frame
The frame is two triangles joined together for maximum strength with minimum materials and weight.

Frame tube
The walls of these tubes are not the same thickness all along. Shallow curves on the inside mean that the tube wall is thinner in the middle, where there is less stress, and thicker at the ends where the most bending strain occurs.

Rear changer
The rear changer has a cage of jockey wheels that moves sideways to shift the chain from one cog to another. This bike has 7 rear cogs, which with the 3 front ones, gives a total of 21 gear combinations.

Front changer
The chain runs through a slot-shaped cage that moves sideways to shift it from one cog to another.

TYPES OF GEARS

Hub gears are contained in an extra-wide rear hub (the central part of the rear wheel). They are changed by a chain that moves in and out of the hub from the side. The chain is worked by a cable attached to a trigger changer on the handlebars. Hub gears usually have only three or perhaps five gear combinations.

Back-pedal gears are also contained in the rear hub. There are two combinations and you change from one to the other by pedalling backwards slightly. In some designs if you back-pedal slightly more you apply the back hub brake.

Derailleur gears as shown here are exposed to rain, mud and grit. But they are easy to clean, adjust and mend and they give the widest variety of gear combinations.

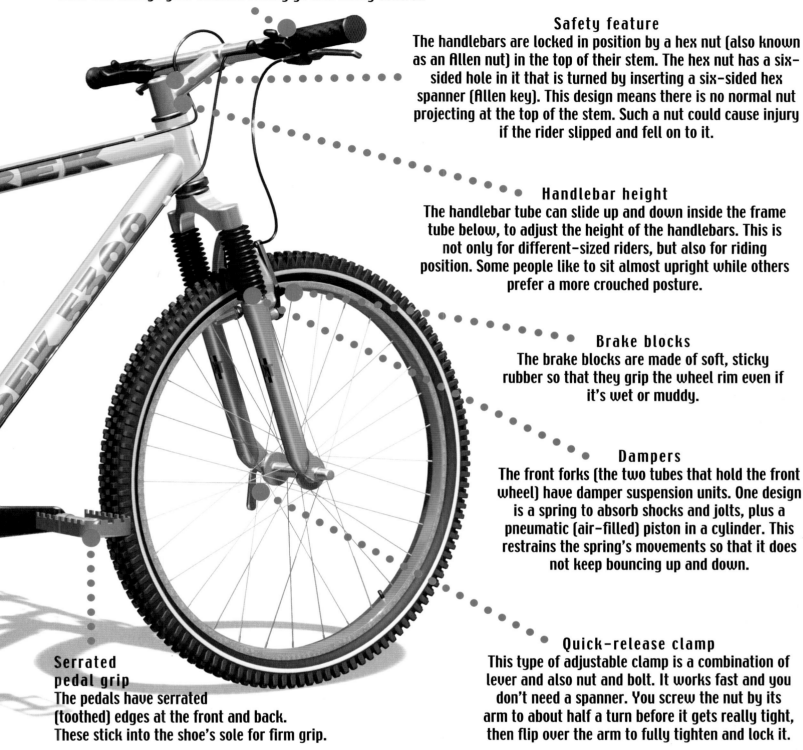

Gear shifts
The gear shift levers or buttons are on the handlebars so the rider can change gear without letting go and losing control.

Safety feature
The handlebars are locked in position by a hex nut (also known as an Allen nut) in the top of their stem. The hex nut has a six-sided hole in it that is turned by inserting a six-sided hex spanner (Allen key). This design means there is no normal nut projecting at the top of the stem. Such a nut could cause injury if the rider slipped and fell on to it.

Handlebar height
The handlebar tube can slide up and down inside the frame tube below, to adjust the height of the handlebars. This is not only for different-sized riders, but also for riding position. Some people like to sit almost upright while others prefer a more crouched posture.

Brake blocks
The brake blocks are made of soft, sticky rubber so that they grip the wheel rim even if it's wet or muddy.

Dampers
The front forks (the two tubes that hold the front wheel) have damper suspension units. One design is a spring to absorb shocks and jolts, plus a pneumatic (air-filled) piston in a cylinder. This restrains the spring's movements so that it does not keep bouncing up and down.

Serrated pedal grip
The pedals have serrated (toothed) edges at the front and back. These stick into the shoe's sole for firm grip.

Quick-release clamp
This type of adjustable clamp is a combination of lever and also nut and bolt. It works fast and you don't need a spanner. You screw the nut by its arm to about half a turn before it gets really tight, then flip over the arm to fully tighten and lock it.

WHY HAVE GEARS?

Imagine a bicycle where you turn the pedals once and the rear wheel turns 10 times. This is a high gear. It's great for speeding downhill where you need little pedalling effort. But you couldn't press the pedals hard enough to turn them when going uphill.

Now imagine a bicycle where you turn the pedals once and the rear wheel turns less than once. This is a low gear. It's great for going up a steep slope, slowly but surely, and with not too much effort. However, you could never turn the pedals fast enough to get up speed when going downhill.

Bicycles have gears for ease and convenience. You can adjust the speed and effort of pedalling to suit you. The bicycle then goes along according to the gearing, usually an average speed on the level, fast downhill or slow uphill. Gears make cycling easier but they don't change the total amount of effort you put in. Low gears make cycling uphill easier. But you are cycling slower and for longer, so your effort lasts longer.

SPEED BIKE

No frame tubes
The frame is one piece of moulded material called carbon fibre composite. It is extremely light and strong, shaped to withstand all the main stresses put on it without any excess material or extra weight.

No freewheel
If you stop pedalling on a sprint or speed bike, the pedals keep turning. There is no freewheel, as on a normal bike, that allows the pedals to stay still while the bicycle rolls along.

ON THE ROAD
Speed bicycles are too specialized to ride on roads. The basic design of the road racer or touring bike, with its down-curved drop-handlebars, has not changed for more than 50 years.

No spokes
As a spoke moves through the air, both turning with the wheel and moving forward with it, this creates air resistance or friction. The solid spokeless wheel cuts out the air friction of the 30–40 normal spokes.

No air-filled tyres
A cycle track is very flat, without lumps and bumps. So the speed or sprint bike needs only thin, solid rubber treads.

No left stays
The back wheel is fixed to one side of the frame, like the front wheel and for the same reason.

No pedal clips
Expert cyclists pull the pedal up as well as push it down, for greater power and speed. Older style pedals had clips and straps that fitted around a cycling shoe. Newer ones have clips that attach to clips on the soles of the shoes, similar to ski bindings that clip ski boots to skis.

BICYCLE SPEEDS
In a road race a cyclist needs air-filled tyres to iron out bumps in the road, gears to cope with the ups and downs of hills and brakes to manoeuvre between competitors or avoid obstacles. But a cycle track is smooth and banked, usually indoors, empty apart from competitors, and exactly the same for every circuit. So the speed or sprint (short race) bicycle is the most stripped-down cycling machine available. Cyclists zoom along at 60 kph (40 mph) or more in races, with top speeds on specially modified cycles of over 100 kph (60 mph).

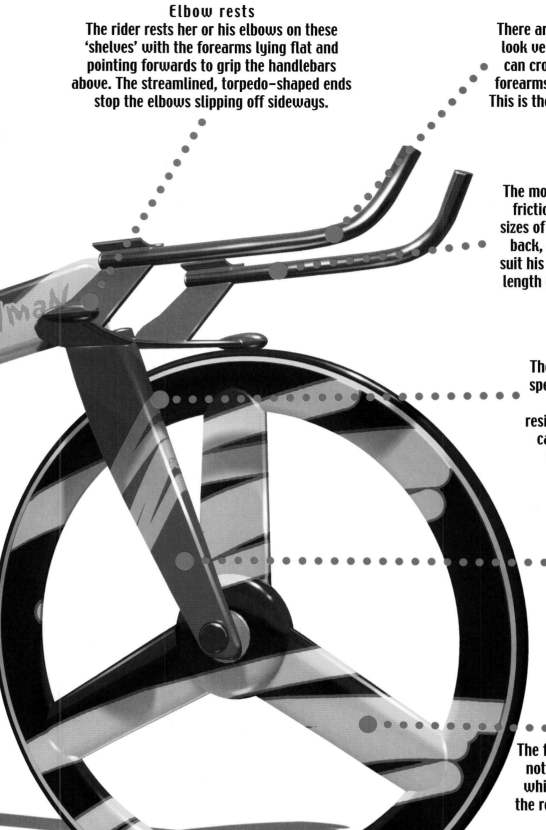

Elbow rests
The rider rests her or his elbows on these 'shelves' with the forearms lying flat and pointing forwards to grip the handlebars above. The streamlined, torpedo-shaped ends stop the elbows slipping off sideways.

No controls
There are no brakes or gears, so the handlebars look very bare. They face forward so the rider can crouch over them, hands at the front and forearms facing forwards with elbows together. This is the best position for streamlined pedalling.

No gears
The moving parts of gear changers would add friction, weight and wear to the cycle. The sizes of the two gear wheels or cogs, front and back, are chosen by the rider at the start to suit his or her own cycling style, the track, the length of the race, the skill of the competitors and the conditions.

No brakes
There is rarely any need to brake on the special oval, banked cycle track. Brakes merely add more weight and air resistance and get in the way. The pedals can be used to slow the bike down by their fixed drive to the rear wheel.

No left fork
On a normal cycle there are two tubes on either side of the front wheel in a Y shape or fork. The sprint or speed cycle has only one, to cut down air resistance. Like other forward-facing parts it has a narrow leading edge and smooth sides for streamlining.

Not many spokes
The front wheel has three thin spokes. It does not have to be as strong as the rear wheel, which must transmit the turning force from the rear gear cog to the ground, so it can have less construction material.

HIGH GEARS

As you cycle along a level road on an ordinary bike, you push the pedals around once and the back wheel turns around about two times. But sprint and speed cycles have very high gear ratios or combinations. On a speed bike one turn of the pedals turns the back wheel around more – four, five or even more times!

TOURING BIKE

Rear view mirrors
Touring means riding long distances on the open road. Large rear view mirrors are vital for safety, to look behind for overtaking cars and bikes, or for emergency vehicles that need to get past.

Brake lever
This applies the front brake.

Accelerator twist grip
The speed of the engine is controlled by the accelerator twist grip, that is, by twisting the hand grip on the handlebar (usually the right one).

Cooling fins
A car has a cooling system with a radiator to take heat away from the engine. Most motorcycles do not. The cylinder, which is the part that gets hot because the fuel explodes inside it, has many metal flanges or fins. These pass excess heat to the air rushing past.

Fuel tank
The large fuel tank is just in front of the rider. It has a smooth curved top to cause minimum injury in case the rider slips onto it. It may have a map-holder on top, too.

Passenger seat
A second person can travel on the bike, on the second or pillion seat. The passenger should not try to lean or balance the bike. He or she should sit upright, grip the handhold-backrest just behind and act as 'dead weight' to let the rider do the balancing.

Rider's seat
The well-rounded, padded seat is very comfortable for long journeys.

Panniers
A motorcycle has no boot like a car. So luggage is stored in bags or cases called panniers. These are on frames, one on each side of the rear wheel. An equal weight of luggage on either side gives good balance.

Foot rest
The passenger can rest his or her feet on flip-down foot rests that fold back up when not in use.

Rear brake
This is worked by a foot pedal on the right side of the bike. The foot pedal on the other side changes gears.

SPEED AND COMFORT

The freedom of the open road with the wind whistling past, the feeling of being part of the scenery or snaking between cars to beat a traffic jam – motorcycle touring as an 'easy rider' can be great fun. But if it is very cold, raining or icy, it is not so wonderful! The touring bike has a long wheelbase (distance between the wheels) that gives better roadholding and a smoother ride over humps and lumps than a short wheelbase. However, the long wheelbase is not so good for manoeuvring around tight corners.

CYLINDERS AND STROKES

The motorbike shown here is a transverse V twin. It has two cylinders, one each side, at an angle to make a V-shape seen from the front. Two cylinders give a smoother ride and are more powerful than one.

There are many other designs. An in-line twin V has the cylinders one behind the other but still in a V shape seen from the side, one pointing up and forward and the other up and backward. There are also four-cylinder engines that are even smoother and more powerful, but also heavier and more complicated, with more to go wrong.

Many smaller off-road or dirt track motorbikes have just one cylinder. The engine may be a two-stroke. This means that the fuel ignites (explodes) and delivers power every two strokes, that is, every up and down movement of the piston. Normal car and motorcycle engines are four-stroke.

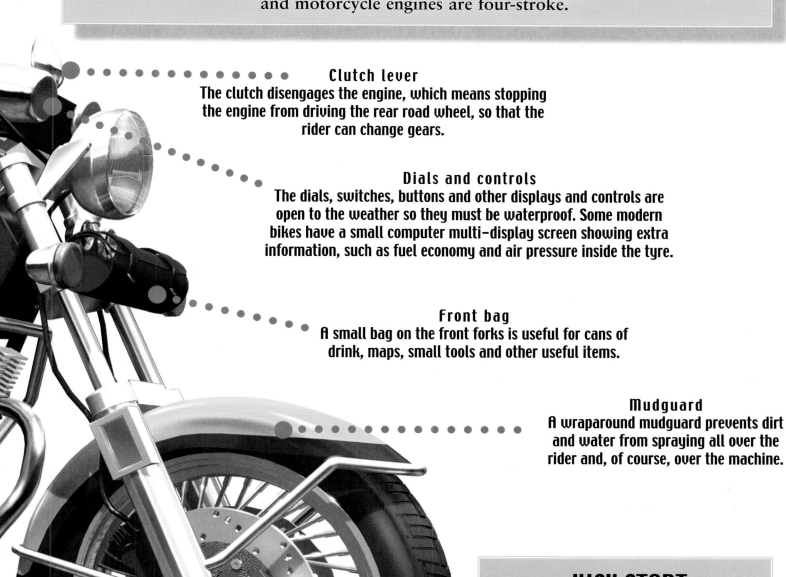

Clutch lever
The clutch disengages the engine, which means stopping the engine from driving the rear road wheel, so that the rider can change gears.

Dials and controls
The dials, switches, buttons and other displays and controls are open to the weather so they must be waterproof. Some modern bikes have a small computer multi−display screen showing extra information, such as fuel economy and air pressure inside the tyre.

Front bag
A small bag on the front forks is useful for cans of drink, maps, small tools and other useful items.

Mudguard
A wraparound mudguard prevents dirt and water from spraying all over the rider and, of course, over the machine.

KICK START

Different motorbikes start in different ways:

• Some motorcycles are started by pushing down hard on the kick start pedal, which starts the engine turning over.

•Others have an electric motor, switched on by turning a key as in a car, to start the engine.

SUPERBIKE

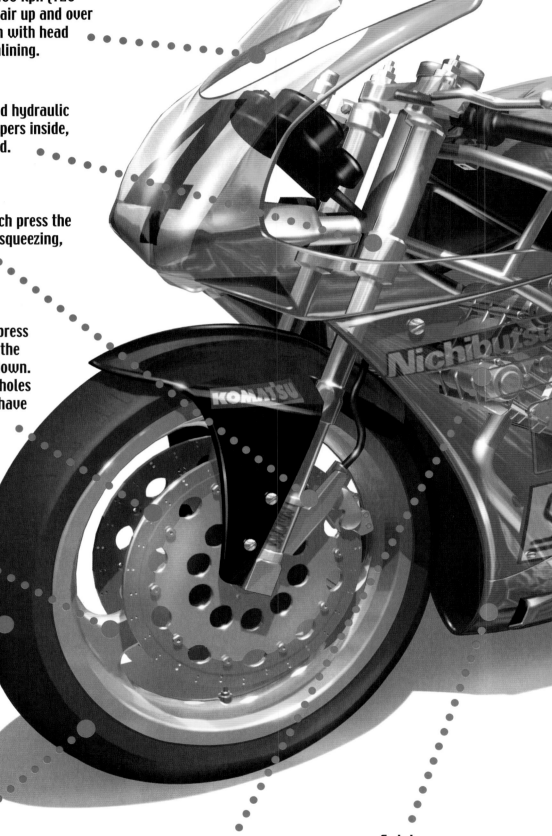

Windshield
The wind is very strong at more than 200 kph (120 mph). The windshield pushes the rushing air up and over the driver, who is also crouched down with head forward into the wind for streamlining.

Front suspension
The front forks are tubes with springs and hydraulic (oil-filled) or pneumatic (air-filled) dampers inside, to smooth out bumps in the road.

Brake calipers
The brake lever works the calipers, which press the brake pads onto the brake disc with a squeezing, scissor-like action.

Brake discs
The brake blocks or pads in the calipers press on to a large metal disc that is fixed to the road wheel and turns with it, to slow it down. The friction makes the disc hot, so it has holes in it for better cooling. Most superbikes have twin discs on the front wheel.

Few spokes
Many modern motorbikes do not have bicycle-type spokes in the wheels. The whole wheel is cast from one piece of metal alloy to make it strong but light. The lighter the wheel, the faster the engine can get it turning.

Slicks
Race tracks and fast roads are usually smooth and free of mud and dirt. So the superbike's tyres, or slicks, do not need tread. They are just plain, soft, sticky rubber to grip the tarmac.

Wraparound
The tyre surface wraps around both sides. This allows the rider to lean over at an amazing angle to balance while going round corners at great speed, with the tyre still gripping the road.

In-line twin V
This engine has two cylinders, one behind the other.

Fairings
A curved plastic or metal cover wraps around the main body of the motorbike to cut down wind resistance.

POWER, WEIGHT AND SPEED

The key to a fast vehicle is its power-to-weight ratio. This compares the weight of the vehicle with the amount of power that its engine produces to drive it along. A superbike might weigh about 170 kilograms (375 pounds) and have an engine that produces 160 horsepower. A family car weighs up to 10 times as much and has an engine that is half as powerful. So its power-to-weight ratio is 20 times less! No wonder superbikes are among the fastest of all vehicles – and so exciting to ride.

Low handlebars
The rider crouches low over the handlebars to minimize wind resistance.

Rider's seat
This is scooped out so that the driver sits as low as possible, hunched over the fuel tank for least wind resistance.

Exhaust
Exhaust gases and fumes from each cylinder flow along pipes that come together into one pipe. They pass through the silencer box before emerging into the air at the back, away from rider and passenger.

Rear suspension
The rear wheel is at the end of a long lever–like arm called a swinging or trailing arm. This pivots with the main chassis just behind the engine. Large springs and hydraulic dampers smooth out bumps and vibrations.

Chain drive
Toothed cogs (sprockets or gear wheels) and a link chain transfer turning power, from the engine between the wheels to the rear wheel. Some bikes have a spinning drive shaft instead of a chain.

Gear pedal
The rider changes gear with a foot pedal by flicking it up and down. The foot pedal on the other side applies the rear brake.

HOW MANY CCS?

A cc is a measure of volume. One cc is one cubic centimetre, that is, a cube roughly the size of a sugar lump. Motorbikes, cars and other vehicles have engines measured in ccs or litres (one litre is 1,000 ccs). The volume that's measured is the amount of air pushed aside as the pistons move their full distance inside their cylinders.

- A small moped or track motorbike is 50 ccs.
- A small racing motorcycle is up to 250 cc.
- A medium motorcycle is 500 ccs.
- A large motorcycle is 750 or 900 ccs.
- There are also superbikes of 1,000 ccs (one litre) and more!
- A smallish family car might have an engine size of 900–1,000 ccs (up to one litre).
- Big luxury cars are 2.5 litres or more.

FAMILY CAR

Rear-wheel drive
Most ordinary family cars are rear-wheel drive, where the engine turns only the two roadwheels at the back. This gives the best combination of balance, roadholding, steering and handling. Some smaller cars are front wheel drive, but the extra parts needed both to turn and to steer the front wheels mean extra weight and wear.

Spare wheel and tyre
The spare wheel is usually under one side of the rear of the car next to the fuel tank. If the boot is full, everything must be taken out to change the wheel.

Air bag
In case of a sudden shock or stop, a plastic bag bursts from a container in front of the driver (usually in the middle of the steering wheel) and begins to blow itself up with gas, all in less than one-tenth of a second.

Rear suspension
Springs and hydraulic dampers (pistons in oil-filled cylinders) allow the car body to sway smoothly as the air-filled tyres and the wheels absorb vibrations, bumps and jolts from the road beneath.

Fuel tank
The tank is usually under one side of the rear of the car next to the spare wheel. In this position the fuel is furthest from the hot engine and least likely to catch fire in an accident.

Differential box
This allows the two rear wheels to be turned by the engine at different speeds while going around corners.

CAT
The exhaust fumes and gases are made safer by a CAT or catalytic convertor. This absorbs and keeps back some of the most dangerous exhaust products.

SMART CARS
More and more cars are fitted with electronic gadgets, sensors and microchips. In the engine they monitor how much fuel is being used and help the driver to be more economical. They keep check on the levels of various fluids, such as petrol or diesel fuel, engine oil, gearbox oil, braking system fluid and hydraulic oils, cooling fluid and even windscreen-washer fluid! They also track engine temperature and oil pressure, and warn when replacements will be needed for brakes and other wearing parts.

A satellite navigation unit using the GPS (global positioning system) can pinpoint the car's position to within a few metres on a local map stored in electronic memory, and display this on a screen. Radio and radar links to speed-warning signs tell the driver about exceeding the speed limit. A hands-free mobile phone provides a link to the outside world.

ABS

The automatic braking system (ABS) stops a car from skidding. Without ABS, brakes suddenly jammed on could lock, so the wheels stop turning but the car carries on in a skid. With no grip on the road it's difficult to bring the vehicle to a controlled halt. With ABS, sensors in the wheels react if the brakes are about to lock, and brake pressure is released slightly. This means that the wheel keeps turning and the tyre holds its grip on the road while being slowed down. ABS kicks in several times each second, making a rattling noise. The result is a fast, safe, controlled, non-skid stop.

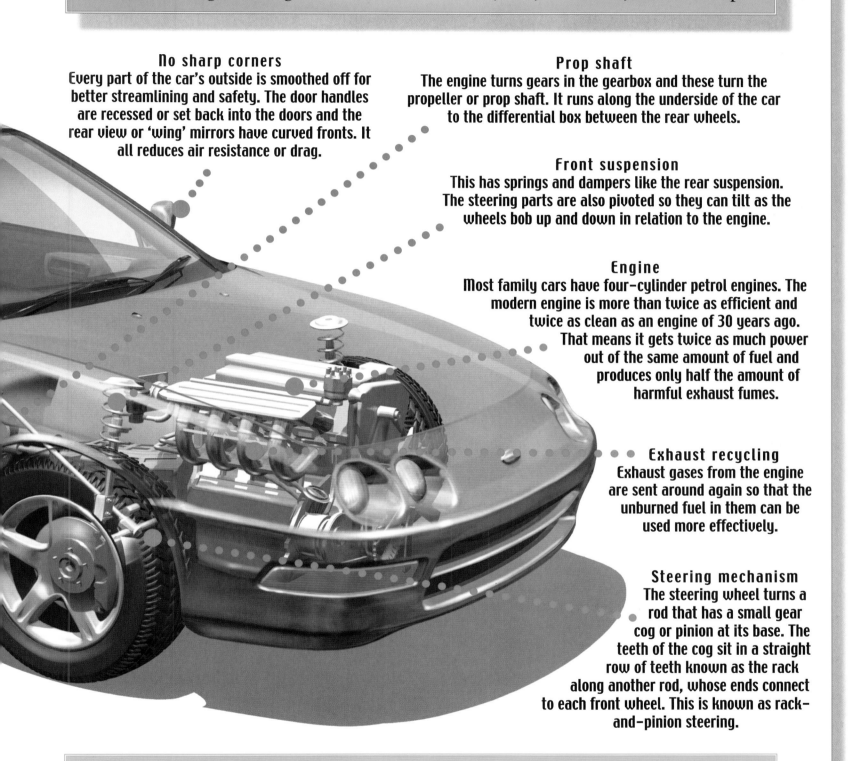

No sharp corners
Every part of the car's outside is smoothed off for better streamlining and safety. The door handles are recessed or set back into the doors and the rear view or 'wing' mirrors have curved fronts. It all reduces air resistance or drag.

Prop shaft
The engine turns gears in the gearbox and these turn the propeller or prop shaft. It runs along the underside of the car to the differential box between the rear wheels.

Front suspension
This has springs and dampers like the rear suspension. The steering parts are also pivoted so they can tilt as the wheels bob up and down in relation to the engine.

Engine
Most family cars have four-cylinder petrol engines. The modern engine is more than twice as efficient and twice as clean as an engine of 30 years ago. That means it gets twice as much power out of the same amount of fuel and produces only half the amount of harmful exhaust fumes.

Exhaust recycling
Exhaust gases from the engine are sent around again so that the unburned fuel in them can be used more effectively.

Steering mechanism
The steering wheel turns a rod that has a small gear cog or pinion at its base. The teeth of the cog sit in a straight row of teeth known as the rack along another rod, whose ends connect to each front wheel. This is known as rack-and-pinion steering.

WHAT'S THE DIFFERENCE?

The differential allows two wheels on either side of a car to rotate at different speeds while still being driven by the engine. Why? Imagine a car turning left. The wheel on the right covers a longer curve or arc than the left one but during the same time. So it must turn faster to travel the extra distance. If both wheels are being driven at the same speed they lose grip and 'skip' or 'hop' so that they can cover their different distances.

The differential allows this to happen. As the wheel on the outside of the corner turns faster, the one on the inside turns more slowly by the same amount. This gives smooth cornering. Nearly all cars and trucks have this system.

F1 RACING CAR

Front wing
The specially shaped wing produces a force that presses the car down on to the track.

Radio aerial
The driver and his racing team can keep in contact by radio.

Tyre
F1 tyres are wide and have hardly any tread pattern. Tyres for use in the wet have more pattern. During a race, the tyres can heat up to 110 °C.

Wheel
Each wheel is held in place by a single screw-on wheelnut, which can be removed very quickly. This is so that the wheels and tyres can be changed rapidly during a race.

Steering wheel
The small steering wheel is fitted with buttons and switches that enable the driver to change gear and do many other things without having to let go of the wheel.

Cockpit
The driver's cockpit is very cramped, with almost no room to move. It is so small that the driver must remove the steering wheel before he or she gets in or out.

Sponsor's name
Running an F1 racing team is incredibly expensive. Most of the money comes from sponsors, who pay the team to advertize their names on the cars.

Fuel tanks
The tanks on either side of the driver have a honeycomb-like mesh inside. This stops the fuel slopping about too fast inside, which would upset the car's delicate balance.

Driver's survival cell
The driver lies in a tube-shaped survival cell or 'cocoon' made of extremely strong but light composite material, with only the head and arms exposed. The cell resists breaking in a crash to protect the driver.

THE CHAMPIONSHIP MACHINE

The Formula 1 racing car can accelerate from 0–160 kph (0–100 mph) and brake back to a standstill, all in less than six seconds. For this, the driver only needs first and second gears out of the six usually fitted. The fastest speeds are over 320 kph (200 mph). A Formula 1 race is usually about 300 kilometres (nearly 200 miles) and takes up to two hours. Every aspect of the car, including steering angles and fuel tank sizes, is reset for each race track. Dozens of sensors inside the car radio information on every aspect of performance back to the team in the pits. This information transfer is known as telemetry. The team can then advise the driver on the return radio link.

CARS WITH WINGS

Just as the wings of a plane lift it upwards into the air, the wings on an F1 car push it down on to the track. This is because of their shape. On a plane, the top of the wing is curved and the underside is flat, which means that the air presses less on the top than on the bottom, so the wing is pushed upward. F1 car wings are mounted the other way up, so that the force pushes them downwards. This helps the car to grip without slowing it down too much, and gives the driver more control when cornering. The wings and the body shape produce so much force that at 240 kph (150 mph) the car could race upside down on a ceiling and not fall off!

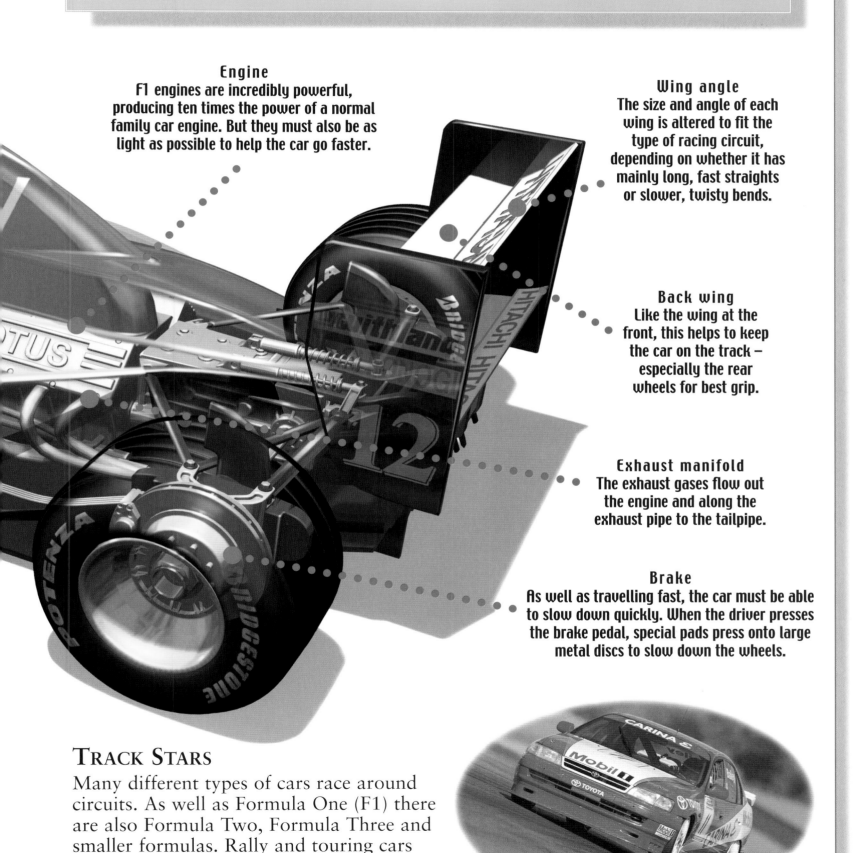

Engine
F1 engines are incredibly powerful, producing ten times the power of a normal family car engine. But they must also be as light as possible to help the car go faster.

Wing angle
The size and angle of each wing is altered to fit the type of racing circuit, depending on whether it has mainly long, fast straights or slower, twisty bends.

Back wing
Like the wing at the front, this helps to keep the car on the track – especially the rear wheels for best grip.

Exhaust manifold
The exhaust gases flow out the engine and along the exhaust pipe to the tailpipe.

Brake
As well as travelling fast, the car must be able to slow down quickly. When the driver presses the brake pedal, special pads press onto large metal discs to slow down the wheels.

TRACK STARS

Many different types of cars race around circuits. As well as Formula One (F1) there are also Formula Two, Formula Three and smaller formulas. Rally and touring cars (right) look more like normal family cars – but they too go much, much faster!

STRETCH LIMOUSINE

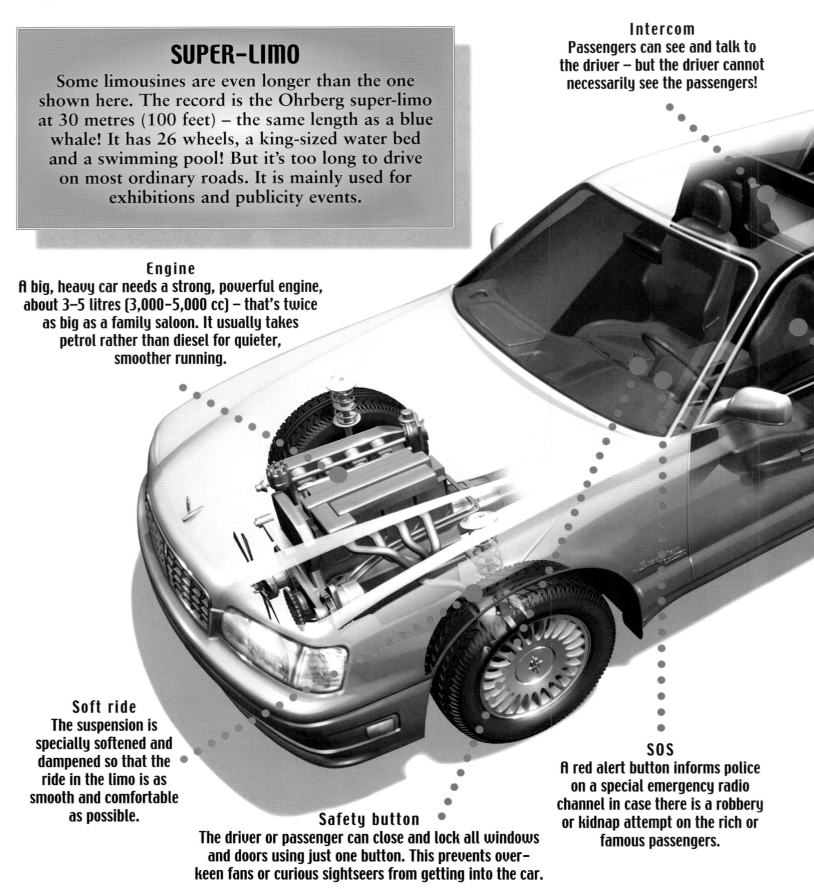

SUPER-LIMO

Some limousines are even longer than the one shown here. The record is the Ohrberg super-limo at 30 metres (100 feet) – the same length as a blue whale! It has 26 wheels, a king-sized water bed and a swimming pool! But it's too long to drive on most ordinary roads. It is mainly used for exhibitions and publicity events.

Intercom
Passengers can see and talk to the driver – but the driver cannot necessarily see the passengers!

Engine
A big, heavy car needs a strong, powerful engine, about 3–5 litres (3,000–5,000 cc) – that's twice as big as a family saloon. It usually takes petrol rather than diesel for quieter, smoother running.

Soft ride
The suspension is specially softened and dampened so that the ride in the limo is as smooth and comfortable as possible.

Safety button
The driver or passenger can close and lock all windows and doors using just one button. This prevents over-keen fans or curious sightseers from getting into the car.

SOS
A red alert button informs police on a special emergency radio channel in case there is a robbery or kidnap attempt on the rich or famous passengers.

THE STRETCHED PART

Originally the 'stretch' limousine was made by taking an existing luxury car, cutting it in half and welding extra panels into the gaps to make it longer. Then a new top-class interior was fitted with leather seats, deep-pile carpets and all the trimmings. Today, various specialized vehicle-makers build limos exactly to the owner's wishes. Some have fold-out beds so that they can become a luxury hotel on wheels!

Mobile office
On long journeys the limo can be a place to work. It may be fitted with a computer linked to the Internet, and a video player so that movie or music star passengers can view their latest scenes.

Radio links
Various aerials and antennae send and receive signals for radio, TV, telephone, Internet and also private encrypted (secrecy-coded) radio and walkie-talkie channels.

Tinted windows
The windows to the passenger compartment are tinted and have a reflective coating. People trying to see in from the outside can only see their own faces. The windows are often bullet-proof, too.

Comforts of home
The limo has a mobile phone, a TV (terrestrial and satellite of course), a stereo system, a courtesy bar, hot drinks and many other comforts.

Expert driver
The driver or chauffeur must be specially trained not only to drive safely and within the law, but also to start and stop very smoothly and to guide the long limo around awkward turns and avoid too-sharp corners.

Keeping cool and quiet
Air conditioning keeps passengers warm in cold weather or cool when it is hot. It also filters out the smoke and fumes from traffic jams. Special body panels and thick windows keep out the noise.

WHO BUYS A STRETCH LIMO?

Whoever wants one and has enough money! However, it is a very expensive 'toy' to leave sitting in the garage. And it may not get through the barrier at the local supermarket car park. This is why 19 out of 20 large limousines are owned by vehicle hire companies. A limo can be rented by the hour, day, week or longer. The driver costs money, too. Big limos are hired for film and music stars, bosses of big companies, royalty, presidents and prime ministers, important politicians and public figures. And also the ordinary family who decide to splash out on a special day, such as a wedding or anniversary.

4WD - FOUR WHEEL DRIVE

Silencer
This box in the exhaust pipe makes the waste gases and fumes from the engine slower and quieter. It may also contain a CAT (catalytic convertor) with special substances that remove some of the most dangerous chemicals in the fumes.

ATTs
All terrain tyres have thicker, chunkier tread than normal road tyres. They give good all-purpose grip on a variety of surfaces, from motorways to ploughed fields.

Chassis
Steel box girders make the car's chassis or framework very strong and rigid, so that it can withstand knocks from rocks and potholes.

Rear door
Some rear doors are hinged to the roof so they lift up in one piece. Others are horizontal two-part so the window section folds up and the lower solid part hinges down to form a tailgate platform. Still others are vertical two-part, hinged at each side so they open in the middle.

Rear drive
The rear drive or half shafts turn the rear road wheels when the vehicle is in RWD or 4WD mode.

Light cages
If a 4WD is used off-road it may skid and bump into trees, posts and other objects. Wire cages around the lights prevent their coverings and bulbs from being smashed. It's easier to straighten out the wire cage than to replace the bulb and cover.

Limited slip diff
This box of gear cogs stops the vehicle from getting bogged down in slippery mud.

Suspension
4WDs have strong, stiff suspension to cope with bumps and lumps on rough ground and also with the heavy loads they may carry.

Prop shaft
The propeller shaft carries the turning force from the engine back to the rear road wheels.

WHY 4WD?

A normal family car is 2WD or two wheel drive – only two of the road wheels are turned by the engine. In small cars it may be the front two (FWD), in larger ones it's the rear two (RWD). In a 4WD (four-wheel drive) vehicle all four road wheels are made to turn by the engine. This allows much more power to get through to the road, giving improved grip or traction. The vehicle has a better grip on slippery mud and ice. There is more control in going up and down very steep hills and getting out of potholes or over rocks and roots. It also allows heavier loads to be carried.

However, 4WD uses up much more fuel. This is because the engine has to turn and work an extra set of road wheel drive parts. So most 4WDs have a lever or button that switches to 2WD for smooth roads, to save fuel and wear and tear.

Head restraint
As a 4WD travels over rough ground the passengers bump and sway about. Shaped restraints help to steady their heads so that they can avoid neck pain and whiplash injuries.

Engine
Most 4WDs have diesel engines. They may be heavier and noisier than petrol engines, but they are usually more reliable and also need less servicing and maintenance.

Drive control
The driver uses a lever or shiftstick to change between FWD, RWD and 4WD.

Front drive
The front drive shafts turn the front road wheels when the vehicle is in FWD or 4WD mode.

Disc brakes
A big, heavy car like a 4WD needs strong brakes, so it is fitted with disc brakes all around. These are power-assisted, which means that the driver's pressure on the foot pedal is greatly boosted by hydraulic pressure supplied by the engine.

EVEN MORE GRIP
Four wheels turning may not be enough in very slippery conditions like ice and snow. So special snow chains are wrapped around the tyres to give even more 'purchase' (grip).

LIMITED SLIP DIFF

In a 2WD vehicle, the wheels on either side of the axle can rotate at different speeds while still being driven by the engine. This is called the diff or differential. But it can cause trouble when off road. Imagine the left back wheel of the car is in a very slippery place such as on ice. It has hardly anything to grip, so it can spin almost freely. The diff allows it to do this, while the right back wheel – which is on dry tarmac and can grip – simply stays still. The vehicle is stuck! This doesn't happen when a vehicle has limited or non-slip diff. Only a limited difference is allowed between the speeds of the two wheels. Beyond this the drive is still applied to the slower wheel, which hauls the vehicle out of the rut, so it's no longer stuck.

PICK-UP TRUCK

Turbo diesel
The turbocharged diesel engine has about twice the power of an ordinary family car engine.

Winch
This is a cable wound on to a reel or drum, with a hook or link on the end. The drum spins easily one way so that the cable can be unwound. Then the drum turns slowly but powerfully to wind it back in. If the pick-up is parked, the winch can haul items towards it. If the pick-up cannot climb a steep hill, the cable can be unwound and attached to something higher up, such as a tree, pole or building. Then the winch turns to pull up the pick-up!

Bull bar
There aren't usually many real bulls to push out of the way. The bull bar is really a large front fender for pushing branches and other items aside or to protect the pick-up in case of a crash.

Clean headlamps
Because pick-ups often travel over soft ground and unmade roads, they get covered in mud. The headlamps have their own water sprayers and wipers to keep them clean.

Stiff suspension
The pick-up's suspension springs and dampers are very stiff. That is, they do not soften the ride very much. This is because pick-ups are built to carry heavy loads over rough grounds, where soft suspension might strain or break.

Ground clearance
All parts on the underside of the pick-up are well above the ground. This is called high ground clearance and prevents damage as the vehicle goes over rocks and roots. There may be sheets of metal, under-pans, covering the undersides of more fragile parts.

4WD
Most pick-ups have four-wheel drive where the engine turns all four road wheels.

THE WORKING PICK-UP

Pick-ups were specially designed as work vehicles for people to carry various odd and awkward loads on short journeys. They can 'pick up' almost anything. They are used by builders, farmers, maintenance engineers, mechanics, road construction workers, foresters, wildlife rangers and many other people. The loads can vary from bricks to bits of wood, tools such as shovels and sledgehammers, concrete mixers, sand and rocks, to caged animals such as chickens, and even sheep with their sheepdog. Most pick-ups have hooks, cleats or similar anchor points around the load bay so that the load can be tied or strapped safely. Some have covers that can be tied over the load bay to protect the contents from rain and snow.

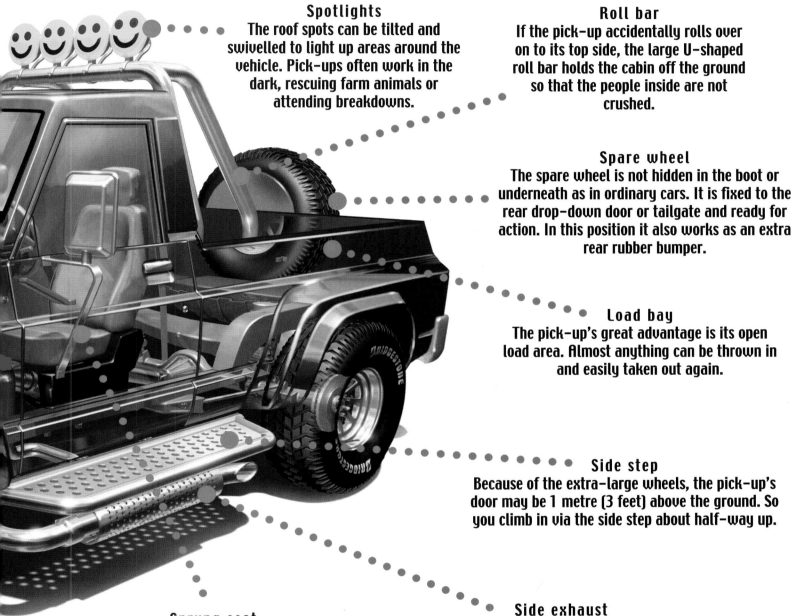

Spotlights
The roof spots can be tilted and swivelled to light up areas around the vehicle. Pick-ups often work in the dark, rescuing farm animals or attending breakdowns.

Roll bar
If the pick-up accidentally rolls over on to its top side, the large U-shaped roll bar holds the cabin off the ground so that the people inside are not crushed.

Spare wheel
The spare wheel is not hidden in the boot or underneath as in ordinary cars. It is fixed to the rear drop-down door or tailgate and ready for action. In this position it also works as an extra rear rubber bumper.

Load bay
The pick-up's great advantage is its open load area. Almost anything can be thrown in and easily taken out again.

Side step
Because of the extra-large wheels, the pick-up's door may be 1 metre (3 feet) above the ground. So you climb in via the side step about half-way up.

Sprung seat
Because pick-ups are built for rough ground and have stiff suspension, the seats have extra springs and padding so that the driver and passenger are not shaken to bits.

Side exhaust
Ordinary cars have their exhaust pipes and boxes along the underside. But the pick-up has them along the sides as part of its high ground clearance for rough terrain.

TYPES OF PICK-UP

Pick-ups are more popular in warmer, drier regions where there is less chance of the load getting wet in the rain. The countryman pick-up has a longer cab so that two or three people can sit on the rear seat behind the driver and front passenger. The flat-bed pick-up has a load bay with fold-down sides or no sides at all, so heavy loads can be slid straight on and off the load platform. The crane pick-up has a small crane and a winch at the back to rescue broken-down cars.

COMBINE HARVESTER

Rotating reel
The large reel at the front pulls the crop down and back, towards and over the cutter bar. Guide pegs at each end help the driver to steer the combine so that no strip of crop is left unharvested.

Cab
The driver sits well forward over the cutter so that he or she can watch for obstacles and guide the combine in an accurate line. The cab is insulated against noise and may have air-conditioning since the weather is often hot and very dusty at harvest time.

Lifters
Sometimes heavy rain knocks the crop over and flattens it near to the ground. The lifters slide under it like the prongs of forks so that it is harvested rather than going underneath the cutter.

Cutter bar
This slices the stalks of the crop almost at ground level. The height of the cutter can be adjusted for harvesting different plants.

Crop auger
An auger is a large screw or corkscrew-shaped blade. The crop auger pulls the cut crop towards the middle of the machine and on to the feeder elevator.

TELEPORTERS
Vehicles with long, tilting, telescopic arms can carry loads and lift them into awkward places.

Feeder elevator
A continually moving conveyor belt carries the cut crop from the front into the body of the combine.

MANY JOBS IN ONE

The combine harvester is named after the fact that it combines or joins together all the jobs normally done when harvesting grain crops, such as wheat, barley, oats and rye. The first combines appeared in the USA in the 1920s, towed and powered by tractors. Self-propelled combines with their own engines became popular in the 1950s. Modern combines have a range of cutting heads, bars and reels to suit different crops, including beans, sweetcorn and sorghum. Each one does the work of up to 100 people using hand-harvesting tools.

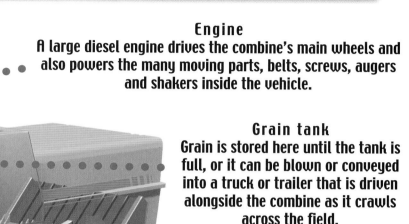

Engine
A large diesel engine drives the combine's main wheels and also powers the many moving parts, belts, screws, augers and shakers inside the vehicle.

Grain tank
Grain is stored here until the tank is full, or it can be blown or conveyed into a truck or trailer that is driven alongside the combine as it crawls across the field.

Baler
A baling attachment can be fitted to the rear of the combine. It presses the straw into box-shaped bales and ties them with twine.

Straw walker or shaker
The shaker rattles to and fro and shakes the straw (stalks) rearwards. Grain and other material fall through the sieve onto the grain pan. Another corkscrew–like auger lifts the threshed, clean grains up into the main storage tank.

Grain pan
The grain is carried backwards and powerful blasts of air from the chaff fan blow the lighter unwanted bits and pieces (chaff) upwards away from it.

Drive wheels
The large wheels under the main part of the machine push the combine along. Smaller wheels at the rear steer the vehicle.

Threshing cylinder
The thresher turns around and shakes the crop so violently that the seeds (grain) fall away from the seed cases, stalks, leaves and other unwanted bits.

COMPUTERIZED COMBINES

Remote sensing satellites far above in space can survey huge expanses of fields that would take a long time to check on the ground. The satellites beam pictures of the fields down by radio. The farmer can tell by the different computer-enhanced colours which areas of crop may be diseased or in need of pesticides, fertilizers or other sprays and which are ready to harvest. This information, plus the size and shape of the area to be cut, are fed into the combine's on-board computer.

The computer works out the best route for harvesting the field. It can also avoid any poor areas that are not worth cutting. The route is displayed on a screen for the driver to follow.

DIGGER

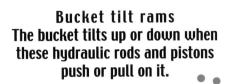

Lights
To get the job done on time the digger and driver may have to work nights. The lights move with the bucket so it is always brightly lit. There are also lights at the rear, and the driver's seat swivels round, too, since a digger spends plenty of time in reverse.

Hydraulic hoses
High-pressure oil is pumped along these flexible pipes into the cylinders to work the rams. The pipes bend so that the digger booms and bucket can move and they have steel mesh inside their walls for extra strength.

Bucket tilt rams
The bucket tilts up or down when these hydraulic rods and pistons push or pull on it.

'Artic'
The digger is articulated – it has a hinge or joint in the middle. It steers not by twisting the wheels but by moving the whole front end, including the bucket, to one side or the other.

Bucket
An average bucket is 2.5–3 metres (7 or 8 feet) wide. It is not always full of earth or rocks. The digger can be used to carry loads, such as bags of cement or blocks of bricks, around the site.

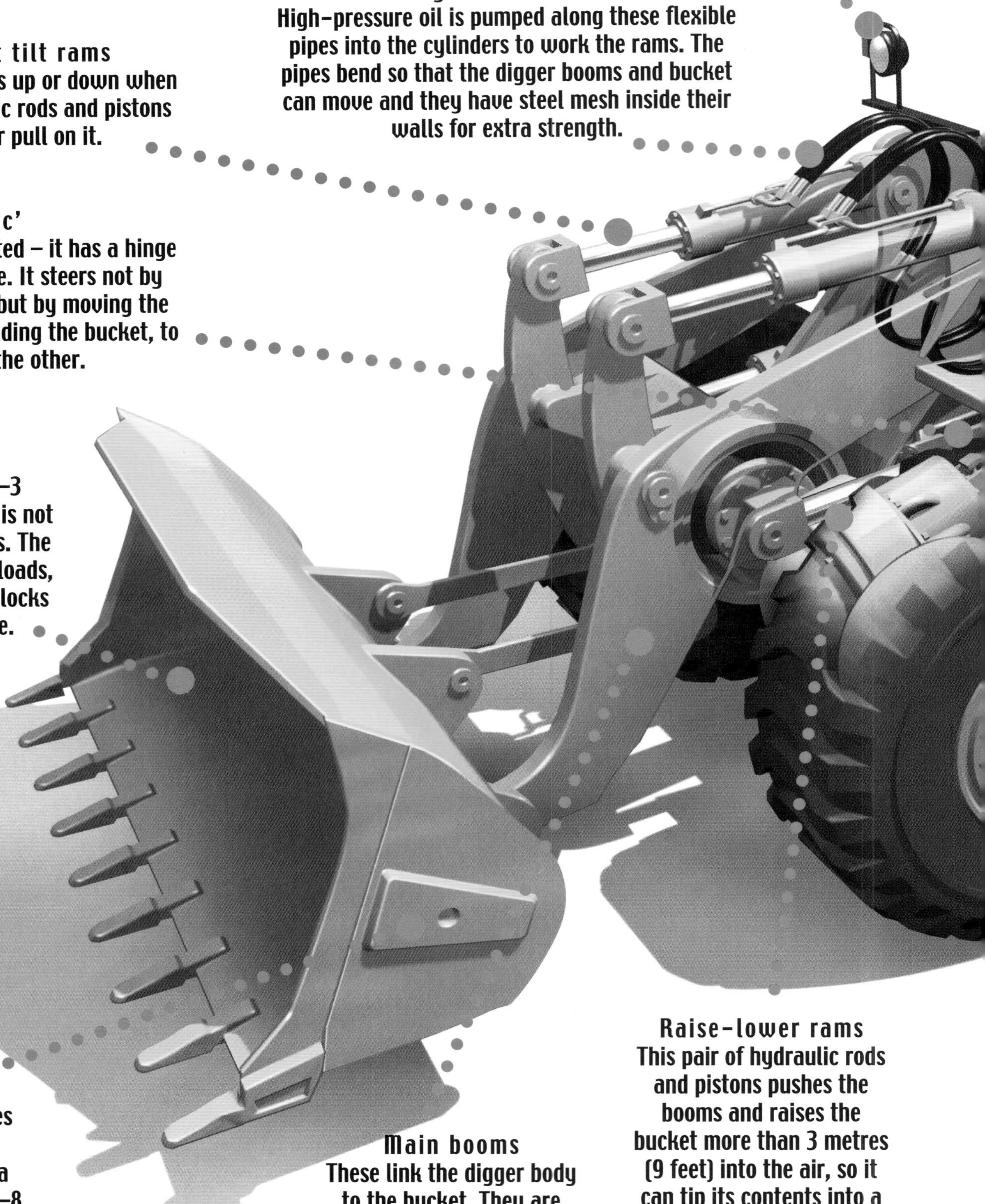

SWL
Most construction machines have SWLs, safe working loads. A digger may have a SWL of 7–8 tonnes (about 7–8 tons) for the bucket.

Main booms
These link the digger body to the bucket. They are moved by hydraulic rams.

Raise-lower rams
This pair of hydraulic rods and pistons pushes the booms and raises the bucket more than 3 metres (9 feet) into the air, so it can tip its contents into a dump truck or earthmover.

BUCKETS OF BUCKETS
The bucket shown here is a typical all-purpose design for gouging into and lifting soil, earth, small rocks, shingle, gravel and sand. There are many other bucket designs for different jobs. A smoothing bucket is lower and wider to scrape a large area level. A basket bucket is made of steel bars like a cage for lifting lighter, looser material such as hay, straw and household refuse.

Cab
The driver sits in an air-conditioned, vibration-proofed and sound-proofed cab. This protects the driver from being deafened and shaken up by a day's work.

Controls
Hand levers or buttons control the bucket's movements. Floor pedals and the steering wheel make the whole digger move about.

Engine
A heavy-duty diesel engine provides the power for turning the wheels and for the hydraulic system to raise and lower the bucket. The engine produces about 180–200 horsepower (almost three times the power of a smallish family car engine).

Massive tyres
A big digger has tyres taller than an adult person. They have deep tread to grip soft ground. Sometimes they are filled partly with water for extra weight and grip.

DIGGERS GALORE
Diggers, excavators and other load-movers find jobs in all kinds of work, from piling up scrapped cars, to scooping up gravel and sand for building, to scraping up sea salt from shallow coastal lagoons.

IT'S ALL DONE BY HYDRAULICS

Many large vehicles and machines rely on hydraulic systems. They use oil under very high pressure. It is pumped along a pipe or hose into a large metal tube-shaped cylinder. Closely fitting inside the cylinder is a rod-shaped piston. As the oil is forced into the cylinder it pushes the piston in front of it. The piston usually has a long metal rod fixed to it and the other end of the rod is linked to the part that moves. The pressure is so great that if a hose sprang a leak, the thin jet of oil spurting out of it would blast a small hole straight through the body of a person standing in the way.

Like our own muscles, hydraulic pistons can only push. For two-way movement there are two pistons that rock the part to be moved like a see-saw. Or two pistons face each other in the same long cylinder and the oil is pumped from one end of the cylinder to the other. This gives push-pull power.

BULLDOZER

Blade controls
These levers control the hydraulic rams to raise or lower the blade and to tilt it up or down.

Dozer controls
There are very few controls for the bulldozer itself. The main ones are two levers that make the tracks work on each side. The dozer has no steering wheel. It turns by slowing or stopping the track on one side while the other track still runs, making the dozer swing or pivot around at its middle.

Track drive
The main cog or sprocket wheel is driven by the engine to make the track run. On some dozers there is a front drive cog, too, and perhaps repeater cogs along the length of the track.

Track
The track is the caterpillar or crawler track, an endless loop of plates joined by pins.

Hydraulic array
The engine supplies the main hydraulic power to the cab, in the form of oil at very high pressure in a pipe. This is divided into many pipes, each with its own control, that send oil to work the various hydraulic rams and systems.

Track pin
Pins link the track plates to each other. If one plate gets bent or broken, the pins can be taken out and a new plate inserted.

Track plate
Some tracks have plates made of very hard and strong rubber, others of metal. The ridge across the track jabs into the ground to give amazing grip.

WHY THE NAME?

The name is a version of the term 'bull dose'. This was a dose of sedative given to a bull, which was more powerful than that needed by a smaller, calmer cow. So giving a 'dose fit for a bull' meant giving an extra-powerful or very strong amount of something. It suited the bulldozer's great size and mighty power.

WHAT DO BULLDOZERS DO?

They are designed to push, scrape and level rough ground and to move piles of rocks, earth, gravel, sand and other loose material. But they can do much more:

- A bulldozer can drive through an area of scrub, young trees or rough ground, flattening everything in its path.

- It can attach a cable or chain to bigger trees and pull them out of the ground, or drag over walls and pylons.

- Two bulldozers with a long steel cable or hawser strung between them can drive either side of a wood or old weak building and make it topple to the ground.

- A bulldozer can also push and move heavy items, such as large steel pipes.

- The bulldozer can rescue other vehicles if they get stuck by dragging them out of ruts or mud on to solid ground.

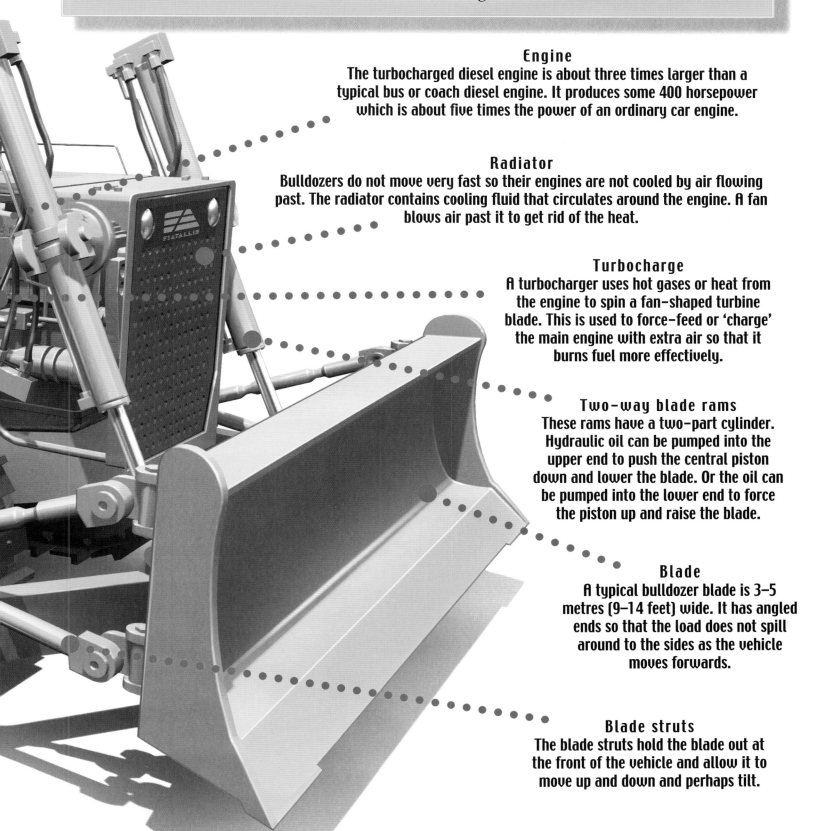

Engine
The turbocharged diesel engine is about three times larger than a typical bus or coach diesel engine. It produces some 400 horsepower which is about five times the power of an ordinary car engine.

Radiator
Bulldozers do not move very fast so their engines are not cooled by air flowing past. The radiator contains cooling fluid that circulates around the engine. A fan blows air past it to get rid of the heat.

Turbocharge
A turbocharger uses hot gases or heat from the engine to spin a fan-shaped turbine blade. This is used to force-feed or 'charge' the main engine with extra air so that it burns fuel more effectively.

Two-way blade rams
These rams have a two-part cylinder. Hydraulic oil can be pumped into the upper end to push the central piston down and lower the blade. Or the oil can be pumped into the lower end to force the piston up and raise the blade.

Blade
A typical bulldozer blade is 3–5 metres (9–14 feet) wide. It has angled ends so that the load does not spill around to the sides as the vehicle moves forwards.

Blade struts
The blade struts hold the blade out at the front of the vehicle and allow it to move up and down and perhaps tilt.

TRANSPORTER

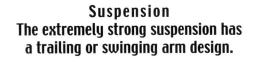

Suspension
The extremely strong suspension has a trailing or swinging arm design.

Securing the load
Before the transporter sets off, this digger will be secured or tied down tightly with chains and very strong straps. Moveable parts such as the bucket must also be secured in case they come loose or swing about.

Trailer unit
The trailer receives its electricity and its hydraulic power to work the brakes, suspension and other systems from the tractor unit via flexible wires and hoses.

Flashing lights
The yellow flashing lights warn other drivers and road users that the vehicle and its load are exceptional.

Wide load
Vehicles over a certain width must have clear signs saying so. The sign warns other drivers that it may be awkward to overtake since the transporter may be wider than one of the lanes on the motorway.

Multi wheels
As many as 20 or more wheels spread the great weight of the load. The digger on this transporter may weigh 20 tonnes (about 20 tons).

THE WEIGHT PROBLEM

The transporter may arrive at a weak bridge, a steep hill, a railway crossing or a similar place where its great weight could cause problems. The weight must be taken into consideration to decide if it is safe to continue.

- MGW or maximum gross weight is the weight of the whole lot – tractor unit, trailer unit, load, fuel, even the driver's sandwiches!

- Axle weight depends on how many axles there are, that is, sets of wheels. The more axles and wheels, the better the weight is spread over a larger area.

- Payload is the weight of just the load, without the transporter.

GIANTS ON THE HIGHWAY

Massive transporters, wide loads, juggernauts and convoys roar through the countryside, carrying every kind of cargo from car spares and washing machines to beds, flowers and chocolate.

Bend in the middle
The articulated joint or link between the tractor and trailer units allows the whole vehicle to bend in the middle, for going around corners more easily.

Tractor unit
The truck at the front is the tractor unit. In this case 'tractor' simply means something that pulls.

Drive wheels
The trailer's wheels are not turned by the engine. Only the wheels on the truck or tractor unit are driven by the engine.

Low load
The load is carried on a low platform slung between the sets of wheels at the front and rear. The lower it is, the more stable it is, and less likely to sway or topple because of a bumpy road or sudden corner.

Ramps
Strong metal ramps may be stored under the trailer. They are brought out and fitted to the back so that loads can be rolled or dragged on to the platform.

Winch and cable
The trailer has a large winch at the front. This winds a steel cable on to a drum slowly and with tremendous power. The winch is used for hauling loads on to the trailer.

PLANNING THE ROUTE

Driving a giant transporter is very different from driving a car! The driver may have to tell the police and other authorities about his or her journey, especially if the load may be dangerous, as with drums of chemicals. The driver must plan the route carefully in advance to avoid problems such as:

- Sharp corners and curves in the road.

- Weak bridges or causeways.

- Low bridges, cables and other places where there is limited height or headroom.

- Places where the ground is soft and may subside (sink or collapse).

- Places where the road surface is bumpy and there could be a risk of grounding.

- Roads or openings with restricted width such as narrow lanes, gateways and driveways.

MONSTER TRUCK

Air horns
Compressed air blasts out of the multi-horns to make a sound heard more than 2 kilometres (1 mile) away.

Cockpit
There are lots of extra dials and controls in the cab, because many running conditions of the highly tuned engine, such as temperatures and pressures, must be closely monitored. The dashboard looks more like a plane cockpit or flight deck.

CB radio
Drivers keep in touch with each other by CB or citizen's band radio. They chat and pass the time of day, discuss the weather and road conditions, or their trucks and loads, and warn each other of traffic jams or accidents.

Gears
There may be 10, 12 or more gears to help the truck pull away uphill with its 40-tonne load or cruise down the motorway at its maximum speed.

Driver's seat
The driver's seat is reinforced and strengthened, with a pilot-like safety harness for a seat belt, to cope with the tremendous acceleration and cornering speed.

Limiter
Working trucks are fitted with speed limiters since in many countries they are not allowed to go as fast as ordinary cars.

Engine
The giant turbocharged diesel engine may be 10 times the size of a family car engine. Some speed trucks are even fitted with jet engines as used on fighter aircraft!

Square shape
This truck has few curves. Its design is flat-sided and squared-off. This makes it look strong and powerful. But it is not so good for speed and fuel economy.

Shiny chrome
On a show truck such as this many of the parts are coated with chrome metal for a shiny, hard-wearing appearance. But that means a lot of polish to keep the vehicle looking clean!

BI-Y J38

TRUCK SHAPES

In the days before power-assisted controls, truck driving was a job for big strong people – usually men. The trucks were designed to look masculine, powerful and even menacing, with box-like shapes. However, these designs are very poor at pushing aside air smoothly. For each kilometre (just over half a mile) that a big boxy truck travels, it must push aside 20 tonnes (about 20 tons) of air. This high amount of resistance or drag uses up huge amounts of fuel. Modern trucks have more curved, streamlined shapes to save fuel.

Exhaust stack
Exhaust fumes are dangerous, even deadly if breathed in, because they contain poisonous gases such as carbon monoxide. They must be vented from an opening higher than all occupied parts of the vehicle. So this exhaust stack is about 4 metres (11 feet) high!

Sleeper
This monster truck has a small room just behind the driver's cab. It has beds, cupboards, a washbasin and a small cooker. On long journeys the driver and co-driver can rest here or pull into an overnight truck stop.

DAYS ON THE ROAD
Drivers may spend days driving a truck from coast to coast, so small personal comforts are very important.

Wheels
The enormous wheels and tyres are chest-high to an adult person. Some trucks have two pairs of front wheels, one behind the other – and both pairs turn with the steering wheel.

Artic link
The truck is designed to haul a trailer fitted with an articulated link, sometimes called the 'fifth wheel'. The front of the trailer hooks into and rests on a large metal disc at the rear of the truck itself, which is known as the tractor unit. This allows the whole vehicle to articulate or bend at the artic link.

Fuel tank
The fuel tank is of shiny chrome (on a working truck it would be dull grey or black). It holds more than 2,000 litres (140 gallons) of diesel fuel, which is 40 times as much as an ordinary car.

Electrics and hydraulics
The rear of the truck has connectors and sockets for the wires and hydraulic hoses on the trailer unit. These allow the driver to control the lights, brakes and other equipment on the trailer.

POWERED EVERYTHING

A large vehicle like this truck is so big and heavy that the steering, brakes and other features are powered or power-assisted. For example, the driver puts on the brakes by pressing the brake pedal. But the driver's leg and foot do not produce all the physical force necessary to press the brake pads on to the brake discs. Pushing the brake pedal works switches called actuators that are connected to the hydraulic system driven by the engine. The hydraulic system's oil-filled cylinders and hoses produce the great force needed to press the brake pads on to the discs.

LUXURY COACH

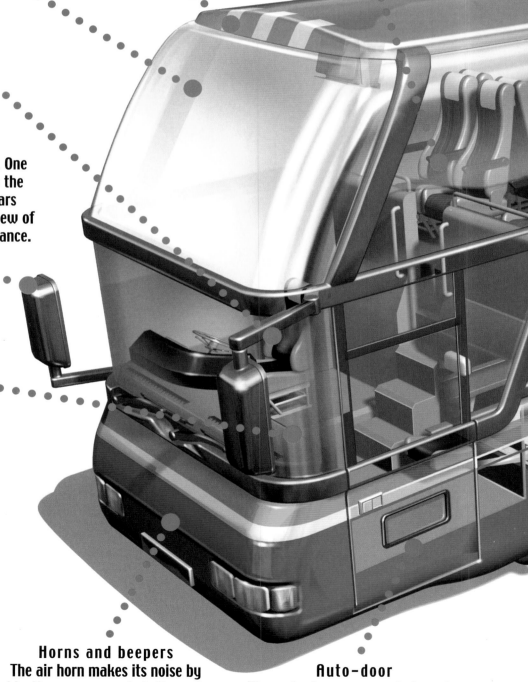

TV and video
A TV screen in the roof at the front shows live programmes or pre-recorded videos for in-coach entertainment. On a big coach there is a repeater screen or second monitor halfway along so the passengers at the back can see, too!

Control console
Like an airplane seat, the luxury coach seat has several controls in the armrest or overhead console. They include a personal reading light, fresh-air blower, socket and volume dial for headphones and a call button to attract the attendant's attention in case of problems.

All-around view
The upper half of the coach is panoramic with windows all around, so that passengers can enjoy the views.

Pilot?
The driver sits at a dashboard display that looks more like the controls of an airplane. There are dozens of buttons, dials and lights, with hi-tech gadgets such as satellite navigation and a direct two-way radio link to base.

Two-view mirrors
The rear view mirrors may have two parts. One shows the side of the coach in close-up so the driver can see passengers getting on or cars overtaking. The other gives a much wider view of the background to show vehicles in the distance.

Courier's seat
The guide or courier may sit in a small seat at the front near the driver. He or she is an expert on the area, speaks the local languages, points our places of interest and gives advice to the passengers.

KILLING TIME
Boredom is a big problem on long road journeys, especially through prairie regions where the only scenery is wheat! Some luxury coaches have fold-down tables in an 'office area' where passengers can work, read and use laptop computers (perhaps for games). There are also TV and videos to watch, radio and recorded music channels to listen to, and books, magazines or games consoles to borrow from the bus library.

Horns and beepers
The air horn makes its noise by blasting compressed air through a trumpet-shaped tube. It's loud! Also as the coach reverses, the warning beepers sound and the lights flash.

Auto-door
The main door opens and closes by hydraulic levers when the driver presses a button. It slides close to the coach's side so it does not knock passengers over.

DRIVER HOURS

All drivers of road PSVs (public service vehicles) such as buses, coaches and taxis have to obey strict guidelines. They can only drive for so many hours, then they must rest for a time. The coach is fitted with a 'tacho' or tachometer. An advanced tacho records the time, the distance the coach has travelled and its speed at various intervals on the route. If it is linked to the global satellite navigation system it can even record every road and turning of the journey! The tacho is in a sealed box and inspectors can examine it at any time to check that the driver is working safely.

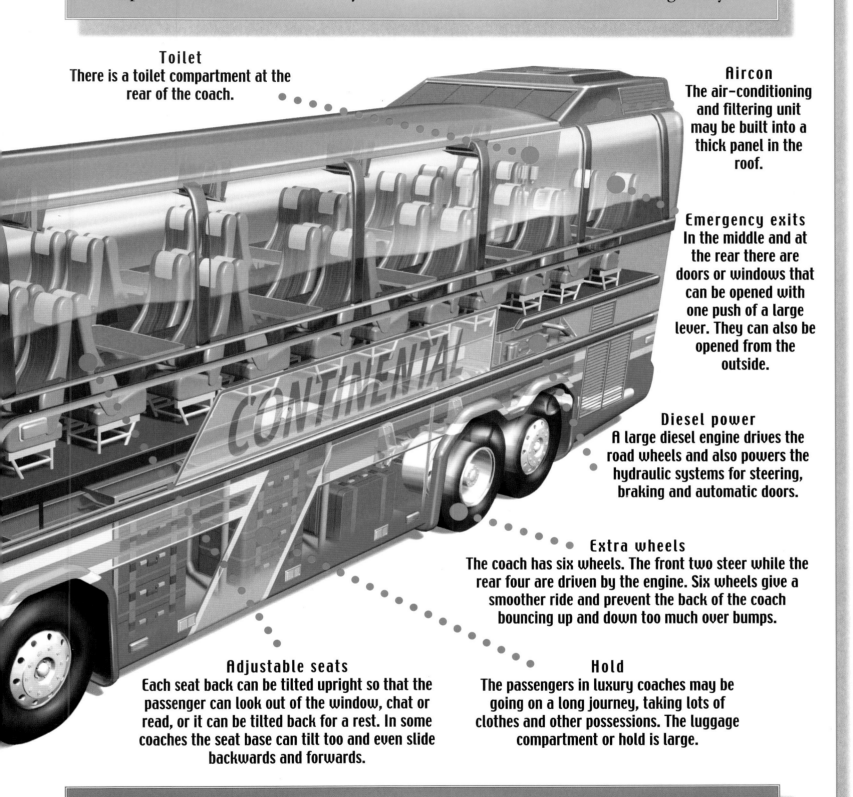

Toilet
There is a toilet compartment at the rear of the coach.

Aircon
The air-conditioning and filtering unit may be built into a thick panel in the roof.

Emergency exits
In the middle and at the rear there are doors or windows that can be opened with one push of a large lever. They can also be opened from the outside.

Diesel power
A large diesel engine drives the road wheels and also powers the hydraulic systems for steering, braking and automatic doors.

Extra wheels
The coach has six wheels. The front two steer while the rear four are driven by the engine. Six wheels give a smoother ride and prevent the back of the coach bouncing up and down too much over bumps.

Adjustable seats
Each seat back can be tilted upright so that the passenger can look out of the window, chat or read, or it can be tilted back for a rest. In some coaches the seat base can tilt too and even slide backwards and forwards.

Hold
The passengers in luxury coaches may be going on a long journey, taking lots of clothes and other possessions. The luggage compartment or hold is large.

FLY-DRIVE

Luxury coaches run many regular passenger routes. They are also hired by companies and organizations for outings or special business trips. Dance troupes, orchestras, rock bands and sports teams also use them. But why drive rather than fly? A coach can pick you up and deliver you to the door. It does not have to wait for air-traffic control clearance at take-off and landing. Passengers can get at their luggage easily. A coach is especially useful for hopping from city to nearby city. Even the best luxury coaches are less expensive than a plane or helicopter. And some people are afraid to fly!

STEAM LOCOMOTIVE

Boiler casing
The main casing is a huge tube or cylinder, a very strong shape to withstand the pressure of the boiling water and steam within. The main boiler section has combustion gas tubes running through it.

Chimney (stack)
This allows smoke and gases from the firebox, to escape into the air.

Superheated steam pipe
After the steam has passed through the superheating pipes it is collected by this larger pipe and taken down to the valves and piston below.

Smoke box
Smoke and hot gases from the firebox pass forwards and collect here before escaping through the chimney.

Combustion gas tubes
Bundles of tubes carry the extremely hot gases from combustion (burning) in the firebox, forwards through the water in the boiler. This heats the water to boiling point.

Valve gear
The valve slides backwards and then forwards to allow the high-pressure steam into one end of the cylinder and then the other.

Valve rod
This rod is linked to the crosshead below and the radius rod behind it. It is pushed to and fro to work the steam valve just in front.

Double acting piston
The piston and its rod slide to and fro inside their tubular case, the cylinder. The piston is alternately pushed from the front and then from the rear as superheated steam is let through by the valve above. This two-way working is called double action.

Crosshead
The crosshead joins the piston rod to the connecting rod and slides back and forth in guide grooves.

Main connecting rod
The 'con rod' is pushed to and fro at the front by the piston and its rod, and makes the central large wheel turn around at its rear end.

THE FIRST STEAM TRAINS

The very first railway trains were pulled by steam locomotives. They ran in the 1800s in England and carried mined coal and rocks. The first passenger steam trains were also hauled by steam locomotives, beginning in 1825 with the Stockton-Darlington railway in northeast England. During the 1830s railroads spread across Europe and North America. This was the Age of Steam. The locomotives were tough, fairly easy to build and maintain, and burned a variety of easily obtained fuels. But they were wasteful of energy since much of the heat escapes through the chimney and their smoke and sparks damaged the countryside.

Steam dome and collector
Steam from the boiling water in the boiler collects here and is forced down into the collector and onwards into the superheating pipes.

Superheating pipes
After steam has been collected in the steam dome it passes through these pipes, which carry it through the combustion gas tubes. This makes the steam even hotter or superheated.

Firebox
Solid fuel such as wood or coal burns to create tremendously hot gases that surge forwards through the combustion gas tubes in the boiler.

Fire door
The crew open this door to add more fuel to the fire, then quickly close it again.

Radius rod
Joined to the eccentric rod behind it by the expansion link, this is pushed to and fro as the wheel turns. It is also linked to the valve gear in front of it, which switches the steam from one side of the piston to the other.

Eccentric rod
Joined to the radius rod in front of it by the expansion link, this is pushed backwards and forwards as the wheel turns. With the radius rod it allows the driver to control the train's speed and also put the locomotive into reverse.

Drive link
This long beam with three pivots transmits the turning force of the central large wheel to the large wheels in front and behind it, so all three are driven and rotate at the same speed.

STEAM TRAINS TODAY

In the early twentieth century the Age of Steam began to fade. The first diesel trains were introduced in Germany in 1913. In the same year, diesel-electric trains came to Sweden and electric trains followed in 1915. But steam locomotives still puff along many of the world's railways. Some are strong and reliable workhorses in remote places where there is little modern engineering equipment to maintain complicated diesel engines and electric motors. Others are tourist attractions.

MOUNTAIN RAILWAY

Pantograph contact
The sliding bar contact picks up electricity from the current wire. The folding arm keeps the bar in good contact with the current wire to keep the electricity flowing and reduce sparks.

Suspension cable and current wire
A strong suspension cable holds up a current wire designed to carry the electric current.

Insulator
Ceramic insulators stop electricity from leaking down the pylon into the ground. They are shaped like stacked cones so that water and ice do not build up on them, causing a short circuit.

Passenger door
Passengers enter and leave by many doors along the side of the car. This makes station stops quicker.

HIGHER AND CHEAPER

Mountain railways are difficult to build and maintain. The track must be fairly straight and may have to be blasted out of the steep rock. It is a constant battle to keep snow and ice off the track and the overhead power wires often ice up, too. A cheaper alternative for some regions, especially tourist resorts and winter sports centres, is the cable car. This is not affected by snow and ice on the ground. It can't work in very windy or stormy weather, but few holidaymakers are out and about in these types of conditions!

Snow shovels
Angled blades push loose snow off the rails and out of the way as the car moves along.

De-icer
Chemical sprays remove ice from the track and rack so the car can keep moving even in very cold conditions.

Motor
The electric motor runs on current picked up from the overhead wire. Sets or trains of gears connect it to the rack drive cog and the main wheels of the car. In some types of electric locomotives the motor can help braking by altering the way electricity flows through it, so that it resists being turned rather than causing a turning motion. This is known as rheostatic braking, and adds to the general braking system so the car does not race away downhill.

Air horns
Very loud horns blow to scare animals off the track or to alert people to the train's approach.

OVER THE SNOW
In one type of cable car the cars are fixed to the cable, which moves around in an endless loop carrying all the cars with it. In another each car has a motor and its wheels move along the stationary cable.

Two cabs
When the train reaches the stop or station at the top of the line, the driver goes to the other end of the car and gets in the cab there, to drive it back down again.

Toothed rack
A strip or rack of teeth runs along the middle of the track between the rails. These are gripped by the rack drive cog on the underside of the train for non-slip propulsion.

Inclined track
The track slants at the same angle all the way up the line. Otherwise the drive cog would not grip the rack.

Wheel cog
This gear wheel is rotated by the motor and in turn makes the main drive wheel spin around. It can also be used as part of the braking system.

Rack drive cog
The teeth of this gear wheel fit between the teeth of the track rack to haul the car up the slope.

SUBWAY TRAIN

GOING UNDERGROUND

The first underground railway system or subway opened in London, England in 1863. The trains were hauled by steam locomotives so they were noisy, smoky and sooty. The tunnels were more like shallow trenches with roofs, which had ventilation shafts along the route. As electricity took over, the London system was converted and many other cities followed.

Subways carry people quickly and avoid the traffic jams and bad weather at ground level. But the tunnels and the elevators or lifts to take people down to the stations are expensive to build. The longest subway network is the London Underground with over 400 kilometres (250 miles) of track, about 190 kilometres (120 miles) actually under ground level.

Traction motor
Each wheel has its own electric motor that turns it around to move the train forward. The motors of all the wheels are linked by electric control circuits so that they all turn at the same speed.

Headlight
The driver can see ahead in the dark tunnel using the headlights, to look out for objects on the track or other problems.

Buffer
These metal discs have hydraulic pistons or strong springs behind them. They are the first part of the train to bump into an object on the line, such as another train, and they absorb or buffer the shock of impact. If they are fitted at each end of each car they also stop the cars in the train from banging into one another as they move along.

Electrified rail
This rail carries electric current to power the train's traction motors, as well as the lights, brakes, ventilation fans, two-way radio and other electrical systems.

Sleeper
Sleepers are wooden or concrete beams bedded into the ground under the track. They give firm, level support to the track and spread the train's weight along the rails and into the ground as it passes.

Hanging rail
Passengers who have to stand can hold on to this rail near the roof, so that they do not fall as the train sways around corners or stops suddenly in an emergency.

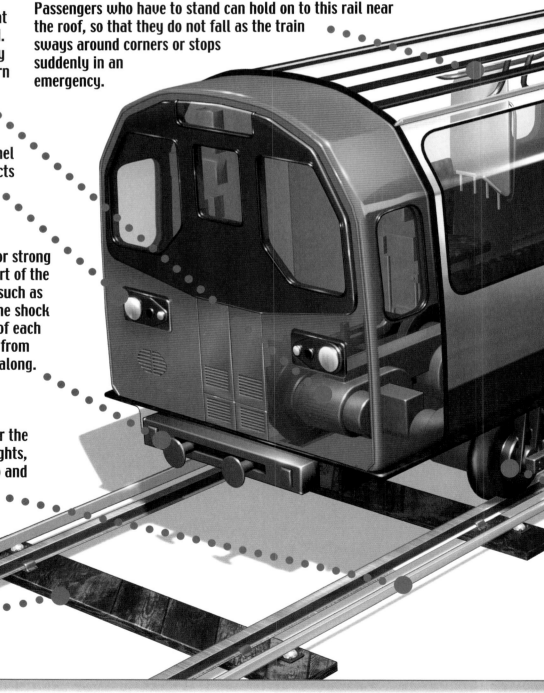

HOW MANY RAILS?

The subway shown here has four rails. The train runs on two. The electricity comes in along a live current rail on one side, and is carried away along the neutral current rail on the other side. Other designs have just one live current rail, called the 'third rail'. They use the running rails to carry the electricity away again.

Every section of track has sensors that monitor how much electricity is passing along the rails. If there is a sudden surge, perhaps due to an accident, the current is switched off within a fraction of a second.

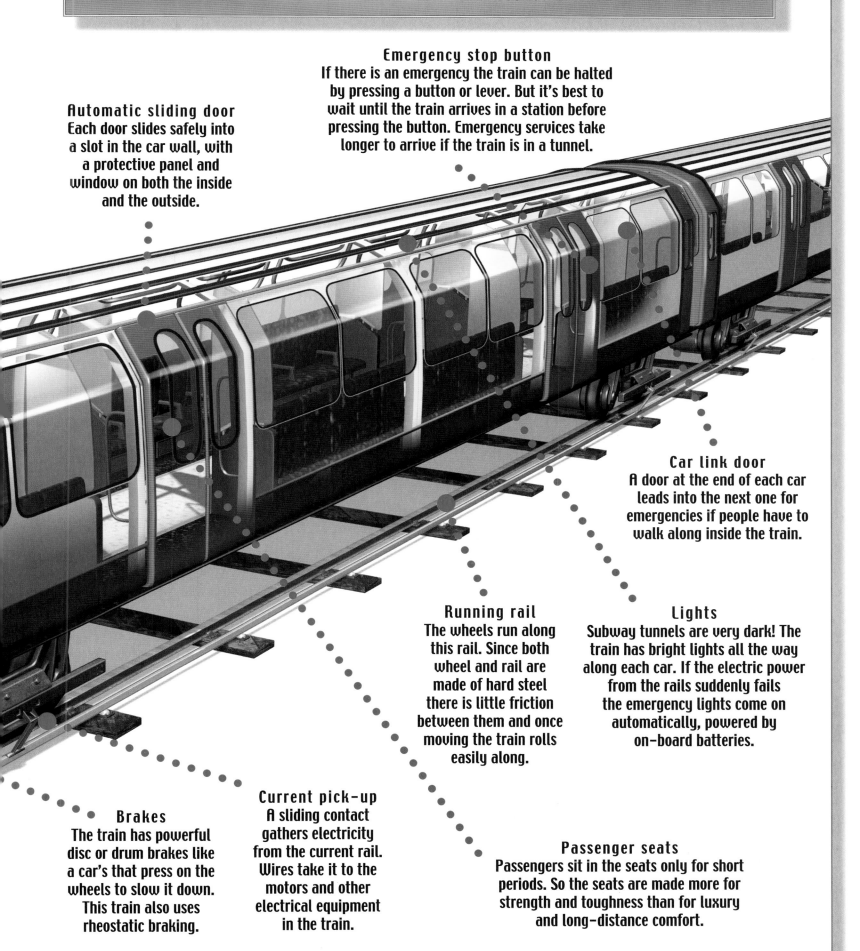

Automatic sliding door
Each door slides safely into a slot in the car wall, with a protective panel and window on both the inside and the outside.

Emergency stop button
If there is an emergency the train can be halted by pressing a button or lever. But it's best to wait until the train arrives in a station before pressing the button. Emergency services take longer to arrive if the train is in a tunnel.

Car link door
A door at the end of each car leads into the next one for emergencies if people have to walk along inside the train.

Running rail
The wheels run along this rail. Since both wheel and rail are made of hard steel there is little friction between them and once moving the train rolls easily along.

Lights
Subway tunnels are very dark! The train has bright lights all the way along each car. If the electric power from the rails suddenly fails the emergency lights come on automatically, powered by on-board batteries.

Brakes
The train has powerful disc or drum brakes like a car's that press on the wheels to slow it down. This train also uses rheostatic braking.

Current pick-up
A sliding contact gathers electricity from the current rail. Wires take it to the motors and other electrical equipment in the train.

Passenger seats
Passengers sit in the seats only for short periods. So the seats are made more for strength and toughness than for luxury and long-distance comfort.

TGV

Suspension (catenary) cable
This cable holds and supports the current wire below it. The suspension cable is made of metals designed to withstand the strain of hanging and being blown about by the wind. The current wire is less strong but made of metals able to carry or conduct electricity very well.

Current (power or trolley) wire
This carries the very high voltages of electric current picked up by the train as it passes below. The current strength may be 25,000 volts or more – 100 times the strength of normal household mains electricity.

Pylon
Tall towers made of steel or concrete beams hold up the electric power lines.

Driver's cab
The driver's display monitors the conditions in the electrical circuits, motors and other equipment. It also monitors the brakes, automatic doors and other machinery further back in the passenger cars.

Drive gear train
Gear wheels slow down the spinning motion of the traction motors and make it more powerful to turn the drive wheels of the power car.

Wheels
Railway wheels have flanges on the inside that project down on to the inner side of the rail, so the wheel does not slip off the rail.

STRAIGHT AHEAD
High-speed trains must have even straighter tracks than normal trains, with very gradual curves, or they would tip over as they went around corners.

FASTER TRAINS
Modern electric passenger trains whizz through city and countryside at tremendous speed. The French TGV (*train à grande vitesse* or very fast train) has reached 515 kph (320 mph) on a special speed run. Other high-speed services that reach 300 kph (190 mph) include Eurostar between England and Continental Europe through the Channel Tunnel, ICE in Germany and the Shinkansen or Bullet trains in Japan.

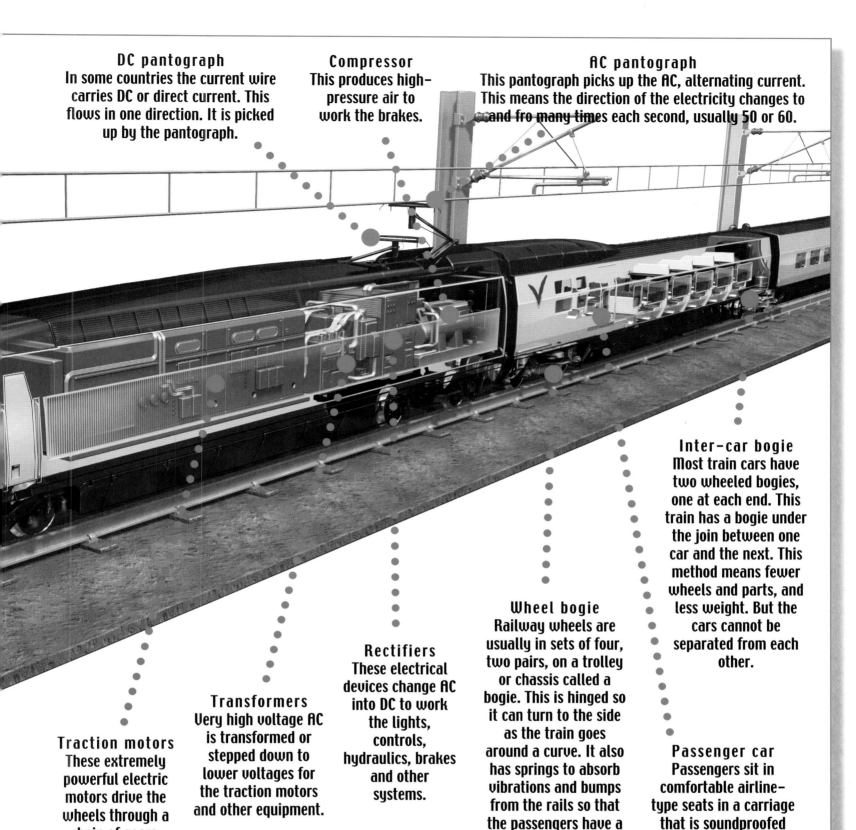

DC pantograph
In some countries the current wire carries DC or direct current. This flows in one direction. It is picked up by the pantograph.

Compressor
This produces high-pressure air to work the brakes.

AC pantograph
This pantograph picks up the AC, alternating current. This means the direction of the electricity changes to and fro many times each second, usually 50 or 60.

Inter-car bogie
Most train cars have two wheeled bogies, one at each end. This train has a bogie under the join between one car and the next. This method means fewer wheels and parts, and less weight. But the cars cannot be separated from each other.

Wheel bogie
Railway wheels are usually in sets of four, two pairs, on a trolley or chassis called a bogie. This is hinged so it can turn to the side as the train goes around a curve. It also has springs to absorb vibrations and bumps from the rails so that the passengers have a smooth ride.

Rectifiers
These electrical devices change AC into DC to work the lights, controls, hydraulics, brakes and other systems.

Transformers
Very high voltage AC is transformed or stepped down to lower voltages for the traction motors and other equipment.

Traction motors
These extremely powerful electric motors drive the wheels through a chain of gears.

Passenger car
Passengers sit in comfortable airline-type seats in a carriage that is soundproofed and air-conditioned.

LOCOMOTIVES

A train is made up of a locomotive, also known as a power car or traction unit, pulling passenger cars, goods (cargo) wagons and other units behind it.
The locomotive or pulling part is powered in various ways:

- By steam power.

- A diesel locomotive or unit has a diesel engine that drives the wheels through a gearbox. It can be heard changing gear like a car.

- A diesel-electric locomotive has a diesel engine that drives an alternator or generator to make electricity, which is fed to electric motors that turn the wheels. Electric motors work well at all speeds, so a gearbox is not needed.

- An electric locomotive uses only electric motors, as in the train shown here.

MONORAIL

Articulations
The train has joints or articulations where it can bend as it goes around curves. These have flexible seals or gaskets.

WHAT'S A MONORAIL?

The 'mono' of monorail means there is only one rail or guide track, instead of the usual two for an ordinary train. This makes the track easier and faster to construct and install.

Monorails carry lots of people quickly over short distances in a busy city. They are quiet, reliable and non-polluting. They must also be able to speed up and slow down quickly between close-together stations or stops.

Pylons
The pylons hold up the track so that it can pass over the city's roads, pavements, canals, public spaces and even low buildings.

Wide aisles
Most monorails take passengers on short trips through cities, like the subway train. More passengers can fit in if they stand in the wide central areas rather than sit. There is also plenty of floor space and perhaps shelved cupboards for suitcases and other luggage.

RMTS

RMTs – rapid mass transits – come in all shapes and sizes:

- Subway or underground trains run below the city.

- Light railways are smaller, lighter versions of a normal railway train, with the usual two tracks.

- The saddlebag-type monorail shown here sits on top of its guide track and uses central wheels for propulsion.

- Other monorails are suspended, that is, the train hangs below the track or beamway. The train's wheels and motors fit inside the hollow beamway.

- Maglev ('magnetic levitation') trains have no wheels. The train floats above the track, pushed up by sets of powerful magnets in the track and train. However, maglev trains have proved too expensive to be practical.

Automatic sliding doors
The doors slide sideways along the car walls so that passengers are not pushed out of the way as they open and close. A safety device in the cab warns the driver if they are not all closed properly, so the train cannot move off.

Driver's cab
Some monorails do not actually need a driver. There are enough computers, signals, radio links, safety devices and backup systems for the driver's cab to remain empty. But most passengers like the reassurance of a real person driving the train.

Signal warnings
On some monorails the signals are not only coloured lights, such as green for go and red for stop, but also radio signals. These beam from trackside boxes and are picked up by the train's receiver and fed into the computer and display.

Controls
The train's controls are monitored by the on-board computer. If the signals are set at stop and the driver tries to continue, the computer flashes and sounds a warning and then takes action itself.

Safety handle
If the driver becomes ill or is injured, he or she lets go of a handle which should be pressed at all times. This automatically stops the train.

Running wheels
The train's weight is taken by running wheels driven by electric motors. The wheels have rubber tyres so that they run quietly and smoothly.

Guide wheels
Rubber-rimmed wheels on either side of the track press against its sides. They keep the train steady and stop it rubbing along the central track or swaying from side to side.

Rubber guides
The wheels press on hard rubber guide linings to reduce noise and vibration even further.

Single track
This track is made from pre-stressed reinforced concrete beams or sections – concrete with reinforcing rods of steel inside to give extra strength and slight flexibility.

Power
Electricity for the motors, doors, brakes and other systems can be gathered by sliding contacts from wires in the track or carried on board as rechargeable batteries.

GOING TO THE SHOW
Smaller-scale monorails and RMTs of various kinds are used in theme parks, airports, seaports, sports stadia, wildlife parks, exhibition centres and big shopping malls. They are purpose-built to carry people between the main event areas and the car parks, ordinary rail stations and other sites.

JETSKI

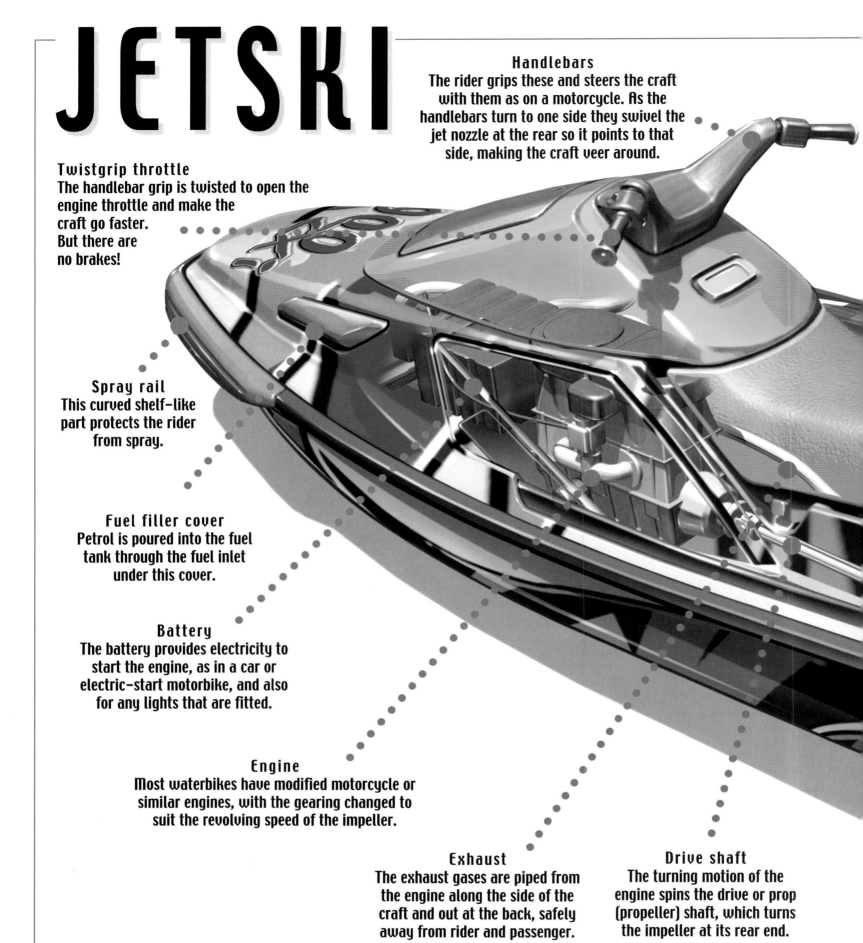

Handlebars
The rider grips these and steers the craft with them as on a motorcycle. As the handlebars turn to one side they swivel the jet nozzle at the rear so it points to that side, making the craft veer around.

Twistgrip throttle
The handlebar grip is twisted to open the engine throttle and make the craft go faster. But there are no brakes!

Spray rail
This curved shelf–like part protects the rider from spray.

Fuel filler cover
Petrol is poured into the fuel tank through the fuel inlet under this cover.

Battery
The battery provides electricity to start the engine, as in a car or electric–start motorbike, and also for any lights that are fitted.

Engine
Most waterbikes have modified motorcycle or similar engines, with the gearing changed to suit the revolving speed of the impeller.

Exhaust
The exhaust gases are piped from the engine along the side of the craft and out at the back, safely away from rider and passenger.

Drive shaft
The turning motion of the engine spins the drive or prop (propeller) shaft, which turns the impeller at its rear end.

TRICKS AND STUNTS

The jetski lends itself to all kinds of tricky riding and exciting stunts. Experts can make the craft leap out of the water and spin around in mid air, or ride up a waterski ramp and turn a somersault. Races are held around marker buoys, often with a line of buoys close together when the rider has to slalom or zig-zag between them. In the group of manoeuvres called 'submarines' the rider makes the craft tilt nose-up, bounce into the air and then dive nose-down under the surface, still holding on. He or she can even turn while submerged and pop up some distance away.

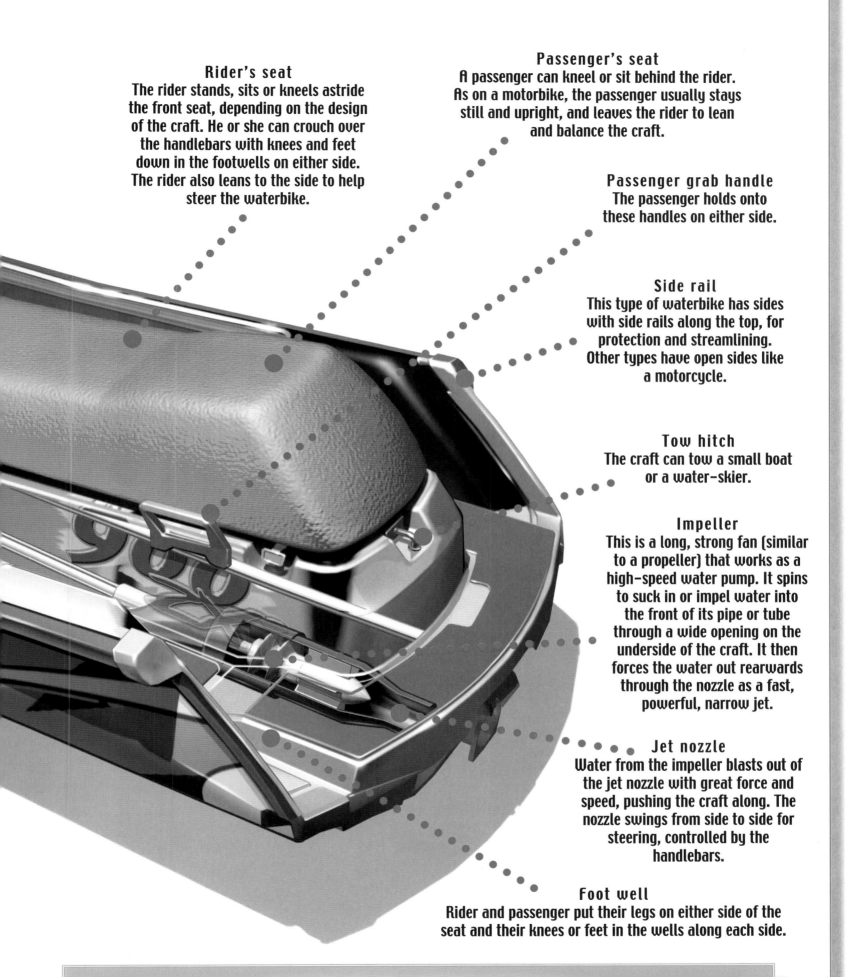

Rider's seat
The rider stands, sits or kneels astride the front seat, depending on the design of the craft. He or she can crouch over the handlebars with knees and feet down in the footwells on either side. The rider also leans to the side to help steer the waterbike.

Passenger's seat
A passenger can kneel or sit behind the rider. As on a motorbike, the passenger usually stays still and upright, and leaves the rider to lean and balance the craft.

Passenger grab handle
The passenger holds onto these handles on either side.

Side rail
This type of waterbike has sides with side rails along the top, for protection and streamlining. Other types have open sides like a motorcycle.

Tow hitch
The craft can tow a small boat or a water-skier.

Impeller
This is a long, strong fan (similar to a propeller) that works as a high-speed water pump. It spins to suck in or impel water into the front of its pipe or tube through a wide opening on the underside of the craft. It then forces the water out rearwards through the nozzle as a fast, powerful, narrow jet.

Jet nozzle
Water from the impeller blasts out of the jet nozzle with great force and speed, pushing the craft along. The nozzle swings from side to side for steering, controlled by the handlebars.

Foot well
Rider and passenger put their legs on either side of the seat and their knees or feet in the wells along each side.

A NEW TYPE OF WATER CRAFT

Jetskis are like water skis with motorbike handles and seats, powered by a waterjet. They are also known as waterbikes or PWC, personal water craft. They were developed in the late 1960s by American motorcycle racer Clay Jacobson and the Japanese Kawasaki motorbike company. Their idea was to combine a motorbike, snowmobile and water skis into a one-person water vehicle that was fun to ride and race, and didn't cause injuries if the rider fell off. The first craft went on sale in 1973.

OFFSHORE POWERBOAT

Cockpit
The driver and co-driver sit in the cockpit with an array of dials, switches, buttons and screens in front of them. They rely on these instruments because the waves and spray mean they can often see little.

Strengthened hull
The offshore powerboat is a brutal machine. It smashes through the ocean waves at speeds of over 150 kph (90 mph). The main body or hull must be light yet extremely strong to withstand the battering, since waves at this speed are like hammer blows. The hull is usually made of aluminium or carbon fibre composite.

Spray rail
This lip or shelf along the hull pushes most of the spray and water aside so it does not break over the boat itself.

THE RACE

Powerboat races may be around a marked-out course or across the open sea from one town or island to another. This type of racing looks glamorous but it is very tiring and stressful.

SAFETY FIRST

Speeding powerboats don't lie in the water and push it aside. They plane or skim over the surface. Only the very rear parts with the screws and rudders dip into the water. However, the boat can't avoid tall waves, and these produce huge shocks as they hit. For this reason the crew must be fit and tough. The driver steers the powerboat, using satellite navigation and many other electronic aids. The co-driver controls the speed of the engines using their throttles and adjusts the boat's trim. Both crew are attached to a 'kill switch' by long cords. If they are accidentally thrown out of their seats the kill switch stops the engine so that the powerboat does not race away out of control across the sea.

F1 BOATS

Offshore powerboats have incredible strength and power for racing across the open sea. And just as Formula One is the top level for racing cars around a special track, Formula One powerboats (smaller than the boat shown here) are the top level on water. They race in sheltered waters around marker buoys, following a course similar to a Formula 1 car circuit, for 50–60 laps. They are small and streamlined catamarans – two long, slim hulls side by side under the main body. F1 boats have outboard engines, fixed on by a hinged bracket at the back. They can reach speeds of more than 250 kph (150 mph).

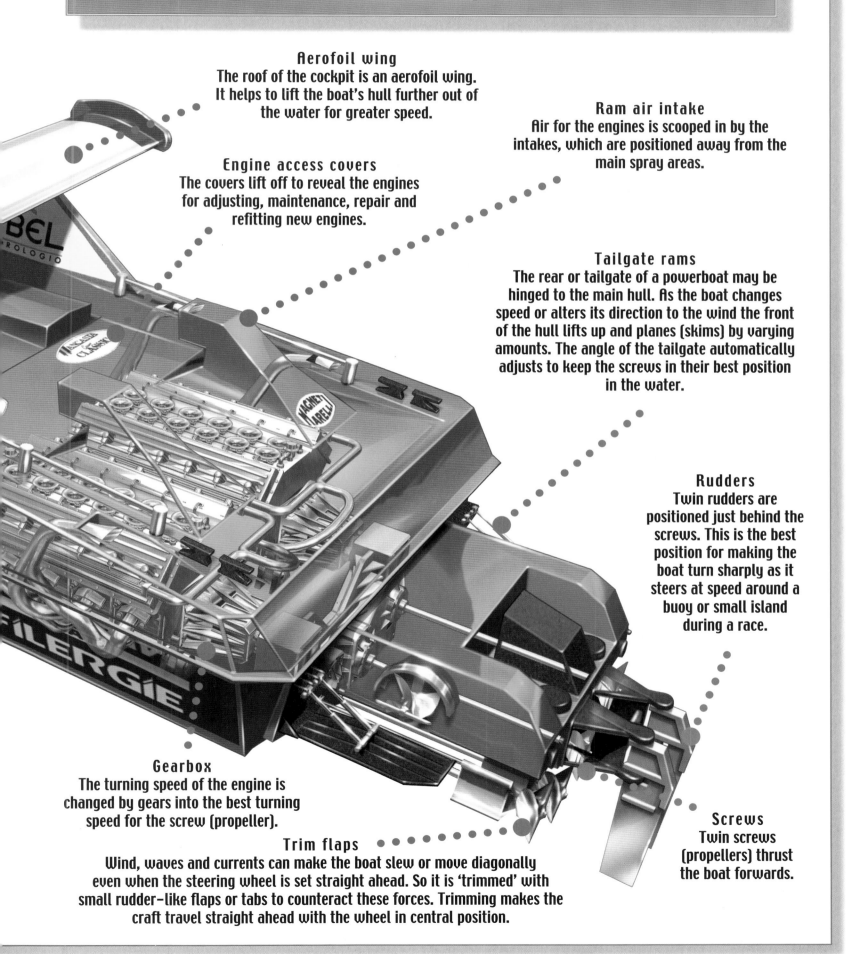

Aerofoil wing
The roof of the cockpit is an aerofoil wing. It helps to lift the boat's hull further out of the water for greater speed.

Ram air intake
Air for the engines is scooped in by the intakes, which are positioned away from the main spray areas.

Engine access covers
The covers lift off to reveal the engines for adjusting, maintenance, repair and refitting new engines.

Tailgate rams
The rear or tailgate of a powerboat may be hinged to the main hull. As the boat changes speed or alters its direction to the wind the front of the hull lifts up and planes (skims) by varying amounts. The angle of the tailgate automatically adjusts to keep the screws in their best position in the water.

Rudders
Twin rudders are positioned just behind the screws. This is the best position for making the boat turn sharply as it steers at speed around a buoy or small island during a race.

Gearbox
The turning speed of the engine is changed by gears into the best turning speed for the screw (propeller).

Screws
Twin screws (propellers) thrust the boat forwards.

Trim flaps
Wind, waves and currents can make the boat slew or move diagonally even when the steering wheel is set straight ahead. So it is 'trimmed' with small rudder-like flaps or tabs to counteract these forces. Trimming makes the craft travel straight ahead with the wheel in central position.

RACING YACHT

Mast
This is a square tube of aluminium alloy, very light but also extremely strong. It holds up the mainsail and jib.

Jib
The jib catches the wind to help propel the yacht along and directs it on to the mainsail too.

Hi-speed winch
Turning the handles of the hi-speed winch pulls on or releases the line to raise or lower the sail.

Jib boom
The boom runs along the bottom or foot of the jib and holds it stretched out.

Jib sheet
This line allows the jib boom to swing to the side by a certain amount so that the jib can best catch the wind.

Side rail
Unlike on most boats, crew members have to move around the yacht's deck even when travelling at full speed in high wind and crashing waves. The rails keep them safely on the boat. They may also be attached by a safety line.

Bunks
The crew members work a shift or rota system and catch up with sleep in the bunks or beds.

SAILING TECHNIQUE
With the sail set at an angle, the boat can sail diagonally into the wind, which is known as tacking. The sailor follows this direction for a distance then swings the sail around to the other side so the craft tacks the other way into the wind. In this way the boat zig-zags into or against the wind. Sailing across or at right angles to the wind is known as reaching. This is the best way to trap the wind and create the sail aerofoil for maximum speed. Sailing in the same direction as the wind, with the sail at right angles to the boat, is called running. Oddly it is the slowest way to sail – you can never move faster than the wind's own speed.

SUCKED ALONG

Wind blows on to the large area of the sail and pushes it, and the boat, along. But sailing is far more complicated than this. The wind bows or bends the sail into a curved shape when seen from above. The curve works like the aerofoil of an airplane's wing to create lower air pressure in front of the sail and higher pressure behind. This means the sail is partly sucked along rather than pushed.

TG-3485

Mainsail
Sails are made of various materials, such as nylon or terylene. They are airproof so they don't let wind through and tearproof so any small nick or cut does not grow.

Wheel
This large wheel can be turned to swing the rudder and help steer the boat.

Aft or main boom
This long strut or pole runs along the bottom of the mainsail and holds its lower edge or foot out straight. It swings outward to either side under the control of a rope or line called the mainsheet.

Cockpit
The steering wheel or helm and main controls and dials are in the middle of the boat towards the rear, where the helmsperson can see the position of the sails and how the wind blows at them.

Vent
This opening allows stale air to leave the living and sleeping quarters.

Main cabin
The crew rest and eat here. There is also a table with maps and charts laid out for navigation.

Auxiliary power
Most yachts have a small engine that turns a screw to drive the craft slowly along. This is useful not only when there is a flat calm, but also for manoeuvring between other boats and when tying up in a port.

Keel
The large flange or keel sticking down from the bottom of the hull stops the yacht from capsizing. It also helps to keep the yacht moving in a straight line as it leans with the wind.

Rudder
The wheel controls the rudder, making it swing left or right to steer the yacht.

CRUISE LINER

Restaurant
Many cruise liners serve excellent food and drinks. In addition to the main restaurant there are also fast-food outlets, snack bars and cafes. You can get a meal or drink any time of day or night.

Bulkhead
A bulkhead is a wall or partition across a boat or ship from side to side. In case of accident the doors and other openings in it can be closed to make it watertight.

Patio deck
Loungers, sun chairs and tables near the restaurant and bar area are for eating, drinking, chatting and enjoying the view.

Pool deck
There's no shortage of water – the swimming pool is topped up from the sea. Of course, the water is filtered and treated with germ-killing chemicals first!

Sun deck
As the liner speeds along, the front end is very windy but the rear deck is usually sheltered. Passengers can laze here out of the breeze.

Rudder
This moveable flap steers the ship. If it swings to the left the water pushes against it and makes the rear of the liner move to the right, swinging the whole liner to the left.

Screw
As the screw or propeller turns it forces water backwards past its angled blades and so pushes the ship forwards.

Engine room
The massive diesel or gas turbine engines are deep in the rear of the liner. Their noise and vibrations are insulated or cut off from the rest of the ship. The heat from the exhaust gases is used for the ship's heating system before the gases are sent through the funnel to the open air.

THE 'BIG SHOP'

A cruise liner for about 2,000 passengers may have almost 1,000 crew to look after them and the ship. That's 3,000 people to feed and supply with drinks. The ship must take plenty of supplies in case the engines fail and it's late back to port. An average shopping list for a two-week voyage might include:

- 12 tonnes (12 tons) of potatoes, pasta and rice
- 25 tonnes (25 tons) of vegetables
- 40 tonnes (40 tons) of fresh fruit
- 25 tonnes (25 tons) of meat and fish
- 30,000 bottles of wine
- 34,000 litres (60,000 pints) of beer and lager

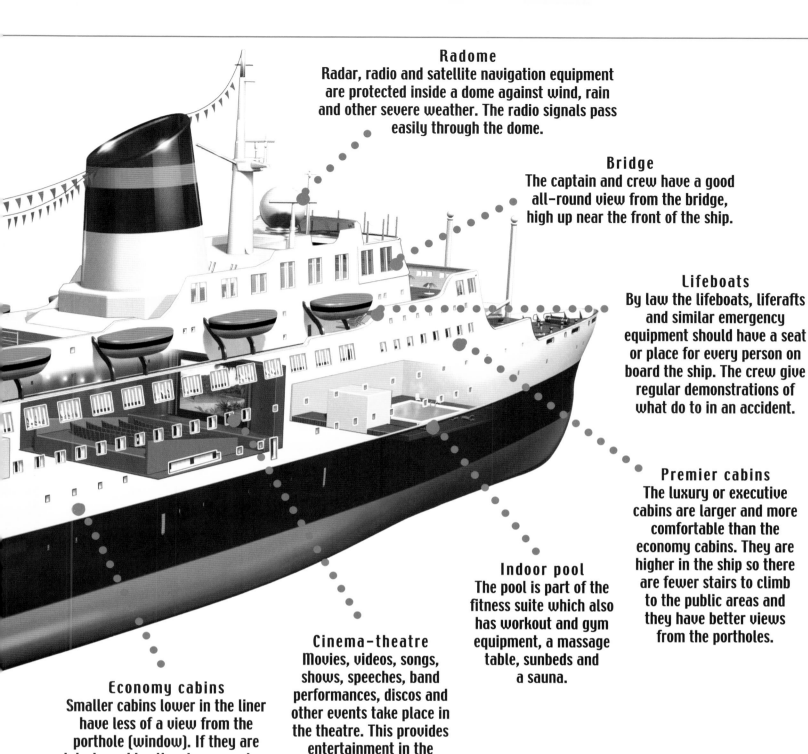

Radome
Radar, radio and satellite navigation equipment are protected inside a dome against wind, rain and other severe weather. The radio signals pass easily through the dome.

Bridge
The captain and crew have a good all-round view from the bridge, high up near the front of the ship.

Lifeboats
By law the lifeboats, liferafts and similar emergency equipment should have a seat or place for every person on board the ship. The crew give regular demonstrations of what do to in an accident.

Premier cabins
The luxury or executive cabins are larger and more comfortable than the economy cabins. They are higher in the ship so there are fewer stairs to climb to the public areas and they have better views from the portholes.

Indoor pool
The pool is part of the fitness suite which also has workout and gym equipment, a massage table, sunbeds and a sauna.

Cinema-theatre
Movies, videos, songs, shows, speeches, band performances, discos and other events take place in the theatre. This provides entertainment in the evenings or when the weather is poor.

Economy cabins
Smaller cabins lower in the liner have less of a view from the porthole (window). If they are interior cabins they have no view at all! This is why they cost less than the premier cabins.

THE FALL AND RISE OF THE CRUISE LINER

During the early twentieth century, when few people travelled by air, the cruise liner was very popular. It was a floating hotel that took holidaymakers to faraway places, which they visited from the liner by boarding smaller boats.

With the rise of jetliners, package holidays and car hire in the mid-twentieth century, people became more adventurous travellers. Cruise ships seemed slow and restricted. You had to go where the captain took you, and for days at a time you were stuck on board with only a limited amount to see and do.

However, the early twenty-first century has seen a revival in luxury cruising, with some of the biggest and best-equipped new ships ever. They are more like floating town centres than floating hotels. Now more than 10 million people enjoy pleasure cruises every year.

HYDROFOIL

HYDROFOIL FERRIES

Around the world, hydrofoil ferries take passengers on short, fast trips. The larger ones carry 300 passengers at speeds of more than 60 kph (40 mph). Jet hydrofoils or jetfoils have water jets or turbines instead of screws. Hydrofoils are especially useful for carrying people between the mainland and nearby islands.

Wheel house
This is where the controls are sited. They are a combination of those from a ship, an airplane and a car.

Wheel
As in a normal boat, the wheel makes the rudder at the rear of the craft swing from side to side for steering at low speed. It also twists the front hydrofoil and its struts from side to side for steering at high speed.

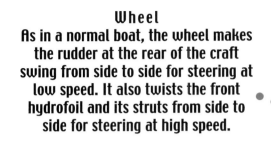

Bow mooring cleats
Ropes or lines from the shore are tied around these cleats when the hydrofoil comes alongside its mooring place or berth, lowering in the water as it slows down.

Hull
The hull sits in the water at low speed but rises above it into the air on the hydrofoil struts as the craft picks up speed.

BOAT ON SKIS

The hydrofoil is an underwater wing. It works in the same way as an airplane wing or aerofoil. Its shape is curved from front to back on top, and flatter from front to back on the underside. As the foil moves forwards, water must flow further over the longer curved upper surface than underneath. So water moves faster above the foil than below. This faster flow creates less pressure above the foil, with the result that the foil is sucked upwards by a force called lift. At high speed the lift is enough to raise the whole craft out of the water. This greatly reduces the water friction or drag along the hull, which slows down a normal boat. It also makes for a smoother ride. But hydrofoils cannot travel in big waves and stormy conditions.

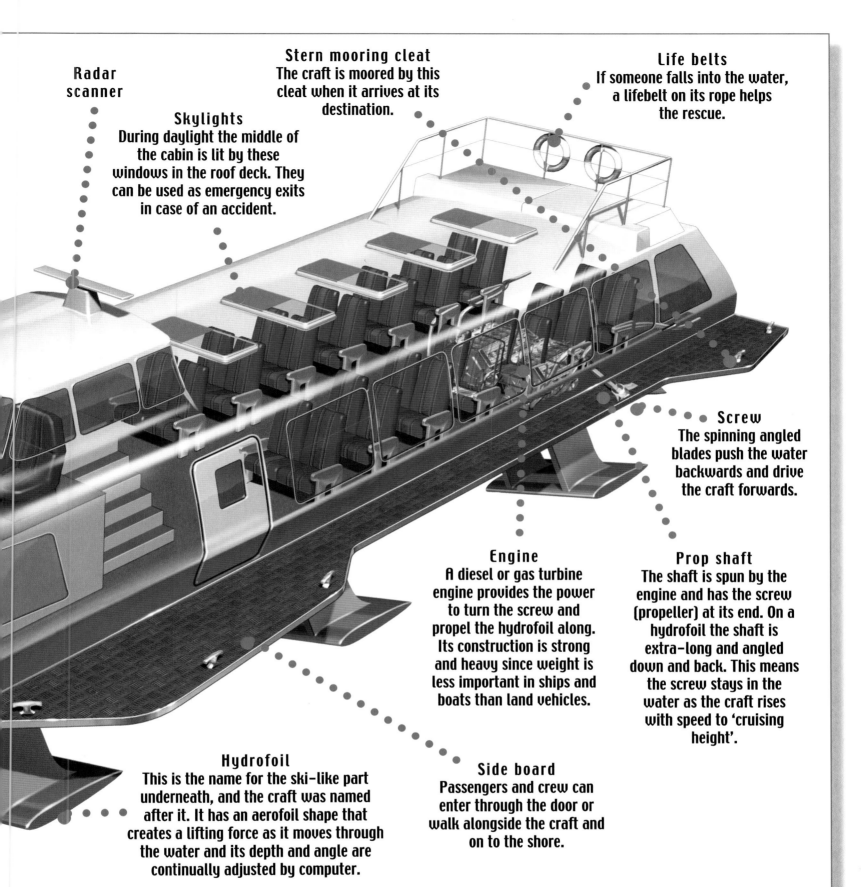

Radar scanner

Skylights
During daylight the middle of the cabin is lit by these windows in the roof deck. They can be used as emergency exits in case of an accident.

Stern mooring cleat
The craft is moored by this cleat when it arrives at its destination.

Life belts
If someone falls into the water, a lifebelt on its rope helps the rescue.

Screw
The spinning angled blades push the water backwards and drive the craft forwards.

Engine
A diesel or gas turbine engine provides the power to turn the screw and propel the hydrofoil along. Its construction is strong and heavy since weight is less important in ships and boats than land vehicles.

Prop shaft
The shaft is spun by the engine and has the screw (propeller) at its end. On a hydrofoil the shaft is extra-long and angled down and back. This means the screw stays in the water as the craft rises with speed to 'cruising height'.

Hydrofoil
This is the name for the ski-like part underneath, and the craft was named after it. It has an aerofoil shape that creates a lifting force as it moves through the water and its depth and angle are continually adjusted by computer.

Side board
Passengers and crew can enter through the door or walk alongside the craft and on to the shore.

HI-TECH HYDROFOILS

The type of hydrofoil shown here is called a submerged-foil. The whole of each hydrofoil stays under the water. Because the foils are not as wide as the boat, there is a risk of the craft tipping over on its side. 'Pingers' along the underside of the craft beam ultrasonic clicks down on to the water surface, which reflects them back to sensors. (This system, called sound-radar or sonar, is also used to measure the depth of the sea-bed, and by bats to fly in the dark.) The on-board computer continually measures the height of the craft and its angle or tilt from front to back and side to side. It then adjusts the angle or tilt of the foils so the craft stays steady and safe.

HOVERCRAFT

Drive propeller shroud
The drive prop is contained in a large tube-shaped shroud. This protects it and makes its turning force more efficient by preventing air from spilling out to the sides.

Drive propellers
These propellers push the hovercraft along. The craft is steered by slowing the propeller on one side compared to the other and also by moving the rudders.

Drive propeller engines
Gas turbine engines are used to power the drive propellers and lift fans. They work in a similar way to jet engines, burning fuel into hot gases. These rush through a fan-shaped turbine with angled blades, making it spin on its shaft.

Belt drive
A flexible endless rubber belt transfers the turning power from the engine shaft to the drive propeller or airscrew.

Rudders
The moveable rudders of a hovercraft work in the same way as those on a plane or boat. They push or deflect the air to one side and make the craft swing around for steering.

Skirt
The tough, flexible rubberized skirt holds air from the lift fans underneath to push the craft upwards. The air makes the skirt balloon out and then spills out around the bottom of the skirt.

Stern side door
Passengers board or embark and leave or disembark through this door.

Lift fan
Large cylinder-like fans suck air from above the craft down through the lift fan air intakes. Then they push it out with great force below the craft, to force it away from the ground or water.

Lift fan air intake
Huge amounts of air flow down through these large intakes towards the lift fans.

Lift fan engine
The lift fans are powered by one or more gas turbine engines under the floor of the passenger cabin.

RIDING ON AIR

Hovercraft and similar craft are known as ACVs, air-cushioned vehicles. Air is pumped to the underneath by large lift fans, where it is partly trapped under a flexible all-around skirt. The increased air pressure below lifts the craft into the air by a small amount. This allows it to move along almost without friction on its cushion of air. The extra power needed to lift the craft is offset by the reduced power needed to move it along. However, the air continually spills out from the lower edge of the skirt so it must be constantly topped up by the lift fans. The first model hovercraft were designed by English inventor Christopher Cockerill in the mid-1950s. The first full-sized hovercraft began its test 'flights' in 1959.

Radio antennae
The crew keep in touch with their base on shore, with other vessels in the area and with satellite navigation via these radio aerials.

Passenger cabin
This hovercraft carries about 50 passengers who sit in airline-type reclining seats. Some hovercraft can take more than 500 passengers.

USEFUL HOVERERS

Hovercraft are especially useful because they can travel over smooth ground and over water. So they do not need to moor at a port or berth. They can glide from the water up a ramp or even on to the beach. This makes loading cars much easier. They can also travel over water that is too shallow or rocky below the surface for boats. The largest hovercrafts weigh more than 300 tonnes (294 tons) and carry more than 400 passengers and 60 cars. They have four gas turbine engines, each 50 times the power of a normal car engine, and cruise at about 140 kph (90 mph) – the fastest large sea-going craft in the world.

But the hovercraft has limits. It has hardly any contact with the ground or water so it can be difficult to steer, and it is pushed about by high winds and rough seas.

Flight deck
Hovercraft are usually run and organized like airplanes rather than boats. The control area where the captain and main crew sit is known as the flight deck rather than the bridge or wheelhouse.

Bow door
This leads to the front area of the cabin and may be used by staff only or as an emergency exit.

Buffer
The skirt acts as a bumper or buffer if the craft is in danger of hitting a wall or or boat.

Life raft
Inflatable life rafts are packed into barrel-like containers. They are easily accessible and at the pull of a lever the raft automatically inflates.

BIG DOORS

Some vehicle ferries have large doors, usually at the bow (front) or stern (rear), that fold down to make ramps for loading the cars, vans and trucks.

SUPERTANKER

THE GIANT IN PORT

Supertankers are so vast and awkward to manoeuvre that they do not come into small harbours. Large terminals are built for them where there is plenty of room and the water is deeper. Small, powerful tug boats push them into position.

Crew gangway
Crew members can quickly reach any part of the deck along the gangways. Often they use bicycles, since the whole ship may be more than 300 metres (800 feet) long.

Pipes
A maze of pipes connects the various tanks and pumps with the connectors for loading or unloading the oil.

Pumps
Various pumps force the oil into the tanks when loading at the oil production platform. They suck it out again when the supertanker reaches its destination – the oil refinery or storage depot.

Mooring winches
Thick cables or hawsers are used to moor the ship against its platform or terminal. They are pulled in by powerful winches and stored below deck on the voyage.

NEDLLOYD ROUEN

Anchor
The huge anchor is lowered to the sea-bed when the supertanker needs to stay in the same place but cannot moor or tie up. The thrusters and main screws may also be used to keep the ship still or 'on station'.

Thrusters
These small propellers or screws in the side of the hull make the boat swing sideways to help with steering.

Valves
The oil is pumped on and off through connectors. Valves inside make sure it flows the correct way.

SAFETY AND POLLUTION

The supertanker may be gigantic, yet it floats easily. Oil is lighter than water and floats on top of it. However, this can cause great problems. A supertanker accident may release vast quantities of thick crude oil that floats on the sea as slicks. It kills fish, sea birds and other marine life. If it washes ashore it can devastate coastal regions and destroy seashore wildlife. Newer tankers have hulls with double skins to prevent them leaking oil in an accident, and very strict fire precautions.

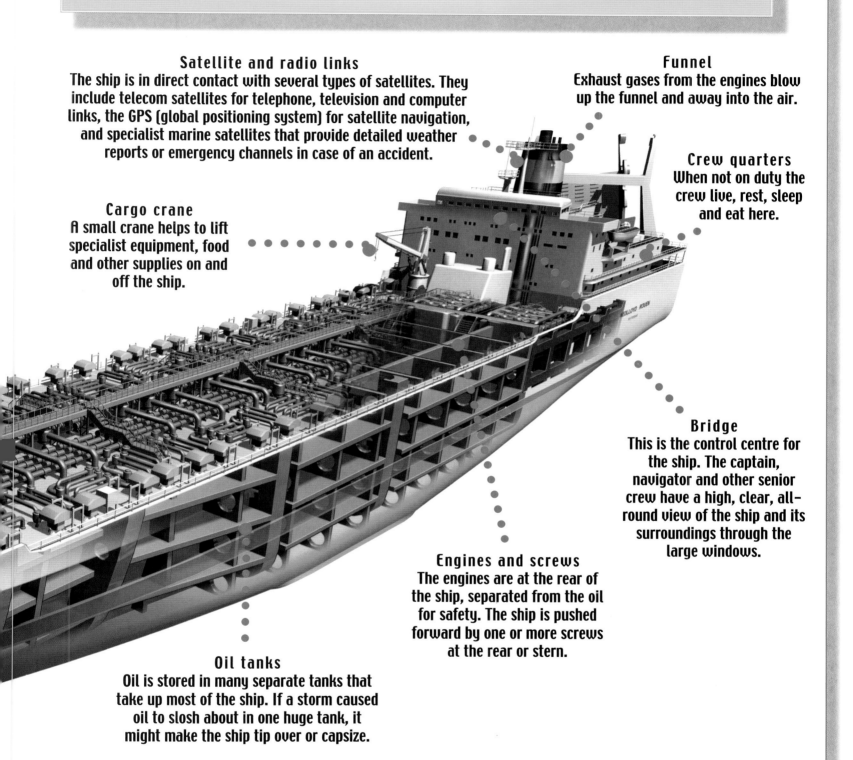

Satellite and radio links
The ship is in direct contact with several types of satellites. They include telecom satellites for telephone, television and computer links, the GPS (global positioning system) for satellite navigation, and specialist marine satellites that provide detailed weather reports or emergency channels in case of an accident.

Funnel
Exhaust gases from the engines blow up the funnel and away into the air.

Crew quarters
When not on duty the crew live, rest, sleep and eat here.

Cargo crane
A small crane helps to lift specialist equipment, food and other supplies on and off the ship.

Bridge
This is the control centre for the ship. The captain, navigator and other senior crew have a high, clear, all-round view of the ship and its surroundings through the large windows.

Engines and screws
The engines are at the rear of the ship, separated from the oil for safety. The ship is pushed forward by one or more screws at the rear or stern.

Oil tanks
Oil is stored in many separate tanks that take up most of the ship. If a storm caused oil to slosh about in one huge tank, it might make the ship tip over or capsize.

GIANTS OF THE SEAS

Crude oil is used to make fuels such as petrol, diesel, kerosene and paraffin, also tars and bitumen for roads, and paints and pigments, plastics, mineral rubber and hundreds of other substances. Many oil reserves are under the sea-bed. Ocean drilling platforms bore holes down to harvest the crude oil. A supertanker takes it on board and carries it to an oil terminal where there are storage tanks and refineries for treatment. Supertankers are the biggest ships on the seas. Some weigh over 300,000 tonnes (294,000 tons), and are more than 300 metres (800 feet) long. They take 3–5 kilometres (2–3 miles) to steer around a corner and 5–10 kilometres (3–6 miles) to stop. They are sometimes called ULCCs, ultra large crude carriers.

FUTURE VEHICLES

Cars and other road vehicles rule our lives. Their increasing numbers demand more roads, bigger car parks, large filling stations and extra safety laws. They also use up valuable natural resources, pollute the air and cause thousands of deaths yearly. We all agree that people should use them less – except of course, ourselves!

THE END OF THE ROAD?

How long can cars and other wheeled vehicles last? Each year millions of new vehicles take to the world's roads. We are using up the Earth's natural resource of petroleum (crude oil) at a frightening rate. Unless we slow down, in less than 100 years the petrol and diesel will run out. Electric cars have been developed over many years but they do not go as far or as fast as petrol-engined cars.

JUST FOR FUN?

Hopefully there are other options. There is amazing growth in telecommunications using computers, videophones, satellites and the Internet. This means that we can see, talk to and send information to people anywhere in the world, instantly. People will have to travel less for business. Mass transport, such as commuter coaches, city trains and ferryboats may have fewer customers. Working vehicles such as trucks and combine harvesters will still be around. Personal vehicles will be used mainly for pleasure.

THE HOVERCAR
A massive breakthrough for the future could be the anti-gravity beam. This would counteract the pull of gravity, so the car could rise up and fly. No wheels! It would be like having your own personal helicopter, but much faster, quieter, safer and more manoeuvrable. This hovercar would be totally computer-controlled to fly along the correct air lanes, avoid other craft and find its way by satellite navigation to your exact destination.

MORE AND MORE

One certainty is that we will continue to develop new kinds of wheeled vehicles and watercraft. Only thirty years ago there were no mountain bikes and no jetskis. Inventors are bound to come up with new ways to transport us and our luggage and cargo, to have fun and to race each other. What might the future have in store? Powered rollerblades? Rocket backpacks? Mini-submarines?

NO NEED FOR WHEELS

One day in the distant future we may learn how to take an object apart atom by atom and send it along some sort of high-energy matter transfer beam to another place, where it can be put back together again. By transporting a person or object like this even through space, there will be no need for vehicles at all. We could go anywhere, anytime. But what about the excitement and fun of travelling through beautiful scenery and exotic lands? The idea of undertaking a journey could even die away. Maybe we'll miss the old-fashioned joy of being stuck in traffic jams!

PLANEX

Space travel may take people to strange new worlds. Imagine PlanEx (Planet Explorer) – a huge armoured vehicle designed to cross almost any terrain as it searches new regions. It might travel under water and also withstand explosions, harmful rays and attack by animals, aliens or germs. Inside it could have living and working areas and enough fuel, air, food, water and other supplies for 10 people for one year. PlanEx may even be in development now! It could soon ready for testing on Earth in deserts and mountainous regions.

SYMBOL OF WEALTH

Many people dream about owning a fast, powerful sports car, a status symbol for leisure and pleasure. While there are still people who want to show off, there will always be powerful sports cars.

ASTONISHING
AIRCRAFT

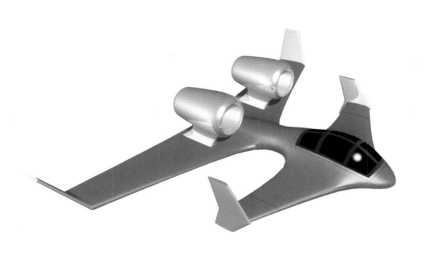

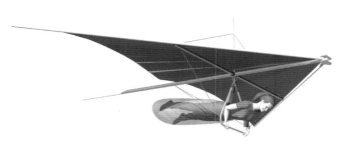

Fantastic Flying Machines 68

Cessna 172 70

Wright Flyer 72

Hang-glider 74

Motorized Glider 76

Breitling Orbiter 3 78

Hindenburg Airship 80

Fokker DR.I Triplane 82

Spirit of St Louis 84

Gee Bee R-2 Super Sportster 86

Boeing 314 Clipper 88

Boeing B-17 Flying Fortress 90

Boeing 747-400 'Jumbo Jet' 92

Concorde 94

Airbus A300-600ST Beluga 96

McDonnell Douglas AH-64 Apache 98

Boeing Vertol Chinook CH-47 100

Sikorsky Sea King 102

Bell Boeing V-22 Osprey 104

Canadair CL-215 106

British Aerospace/Boeing Harrier 108

A-10 Thunderbolt 110

Daedelus Pedal-powered Plane 112

Grumman Hawkeye 114

North American X-15 116

Apollo 11 Saturn V Rocket 118

Space Shuttle 120

Cassini/Huygens Space Probe 122

Fantastic Future 124

FANTASTIC FLYING MACHINES

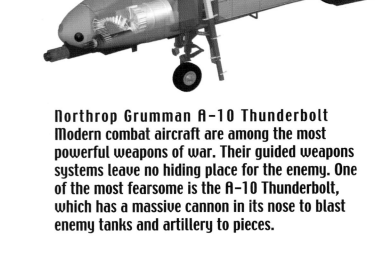

DREAMS OF FLIGHT

For thousands of years, people marvelled at the grace and ease with which birds fly through the air and dreamed of joining them. Some bold inventors made wings of feathers and leapt off high places, flapping wildly in their efforts to share the freedom of the skies. All, needless to say, failed in their attempts. Others tried to design more complicated muscle-powered flying machines. But our arms are not strong enough to keep our heavy bodies in the air. Some aviation pioneers managed to get airborne using gliders and gas-filled balloons, but they were still at the mercy of the wind. Only when people decided to use the petrol engine to power their flying machines did true flight become a reality.

Northrop Grumman A-10 Thunderbolt
Modern combat aircraft are among the most powerful weapons of war. Their guided weapons systems leave no hiding place for the enemy. One of the most fearsome is the A-10 Thunderbolt, which has a massive cannon in its nose to blast enemy tanks and artillery to pieces.

AN AIRCRAFT FOR EVERY JOB

It is about 100 years since the Wright brothers' petrol-powered *Flyer* made the first ever controlled, powered flight by an airplane. Today, there are countless different types of aircraft, from hang-gliders, helicopters and airships, to airliners, bombers and space planes. Some aircraft carry passengers and others carry cargo across the globe. Some are built for war, while others perform daring rescue missions. Some are working planes, but others exist purely for the fun of flying. This book shows you some of the most amazing planes around today, and looks at what makes them tick.

Sikorsky Sea King
Helicopters get their lift from their whirling rotor blades, allowing them to take off and land vertically, and even hover in mid-air. This makes them ideal for rescue work. Some helicopters, such as the Sikorsky Sea King, are used for rescuing people in danger at sea.

GETTING AIRBORNE

The Earth's gravity pulls all objects down towards its surface. To get off the ground, an airplane has to overcome gravity. The plane's engine provides it with thrust that drives it forwards along the runway. Air flowing over the wings produces an upward force called lift. The plane leaves the ground when the upward pull of its lift is greater than gravity's downward pull. Friction with the air creates a backward force called drag. For the plane to move forward, its thrust must be strong enough to overcome drag.

SHAPED FOR FLIGHT

An airplane's wings create lift because they have a special shape called an aerofoil. The wings have a curved upper surface, which makes air flow faster over the top than underneath. This causes a difference in air pressure that sucks the wings upwards, lifting the plane into the air. It is the force of lift that pulls the wings upwards.

Boeing 747
This Jumbo (below) is used to transport the Space Shuttle to the launch site. You can see the metal girders on its back to which the Shuttle is attached for flight.

Space travel
Having mastered the skies, people's attention turned to space. In 1969, the Apollo 11 astronauts became the first people to set foot on the Moon. They were launched into space by a disposable Saturn V rocket (above). Today, the reusable Space Shuttle makes regular trips into space, carrying out research and repairs to satellites.

CESSNA 172

Flaps
The flaps slide back and down to increase lift at slow speeds, especially when taking off and landing.

Wings
The wings produce lift. Most wings have a skin of metal panels. These are attached to a skeleton of long supports called spars, strengthened by ribs running at right angles. The place where the wing attaches to the fuselage is called the wing root.

Trailing (rear) edge of wing

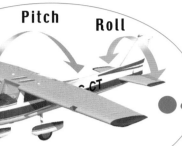

3-D movement
The three main movements made by an airplane are called pitch, roll and yaw. Pitching is the up-and-down movement of the nose, when the plane climbs or dives. Yawing is the left-to-right movement of the nose, when the plane turns left or right. Rolling is the side to side motion, when the plane tilts or banks in a turn.

Engine
The Cessna 172 has a 160-horsepower four-cylinder engine and a top speed of 220 kph (136 mph). Most light aircraft are still powered by piston engines, in which the fuel is burnt in cylinders, driving pistons that turn the propeller. Some airplanes have turboprop engines, in which compressed air and fuel are burnt and the hot waste gases are used to turn a set of turbine blades. The turbine then drives the propeller. Many larger aircraft are powered by jet engines.

Propeller
The engine turns the propeller, which is like a set of rotating wings that pushes the air backwards and gives the plane thrust.

Wheels
The wheels and the struts that link them to the plane are called the undercarriage. The Cessna has a tricycle undercarriage, with one nose wheel and two under the fuselage.

Cockpit
This is where the pilot sits. The control column (joystick) is pushed left or right to move the ailerons, and back and forth to move the elevators. Foot pedals push the rudder left and right.

PLANE CONTROL

A car driver turns the steering wheel to go left and right. But flying a plane is rather more complicated. Not only can the plane move left and right, but it can also tip up and down and tilt from side to side. Special movable surfaces on the tail and wings, called control surfaces, change the flight path by altering the flow of air over the plane. Control surfaces include flaps, ailerons, elevators and rudders. In gliders and some light aircraft, they are moved by wires. In larger aircraft, they are moved hydraulically – that is, by the pressure of an oily fluid pumped through hollow cables. In the most sophisticated aircraft, the surfaces are controlled by computers, in a system known as 'fly-by-wire', and sometimes moved by electric motors. Most airplanes fly using a combination of several control surfaces.

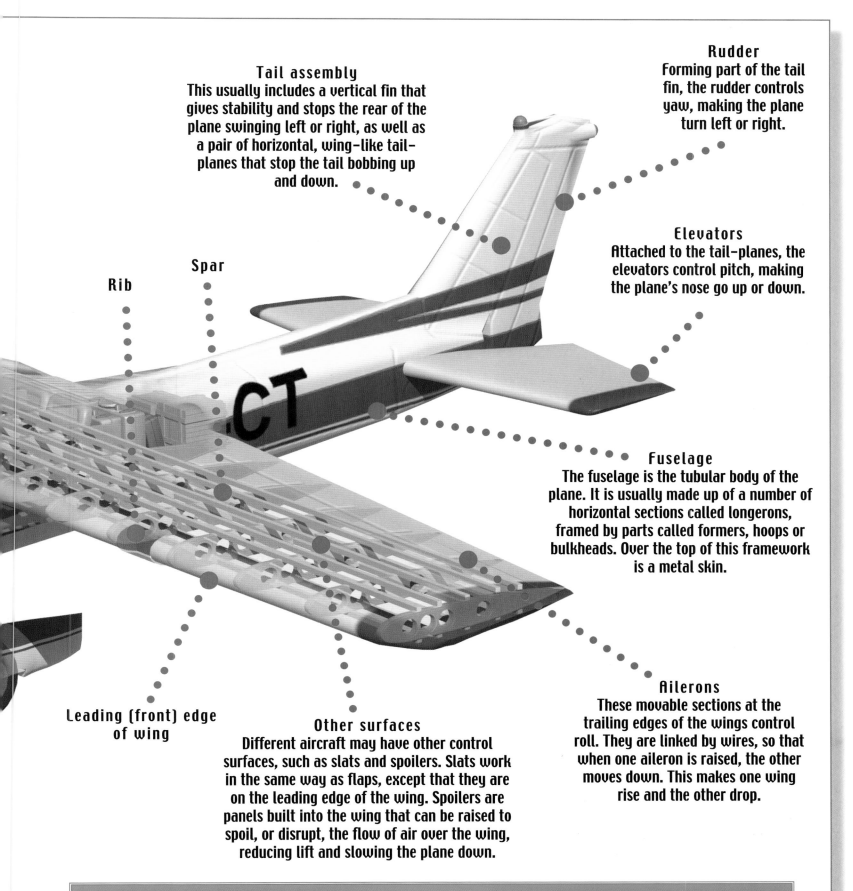

Tail assembly
This usually includes a vertical fin that gives stability and stops the rear of the plane swinging left or right, as well as a pair of horizontal, wing-like tail-planes that stop the tail bobbing up and down.

Rudder
Forming part of the tail fin, the rudder controls yaw, making the plane turn left or right.

Spar

Rib

Elevators
Attached to the tail-planes, the elevators control pitch, making the plane's nose go up or down.

Fuselage
The fuselage is the tubular body of the plane. It is usually made up of a number of horizontal sections called longerons, framed by parts called formers, hoops or bulkheads. Over the top of this framework is a metal skin.

Leading (front) edge of wing

Other surfaces
Different aircraft may have other control surfaces, such as slats and spoilers. Slats work in the same way as flaps, except that they are on the leading edge of the wing. Spoilers are panels built into the wing that can be raised to spoil, or disrupt, the flow of air over the wing, reducing lift and slowing the plane down.

Ailerons
These movable sections at the trailing edges of the wings control roll. They are linked by wires, so that when one aileron is raised, the other moves down. This makes one wing rise and the other drop.

PLANE FOR SALE

Light aircraft are small planes, usually privately owned and mainly used for leisure flying and training. Most are propeller-driven, have a single engine, and normally have a maximum of four seats. The Cessna company of the USA has been a world leader in light aircraft since World War II. Their model 150 has been used to teach more pilots to fly than any other plane in history. More than 35,000 of its descendant, the 172 Skyhawk, have been made to date. The simple, reliable and relatively cheap 172 can accommodate four people and their baggage. This all-metal plane, with its braced, high wing may look dull, but no other light aircraft can compete with it for price, comfort, range, speed and ease of operation.

WRIGHT FLYER

Propellers
The two rear-mounted wooden propellers turned in opposite directions, to make sure that the forces pushing the *Flyer* forwards were balanced. In later airplanes, these 'pusher' propellers were replaced by 'puller' propellers at the front of the plane, which were more efficient.

Engine
The Wrights could not find an engine light and powerful enough for the *Flyer*, so they built their own! The four-cylinder engine weighed 81 kilograms (37 pounds) and produced about 12 horsepower (an average family car engine gives about 80 horsepower).

Pilot's cradle
The pilot lay across the lower wing in a cradle positioned alongside the engine to balance its weight. Cables from the cradle controlled the rudder and wing-warping. The pilot steered by moving his body from side to side, so that the cradle pulled on the control cables.

Elevators
By adjusting the pitch of these mini-wings at the front of the airplane, the pilot could make the *Flyer* climb or descend. On modern airplanes, the elevators are usually at the rear.

Landing runners
The *Flyer* had no undercarriage, but landed on runners, which skidded across the sand.

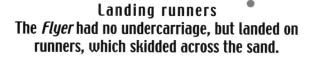

FIRST FLYERS

On 17 December 1903, Orville and Wilbur Wright, two bicycle engineers from Dayton, Ohio, USA, launched the *Flyer* from sand dunes above the windswept beach at Kitty Hawk, North Carolina. Mounted on a small trolley and with Orville at the controls, the *Flyer's* engine kicked into life, spinning the propellers. Orville released the brake and the *Flyer* raced along the 18-metre (50-foot) take-off track, straight into the wind. There were cheers as the *Flyer* lurched up into the air. It rose to a height of about 3 metres (9 feet) and travelled for 36 metres (100 feet) before plunging down on to the sands. It was little more than a 'hop', but it marked the beginning of the age of the airplane.

WING-WARPING

For the Wright brothers getting an airplane into the sky was only half the challenge. The question remained, how do you steer it once it's airborne? The Wright brothers used a vertical rudder to make the body of the *Flyer* swing to the left or right, but to tilt the wings so that the aircraft could bank, or 'roll', in a smooth turn was more difficult. Wilbur designed a system of control wires that twisted the rear edge of the wingtips slightly when pulled. This 'wing-warping' changed the flow of air over the wings and tilted them, so that the *Flyer* could bank. Today, hinged ailerons do the same job.

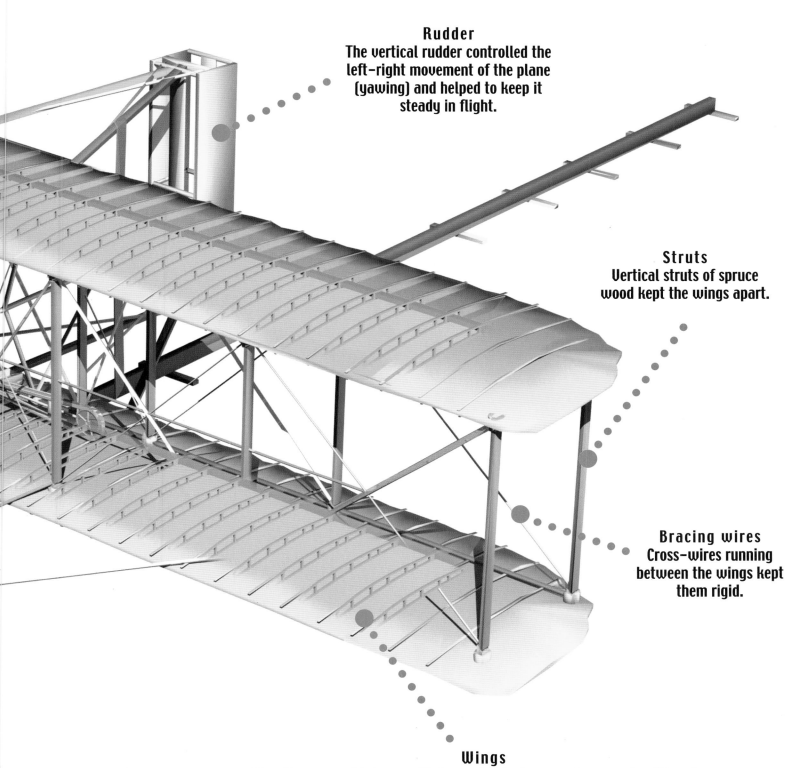

Rudder
The vertical rudder controlled the left–right movement of the plane (yawing) and helped to keep it steady in flight.

Struts
Vertical struts of spruce wood kept the wings apart.

Bracing wires
Cross-wires running between the wings kept them rigid.

Wings
The *Flyer* was a biplane, with two sets of wings, each measuring 13 metres (36 feet) long and 2 metres (6 feet) wide, covered with muslin fabric. Their wooden frame consisted of poles of spruce strengthened by cross-ribs of ash. The ribs were curved, to give the wings an aerofoil shape.

HANG-GLIDER

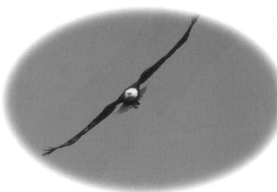

HITCHING A RIDE

In hitching a ride on rising thermals, hang-gliders are copying soaring birds such as eagles, condors and albatrosses. Flapping wings can be tiring work, so soaring on thermals gives the birds rest and saves energy – as well as giving them a high vantage point from which to spot prey on the ground below.

Guy lines
Steel bracing wires secure the wing and help it to keep its shape.

Battens
These rods slip into channels along the wing, stiffening it and giving it an aerofoil shape, to generate maximum lift.

Centre-line beam
This helps to balance the wing.

Body-bag
The insulated body-bag, a long fabric shell, clips to the top of the A-frame. It keeps the pilot warm and stops the pilot's legs from dangling around, giving him or her a streamlined shape.

Microlight
A microlight is a hang-glider with a small motor and rear-mounted 'pusher' propeller. The motor and propeller are attached to a streamlined fibreglass tricycle, which can carry one or two people. Ultralights are microlights with rigid wings.

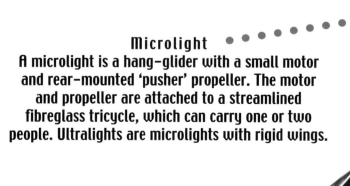

FLYING WING

The closest you will ever come to flying like a bird is to take to the air in a hang-glider. These kite-like craft are basically large wings, made of fabric stretched over a simple frame. There is no fuselage, so the pilot hangs underneath the wing in a special harness called a body-bag. The whole structure is so simple that it can be put together or folded away in a few minutes. When dismantled, it can easily be carried on the roof-rack of a car. Hang-gliders are leisure craft, used for racing, performing stunts or just enjoying the thrill of soaring above the ground.

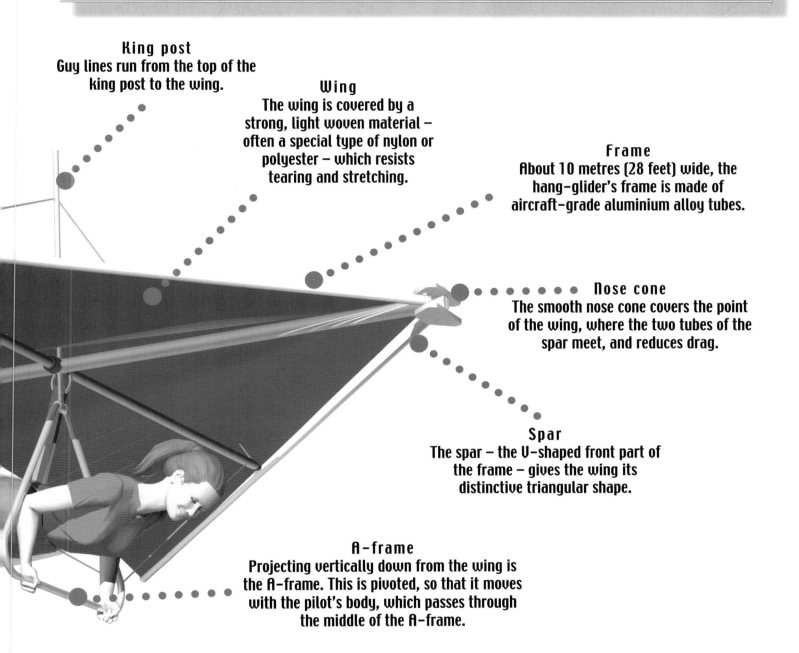

King post
Guy lines run from the top of the king post to the wing.

Wing
The wing is covered by a strong, light woven material – often a special type of nylon or polyester – which resists tearing and stretching.

Frame
About 10 metres (28 feet) wide, the hang-glider's frame is made of aircraft-grade aluminium alloy tubes.

Nose cone
The smooth nose cone covers the point of the wing, where the two tubes of the spar meet, and reduces drag.

Spar
The spar – the U-shaped front part of the frame – gives the wing its distinctive triangular shape.

A-frame
Projecting vertically down from the wing is the A-frame. This is pivoted, so that it moves with the pilot's body, which passes through the middle of the A-frame.

KEEPING CONTROL

To launch a hang-glider, the pilot runs into the wind from the top of a steep hill and is lifted by the wing. There are no rudders, ailerons or elevators, so the pilot holds the control bar and steers by moving his or her body, which in turn moves the wing. Pushing the bar forward makes the hang-glider climb, pulling on it makes it descend. Turns are made by shifting the body from side to side.

Experienced pilots soar on currents of rising warm air called thermals. To cover long distances, the pilot makes the hang-glider climb on one thermal, then glides down and rises again on the next thermal, and so on. By hitching rides on thermals, a hang-glider can stay airborne for more than two hours and travel over 150 kilometres (90 miles).

MOTORIZED GLIDER

Power plant
The 54-horsepower, two-stroke engine and propeller, weighing less than 50 kilograms (23 pounds), are raised for take-off but then retracted back into the fuselage. In flight, doors close over the engine housing to keep the fuselage streamlined.

Materials
Modern gliders are made out of tough, lightweight materials such as fibreglass, carbon-fibre and kevlar. Older gliders were either wood or metal.

Canopy
The cockpit canopy, made of clear plastic such as perspex, gives an excellent all-round view. To get in and out, the pilot lifts up the canopy, which is hinged at the front end.

Nose tow hole
The towing cable attaches here.

Cockpit
This glider has a single seat. Training gliders have more bulging canopies, two seats and dual controls, so the instructor can take over the flight if necessary.

Seat
The semi-reclining seat keeps the pilot's body low in the cockpit, allowing the canopy to follow the smooth lines of the fuselage.

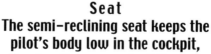

RIDING AIR CURRENTS

A glider cannot glide upwards, or even maintain level flight, so the pilot keeps the nose pointed just below the horizon and glides downwards. But the plane can still climb, even in this downward-pointing position, by soaring on air currents that rise faster than the plane sinks. These air currents include thermals and slope winds (winds deflected upwards by a hillside), and they allow a glider to stay aloft for many hours.

Main wheel
The glider has a single, retractable wheel under the fuselage. Having just one wheel means that when it is at rest, one wing touches the ground, so a helper is needed to hold up the wing during the first part of the take-off. There may be a small wheel or skid under the tail to prevent damage on landing. Some gliders also have a nose wheel.

Fuselage
The fuselage is a slim, tapering tube, moulded to give a smooth, low-drag surface. Near the tail it may have a diameter of less than 30 centimetres (1 foot).

Tail
The high tail usually consists of a horizontal stabilizer (the tail-plane) on top of a vertical fin. This T-shaped design not only improves aerodynamic performance, but also protects the stabilizer from being damaged if the glider has to make a forced landing.

Trim tab
This is a small, hinged surface attached to the rear of the elevator, to 'fine-tune' aerial manoeuvres.

Airbrakes
Flat, oblong surfaces emerge from the wings at right angles to steepen the descent for landing. They extend to disturb the flow of air over the wings, decreasing lift and increasing drag.

Flaperons
Instead of separate flaps and ailerons, each wing has a single, very long control surface called a 'flaperon'.

Wings
The long wings are much narrower than the wings of conventional airplanes. At their tips, all wings lose some of their lifting power because of air turbulence. The longer the wing, the less this turbulence affects the plane's flight.

Ballast tanks
Inside the wings are flexible tanks that hold water ballast, which adds weight and allows the glider to fly faster. The water is jettisoned for circling slowly or for landing.

GETTING AIRBORNE

Being engine-less airplanes, gliders need help to get them moving so that the air flowing over the wings generates enough lift for take-off. Gliders may be launched by being towed into the air by a light airplane called a 'tug'. The glider is tied to the plane by a long cable, which the pilot releases at the desired height by pulling a knob in the cockpit. A winch-launch uses a powerful winch to pull the glider along. The cable, up to 2 kilometres (1.25 miles) long, may have a small parachute to slow its descent after release. In an auto-tow, a car tows the glider along like a kite until it gets airborne. Motorized gliders have retractable engines that are used only for take-off and in emergencies.

BREITLING ORBITER 3

Burners
The six burners, separated from the capsule by a protective heat shield, generated hot air.

Gas valves
If the pilots wanted to level off or descend, they expelled helium through valves in the top of the gas tanks.

Stores of food, water, and emergency equipment

Cockpit
Using switches on the cockpit's instrument panel, the pilots could operate the burners, change fuel tanks and jettison empty tanks from inside the capsule. For communicating with their base in Geneva, Switzerland, and air-traffic control centres around the world the cockpit was equipped with satellite telephone, radios and a laptop computer to send faxes.

Capsule details
The cramped capsule was made of kevlar (a super-tough plastic) and carbon-fibre. It was well insulated to protect the pilots from the freezing outside temperatures, which sometimes plummeted to −58 ° C. The capsule included sleeping quarters, food and water stores, a toilet and mini-kitchen, oxygen for breathing, and an air-filtering system.

LIGHTER-THAN-AIR CRAFT

The first ever sustained flight was made in 1783 by the French Montgolfier brothers' hot-air balloon. The balloon's envelope was made of paper and hot air was produced by burning straw.

Balloons are basically bags or 'envelopes' of hot air or gas such as hydrogen or helium. In a hot-air balloon, burners heat the air inside the envelope. The air expands as it is heated, which makes it lighter than the air outside and gives the balloon lift. A gas balloon contains gas that is naturally lighter (less dense) than air, so it floats in the atmosphere. Hot-air balloons burn propane or kerosene for fuel. Today, scientists use balloons to carry instruments that gather information about the weather. Other balloons, used for racing and leisure trips, have a basket attached beneath the envelope to carry passengers.

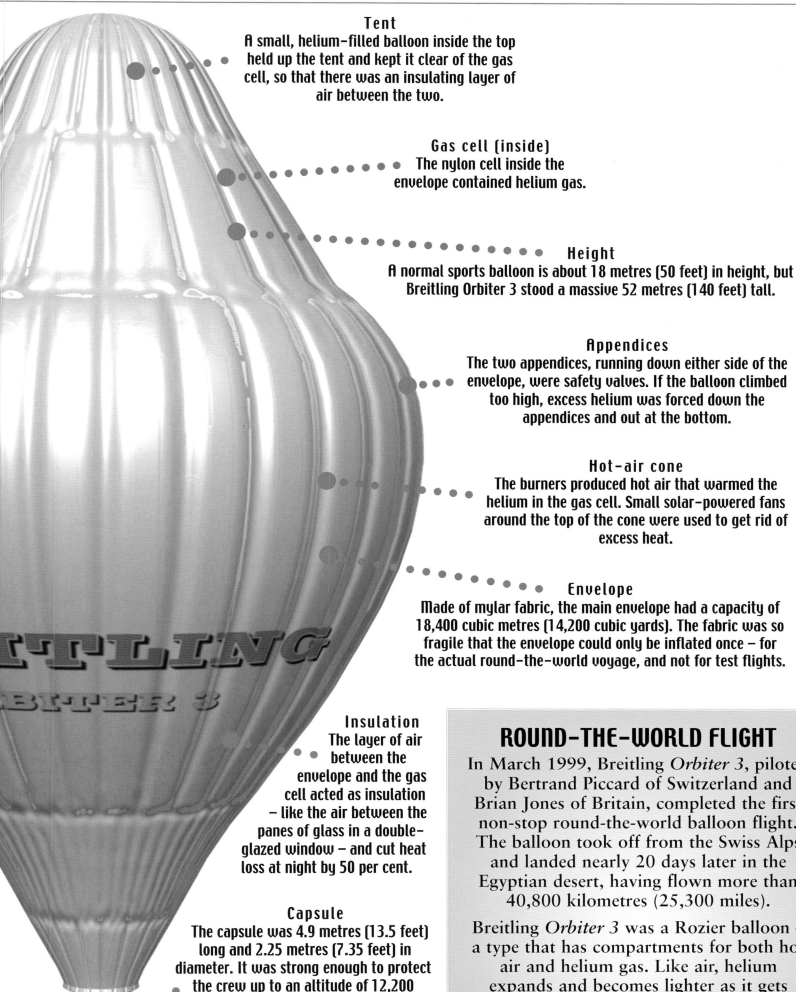

Tent
A small, helium-filled balloon inside the top held up the tent and kept it clear of the gas cell, so that there was an insulating layer of air between the two.

Gas cell (inside)
The nylon cell inside the envelope contained helium gas.

Height
A normal sports balloon is about 18 metres (50 feet) in height, but Breitling Orbiter 3 stood a massive 52 metres (140 feet) tall.

Appendices
The two appendices, running down either side of the envelope, were safety valves. If the balloon climbed too high, excess helium was forced down the appendices and out at the bottom.

Hot-air cone
The burners produced hot air that warmed the helium in the gas cell. Small solar-powered fans around the top of the cone were used to get rid of excess heat.

Envelope
Made of mylar fabric, the main envelope had a capacity of 18,400 cubic metres (14,200 cubic yards). The fabric was so fragile that the envelope could only be inflated once – for the actual round-the-world voyage, and not for test flights.

Insulation
The layer of air between the envelope and the gas cell acted as insulation – like the air between the panes of glass in a double-glazed window – and cut heat loss at night by 50 per cent.

Capsule
The capsule was 4.9 metres (13.5 feet) long and 2.25 metres (7.35 feet) in diameter. It was strong enough to protect the crew up to an altitude of 12,200 metres (33,600 feet). The capsule was designed to float on landing in water.

Fuel tanks
Hanging from a titanium frame were 32 fuel tanks, arranged in two groups, one on either side of the capsule.

ROUND-THE-WORLD FLIGHT

In March 1999, Breitling *Orbiter 3*, piloted by Bertrand Piccard of Switzerland and Brian Jones of Britain, completed the first non-stop round-the-world balloon flight. The balloon took off from the Swiss Alps and landed nearly 20 days later in the Egyptian desert, having flown more than 40,800 kilometres (25,300 miles).

Breitling *Orbiter 3* was a Rozier balloon – a type that has compartments for both hot air and helium gas. Like air, helium expands and becomes lighter as it gets warmer. In daylight, the Sun's rays warmed the helium and gave extra lift, while the burners were used at night to keep the helium at a steady temperature. The burners were also operated in short bursts during the day to make the balloon rise quickly.

HINDENBURG AIRSHIP

Gas bags
The *Hindenburg* contained 16 air-tight gas bags, made from 1.5 million ox bladders. Wire mesh separated them from the outer fabric and metal framework. The gas bags contained nearly 200,000 cubic metres of highly inflammable hydrogen gas, which made the airship lighter than the air around it and gave it lift.

Framework
The spindly framework, made of a strong aluminium alloy called duralumin, consisted of a series of vertical hoops linked by ribs running crossways and strengthened by bracing wires.

Outer fabric
The outer fabric was cotton, specially treated so that it was airtight and reinforced where it stretched over the metal framework. Minor tears could be repaired in the air by lowering engineers down the sides of the ship on ropes.

Fuel and water tanks
The fuel tanks could carry enough diesel for a trip of more than 17,000 kilometres (10,550 miles). As well as water for the passengers and crew, the water tanks also held water as ballast. To take off, some ballast was released and the airship rose.

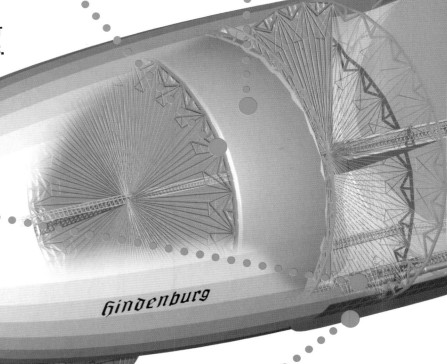

Control gondola
The nerve centre of the *Hindenburg* was the small control car, where officers kept the airship on course.

Passenger decks and crew's quarters

THE AIRSHIP AGE

Airships are lighter-than-air craft which have engines and steering mechanisms. Early airships, built in the late nineteenth century, were cloth-covered, cigar-shaped gas bags, which kept their shape because the gas inside was under high pressure. If the bag sprung a leak, the shape was lost and the airship became difficult to control. So a new type of airship, the 'rigid' was developed, with a strong internal framework made of lightweight metal alloys.

Rigid airships were used in World War I for reconnaissance missions and bombing raids. After the war, they were used to carry passengers on long-distance journeys. In the mid-1930s, airships established the first regular transatlantic air services. Airship travel was expensive and only a small number of passengers could be carried at a time. But airships crossed the Atlantic twice as quickly as the great ocean liners, and the passengers enjoyed an equal level of comfort.

MONSTER OF THE SKIES

Measuring 245 metres (670 feet) long – three times the length of a modern jumbo jet – the German airship *Hindenburg* was the largest craft ever to take to the skies. On a 50–65-hour transatlantic trip it could carry up to 50 passengers in spacious and luxurious accommodation. The crew usually numbered between 50–60, including 10–15 stewards to look after the passengers' needs.

The *Hindenburg* flew for the first time in 1936, and made 18 successful transatlantic trips in all. It took off on its last voyage from Frankfurt, Germany, on 3 May 1937. Disaster struck when it arrived at Lakehurst, New Jersey, USA, on 6 May. Suddenly, the *Hindenburg* caught fire and exploded in a ball of flame, killing 35 of the 97 people on board. The tragedy signalled the end of the airship age, and these vast giants of the skies were soon replaced on transatlantic voyages by flying-boat airplanes.

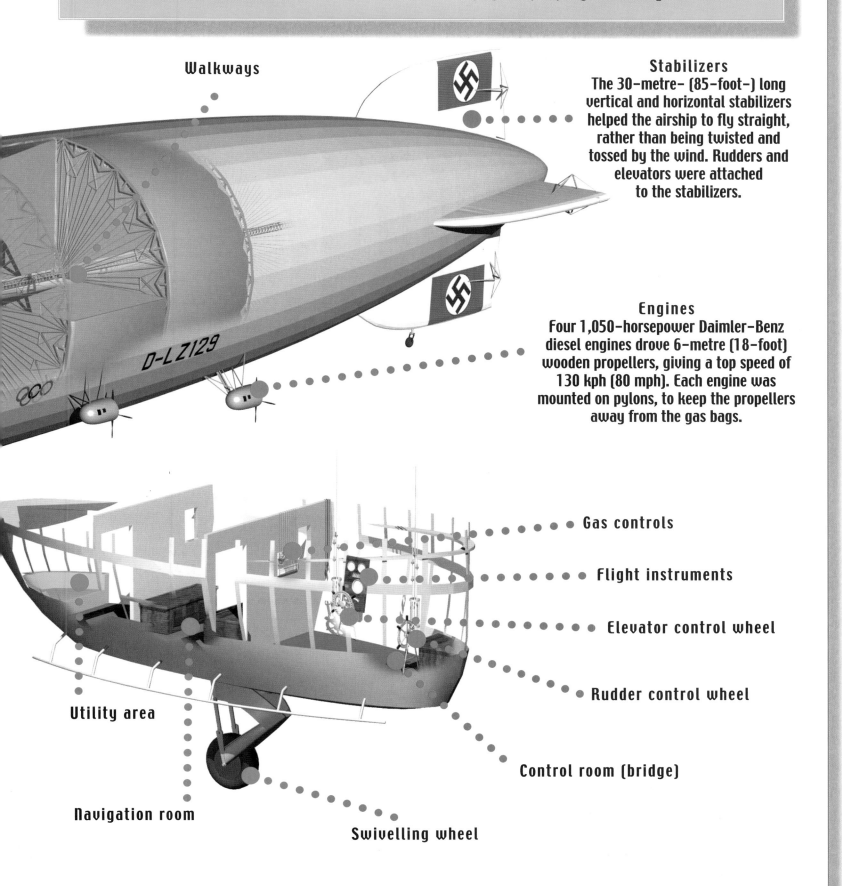

Walkways

Stabilizers
The 30-metre- (85-foot-) long vertical and horizontal stabilizers helped the airship to fly straight, rather than being twisted and tossed by the wind. Rudders and elevators were attached to the stabilizers.

D-LZ129

Engines
Four 1,050-horsepower Daimler-Benz diesel engines drove 6-metre (18-foot) wooden propellers, giving a top speed of 130 kph (80 mph). Each engine was mounted on pylons, to keep the propellers away from the gas bags.

Gas controls

Flight instruments

Elevator control wheel

Rudder control wheel

Control room (bridge)

Utility area

Navigation room

Swivelling wheel

FOKKER DR.I TRIPLANE

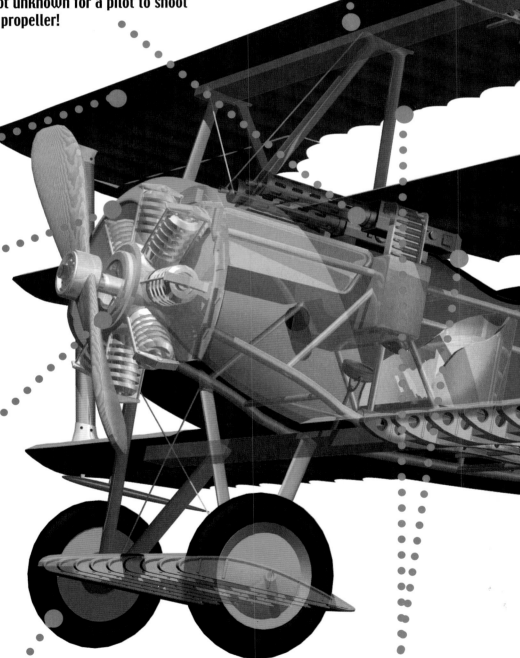

Wing-span
The span of the longest wing set – the upper one – was only just over 7 metres (20 feet). Having three tiers of short wings made the Fokker DR.I very manoeuvrable in aerial battles.

Guns
The Fokker had two fixed, forward-firing Spandau machine guns mounted above the engine. World War I fighters used a timing device called an interrupter, which allowed the guns to fire between the spinning propeller blades. However, interrupters were not fail-safe, and it was not unknown for a pilot to shoot off his own propeller!

Wings
The Fokker DR.I had three sets of wings of different sizes, with the upper set being the longest and the lower set the shortest. The wings were made of fabric over a plywood frame.

Engine cowling
This metal cover prevented the pilot and plane from getting covered with oil thrown out by the engine.

Engine
The DR.I's power plant was a 110-horsepower Oberursel UR II or Le Rhone nine-cylinder rotary engine. The cylinders were arranged in a ring and rotated with the propeller around a stationary crank shaft. The engine was started by a mechanic on the ground spinning the propeller.

Undercarriage
The two landing wheels were mounted on rigid struts. Unlike the wheels of most modern planes, they could not be withdrawn into the fuselage after take-off.

Wing cut-outs
To improve the pilot's view from the cockpit, curves were cut out of the upper and middle wings.

THREE-WINGED FIGHTER

Germany's Fokker DR.I triplane entered service in 1917, and for a while it proved unbeatable. The DR.I had three sets of wings, while most other fighters of the time were biplanes or monoplanes. Although its top speed was slower than other fighters', the DR.I could climb quicker and was unmatched in manoeuvrability – two qualities that gave it a crucial advantage in tight dog-fights.

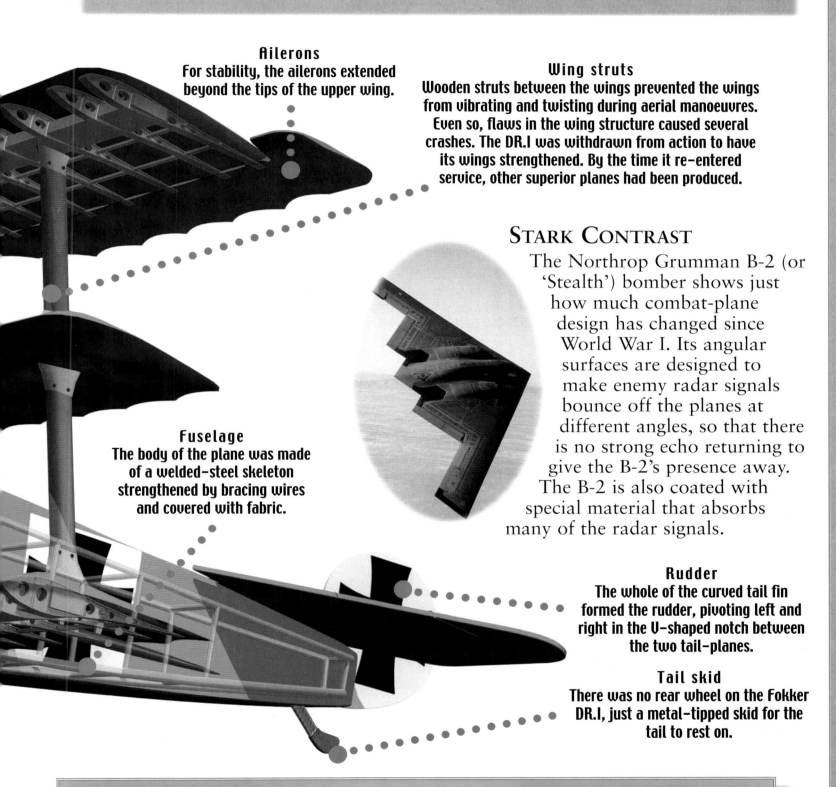

Ailerons
For stability, the ailerons extended beyond the tips of the upper wing.

Wing struts
Wooden struts between the wings prevented the wings from vibrating and twisting during aerial manoeuvres. Even so, flaws in the wing structure caused several crashes. The DR.I was withdrawn from action to have its wings strengthened. By the time it re-entered service, other superior planes had been produced.

STARK CONTRAST
The Northrop Grumman B-2 (or 'Stealth') bomber shows just how much combat-plane design has changed since World War I. Its angular surfaces are designed to make enemy radar signals bounce off the planes at different angles, so that there is no strong echo returning to give the B-2's presence away. The B-2 is also coated with special material that absorbs many of the radar signals.

Fuselage
The body of the plane was made of a welded-steel skeleton strengthened by bracing wires and covered with fabric.

Rudder
The whole of the curved tail fin formed the rudder, pivoting left and right in the U-shaped notch between the two tail-planes.

Tail skid
There was no rear wheel on the Fokker DR.I, just a metal-tipped skid for the tail to rest on.

THE RED BARON

The German flyer Manfred von Richtofen was the most successful fighter pilot of World War I, shooting down a total of 80 aircraft. He was known as the Red Baron, because of the bright red Fokker DR.I triplane he flew. Von Richtofen's squadron, all in brightly coloured DR.Is to startle the enemy, ruled the skies and were nicknamed the 'Flying Circus' by Allied pilots. Von Richtofen was killed on 21 April 1918, when his triplane crashed to the ground after being attacked simultaneously by anti-aircraft guns and a Sopwith Camel fighter flown by Canadian pilot Roy Brown.

SPIRIT OF ST LOUIS

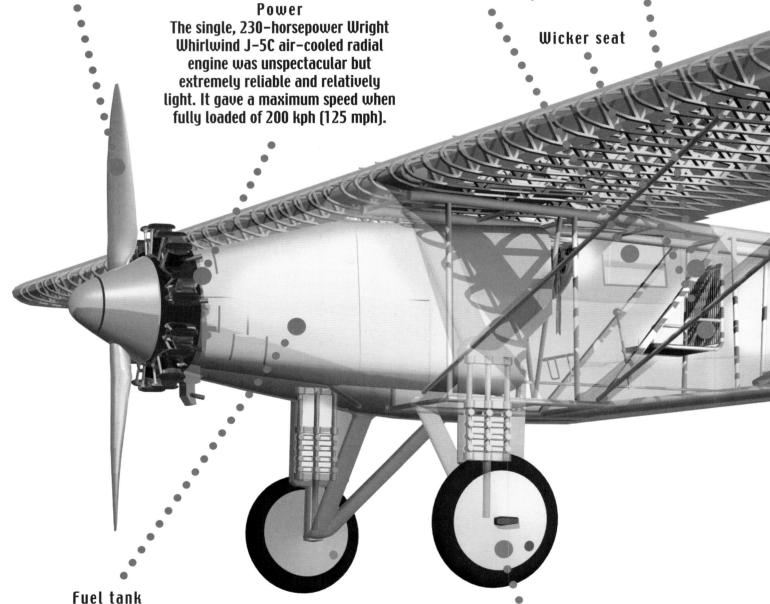

Cockpit
To accommodate the fuel tank, the cockpit had to be moved further back along the fuselage than normal.

Windows
There were only two small side windows, one on either side of the cockpit. When he felt drowsy, Lindbergh would open a window to get a blast of icy air to wake himself up.

Wicker seat

Propeller
The 2.7-metre- (7.4-foot-) diameter propeller had two blades made of duralumin – a strong, lightweight aluminium alloy.

Power
The single, 230-horsepower Wright Whirlwind J-5C air-cooled radial engine was unspectacular but extremely reliable and relatively light. It gave a maximum speed when fully loaded of 200 kph (125 mph).

Fuel tank
The huge fuel tank, immediately behind the engine, blocked direct forward vision. It could hold 1,700 litres (121 gallons) and gave the plane an astonishing range of 6,600 kilometres (4,090 miles).

Undercarriage
The two fixed, spoked wheels were covered with cotton to make them more streamlined.

LEGENDARY AIRCRAFT

In 1927, this single-engine monoplane carried American Charles Lindbergh on the first solo non-stop flight across the Atlantic. Funded by a group of businessmen, Lindbergh asked the Ryan company of San Diego to build him a plane that would win the US$25,000 prize offered to the first pilot who could fly the Atlantic single-handed. The *Spirit of St Louis* was based on Ryan's standard M-1 five-passenger aircraft, modified to Lindbergh's specifications. The plane was stripped down to the bare essentials, so that it could carry as much fuel as possible.

Already tired from a sleepless night, Lindbergh took off from the muddy Roosevelt airfield, New York, at 7.54 am on 20 May...

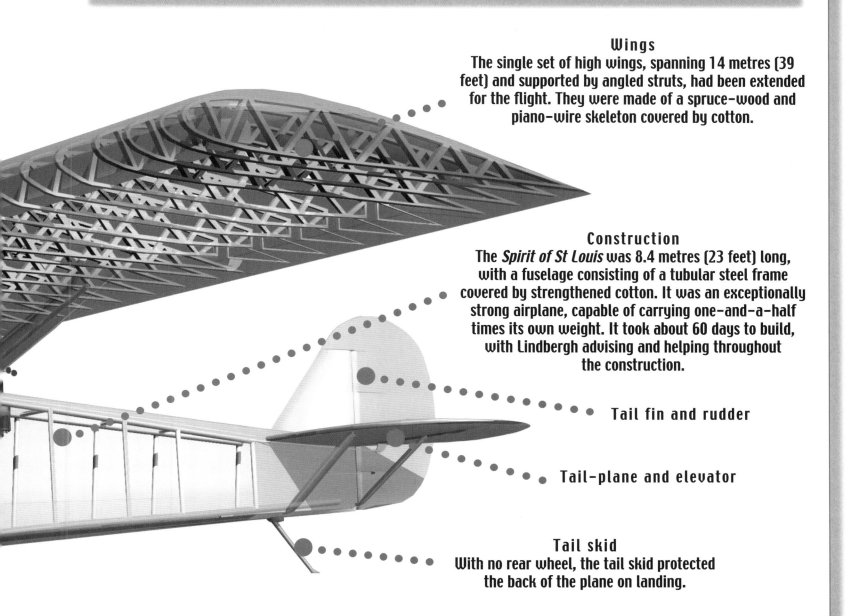

Wings
The single set of high wings, spanning 14 metres (39 feet) and supported by angled struts, had been extended for the flight. They were made of a spruce-wood and piano-wire skeleton covered by cotton.

Construction
The *Spirit of St Louis* was 8.4 metres (23 feet) long, with a fuselage consisting of a tubular steel frame covered by strengthened cotton. It was an exceptionally strong airplane, capable of carrying one-and-a-half times its own weight. It took about 60 days to build, with Lindbergh advising and helping throughout the construction.

Tail fin and rudder

Tail-plane and elevator

Tail skid
With no rear wheel, the tail skid protected the back of the plane on landing.

GRUELLING VOYAGE

The *Spirit of St Louis* was not easy to fly, as it was nose-heavy when fully loaded, and the wings lost much of their efficiency in turbulent air. It had only basic navigation equipment and flight instruments. Fortunately, Lindbergh was skilled and experienced in the air, having flown with the US Army before becoming a stunt flyer and then a long-distance airmail pilot.

Lindbergh finally reached Paris, France, at 10.24 pm on 21 May, after 33 hours and 30 minutes in the air – and 150,000 people at Le Bourget airfield welcomed him as a hero.

GEE BEE R-2
SUPER SPORTSTER

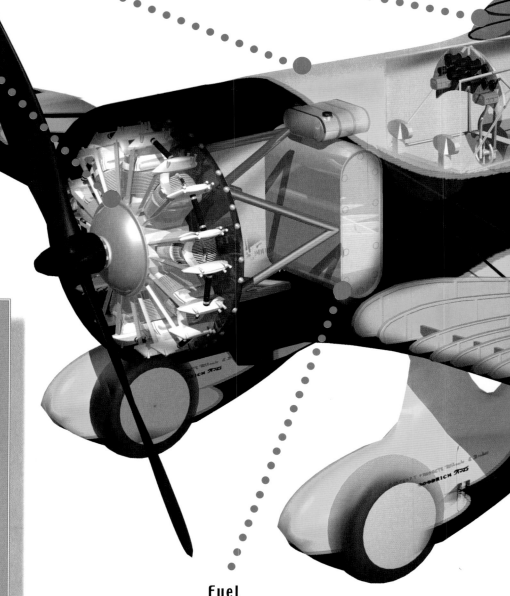

Fuselage
The fuselage, made of metal and wood, was only 5.4 metres (15 feet) long.

Flying engine
The R-2 had a 535-horsepower Pratt and Witney R985 engine stuffed into its nose, giving it a top speed of 413 kph (256 mph). The R-1 had a larger 800-horsepower Pratt and Witney R1340 Wasp engine.

Performance
The Super Sportsters performed superbly in knife-edge turns (with the plane tipped on its side) and even upside down. But landing and looping manoeuvres were a little hair-raising for the pilots.

Balancing act
To balance the engine's weight, the pilot and cockpit had to be at the other end of the plane, tucked at the base of the short tail fin.

Fuel
The tank held about 1,150 litres (82 gallons) of fuel, compared to the 605 litres (43 gallons) carried by the R-1.

FLYING FOR FUN

After the end of World War I, many pilots turned their flying skills to entertaining the public at airshows. During the 1920s air races were all the rage, with daredevil pilots risking all for big-money prizes. A new breed of airplane emerged, designed purely for speed. Ever larger engines were crammed into smaller and smaller fuselages.

Among the most famous race planes were America's Gee Bee Super Sportsters, built by Granville Brothers of Springfield, Massachusetts. The four brothers began making two-seat biplanes for private use, but then switched to racers. The most famous of these were the R-1 and R-2 Super Sportsters.

The R-1 was little more than an enormous engine bolted on to a tiny body. In 1932, Major James Doolittle piloted the R-1 to victory in the Thompson Trophy race, flying laps around a circuit marked out by pylons. The R-1's sister plane, the R-2, looked almost identical. It had a slightly less powerful but more fuel-efficient engine than the R-1 and a larger fuel tank, allowing it to fly long-distance races with fewer refuelling stops. This gave it a better average speed.

All the Granville Brothers' racers were successful, but only the most skilled flyers could handle them. Over the space of four years, seven Gee Bee racers crashed, killing five pilots, leading to the company ceasing production.

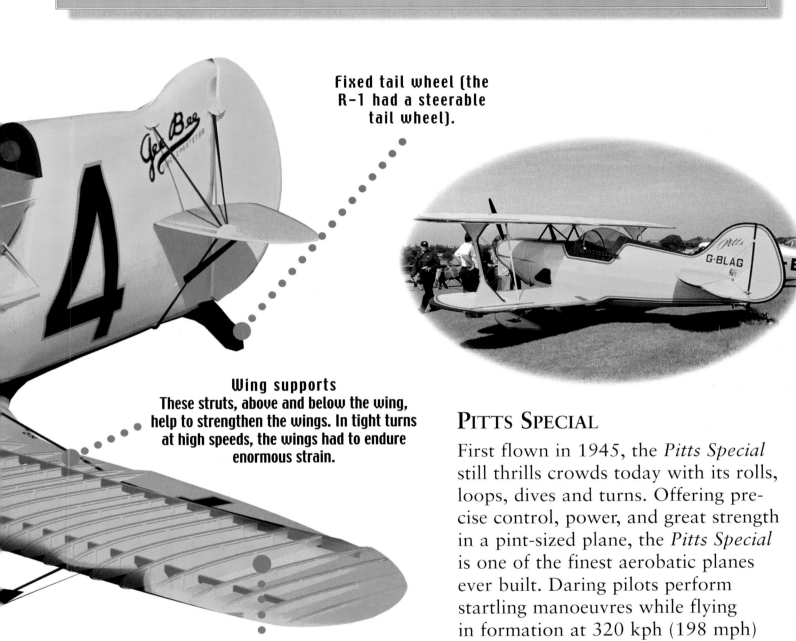

Fixed tail wheel (the R-1 had a steerable tail wheel).

Wing supports
These struts, above and below the wing, help to strengthen the wings. In tight turns at high speeds, the wings had to endure enormous strain.

Clipped wings
The R-2's wing-span was just 7.6 metres (21 feet).

PITTS SPECIAL

First flown in 1945, the *Pitts Special* still thrills crowds today with its rolls, loops, dives and turns. Offering precise control, power, and great strength in a pint-sized plane, the *Pitts Special* is one of the finest aerobatic planes ever built. Daring pilots perform startling manoeuvres while flying in formation at 320 kph (198 mph) with the wing-tips often no more than 3 metres (8 feet) apart!

FATAL FLIGHTS

The planes were said to be dangerous – and they were. Both the R-1 and R-2 crashed in 1933. The parts were salvaged and reused in the form of the R-1/R-2, which had a larger fuel tank set further back than before. This upset the plane's balance, making it impossible to control – it crashed on its first flight killing its pilot, Allen Granville.

BOEING 314 CLIPPER

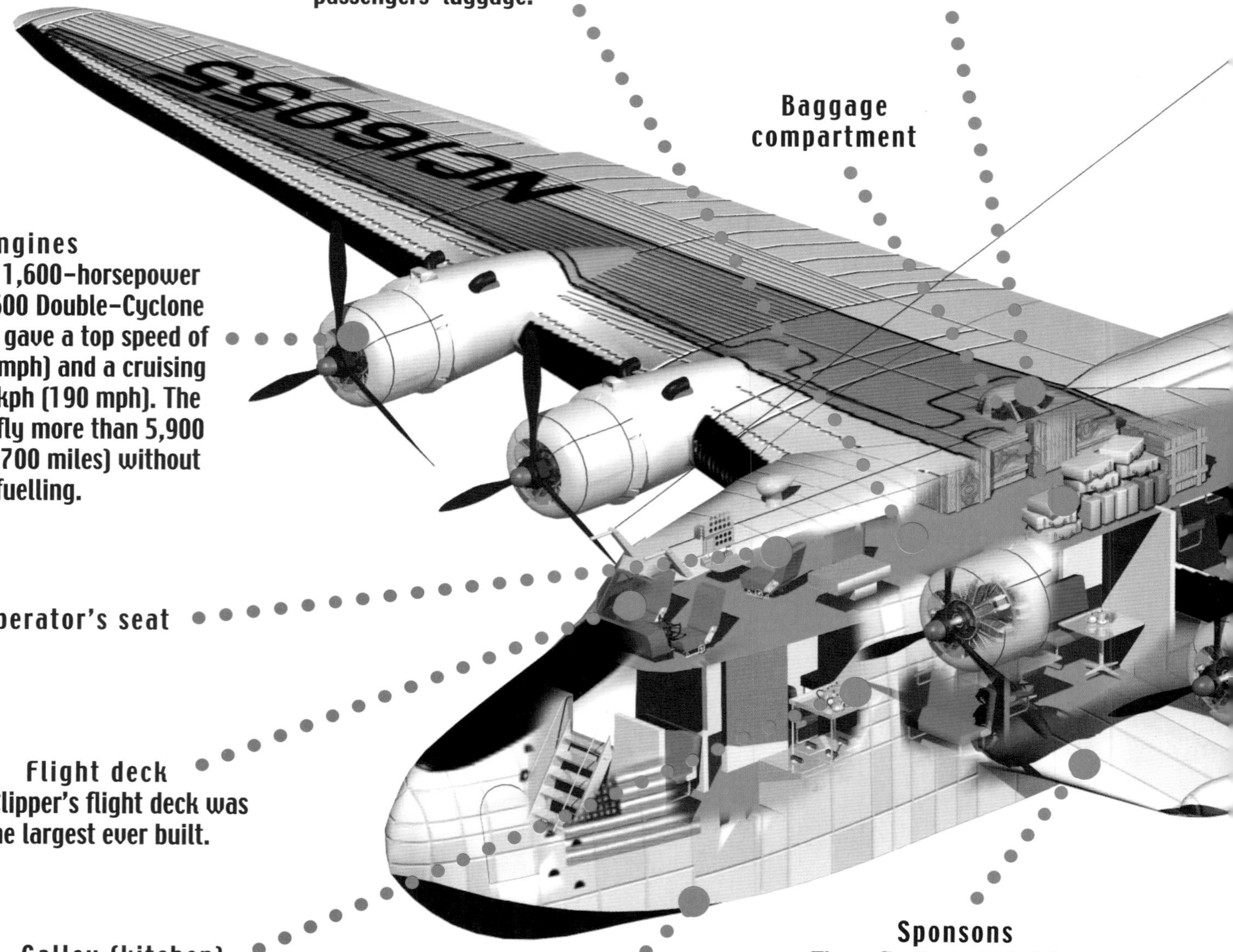

Navigation dome
To check the plane was on course on long ocean flights, where there were no familiar landmarks or coastlines, navigators would look out of this dome and note the positions of stars.

Upper deck
This contained the flight deck, the crew's quarters, and compartments for cargo and the passengers' luggage.

Baggage compartment

Engines
Four massive 1,600-horsepower Wright GR-2600 Double-Cyclone radial engines gave a top speed of 340 kph (210 mph) and a cruising speed of 302 kph (190 mph). The Clipper could fly more than 5,900 kilometres (3,700 miles) without refuelling.

Radio operator's seat

Flight deck
The Clipper's flight deck was the largest ever built.

Galley (kitchen)
The in-flight food was of the highest order. Chefs recruited from top hotels oversaw preparation at the flying boat terminal and the meals were cooked in the galley during the flight. At mealtimes, the tables were set with fine china and silver cutlery. Two waiters served the hungry diners.

Fuselage
The all-metal fuselage, nearly 6 metres (9 feet) deep and shaped like the hull of a ship, was designed to float and move easily through the water.

Sponsons
These floats projected from the sides of the plane and balanced the aircraft on the water. They helped to give extra lift in the air, and were also used to hold fuel. Most other flying boats and seaplanes had floats under the wings.

PLANES THAT FLOAT

The huge flying boats of the late 1930s sped across the water on their take-off run. They established the first long-distance airline routes across the world's oceans. These journeys were beyond the range of conventional airplanes, which could not carry enough fuel. But flying boats were able to cross oceans by refuelling at harbours and islands as they went. The largest commercial flying boat was the Boeing 314, which entered service in March 1939.

During World War II (1939–1945), flying boats were used to hunt enemy submarines and rescue pilots. After the war, the flying boats found themselves competing with fast, reliable airliners on long-distance passenger routes. As the flying boats were much more expensive to run, they were gradually phased out.

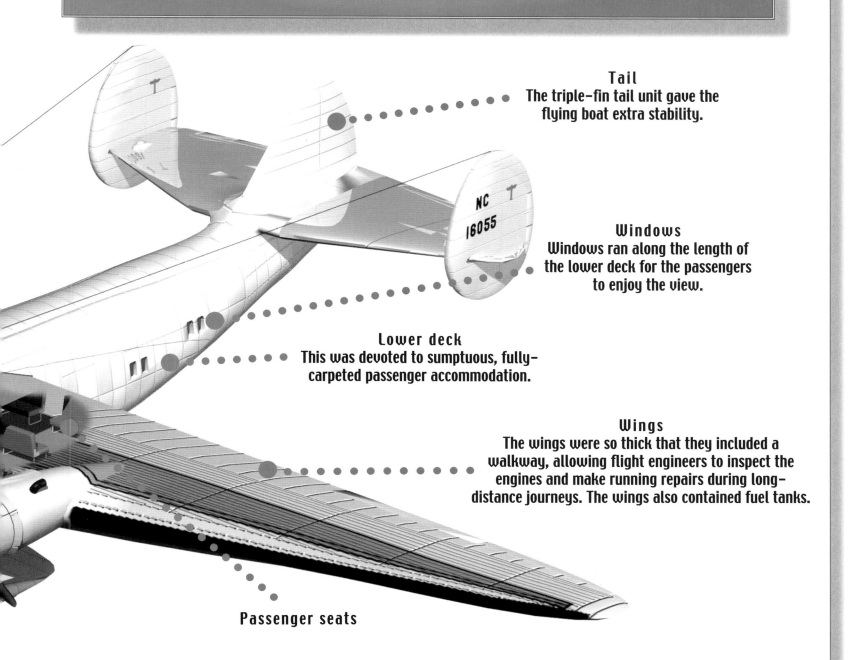

Tail
The triple–fin tail unit gave the flying boat extra stability.

Windows
Windows ran along the length of the lower deck for the passengers to enjoy the view.

Lower deck
This was devoted to sumptuous, fully–carpeted passenger accommodation.

Wings
The wings were so thick that they included a walkway, allowing flight engineers to inspect the engines and make running repairs during long–distance journeys. The wings also contained fuel tanks.

Passenger seats

THE MIGHTY CLIPPER

America's Boeing 314 was designed to carry around 75 day passengers, or 35–40 in sleeping berths on long-distance flights. The 10-man crew included two pilots, a navigator, a flight engineer, a radio operator, the ship's master (an officer who commanded the plane but did not fly it) and a relief crew of four.

Pan American Airways operated a fleet of Boeing 314s – called 'Clippers' after the fast sailing vessels of the nineteenth century – on routes across the Atlantic and Pacific. A Clipper's transatlantic journey from New York to Europe took about 24 hours, including two stops en-route. The flight across the Pacific, from San Francisco to Hong Kong, took five or six days, with rest and refuelling stops on Hawaii and other Pacific islands.

BOEING B-17 FLYING FORTRESS

Engine power
The B-17 had four turbocharged, air-cooled Wright R-1820-97 Cyclone engines. They were radial engines, which means that their nine cylinders were arranged in a circle around the crankshaft. Each gave 1,200 horsepower, allowing the B-17 to reach a maximum speed of just over 460 kph (285 mph). The cruising speed with a full bomb load was around 240 kph (150 mph).

Bombardier
Sitting in the nose of the plane, the bombardier used a bomb-sight to look through the flat viewing panel in the plastic cone and make sure that the bombs were released at just the right moment. Under fire from anti-aircraft guns or enemy fighters, the bombardier needed a steady nerve to hit the target.

Nose cone
This was made of single-piece moulded plastic and fitted with machine guns, one on either side.

Chin turret
The twin guns were remote-controlled from inside the nose cone.

Astro-navigation dome
For night-flying missions, the navigator would look out of this dome to check star positions.

Dorsal gun-turret
Mounted on top of the flight deck, this turret gave protection against fighters diving out of the Sun.

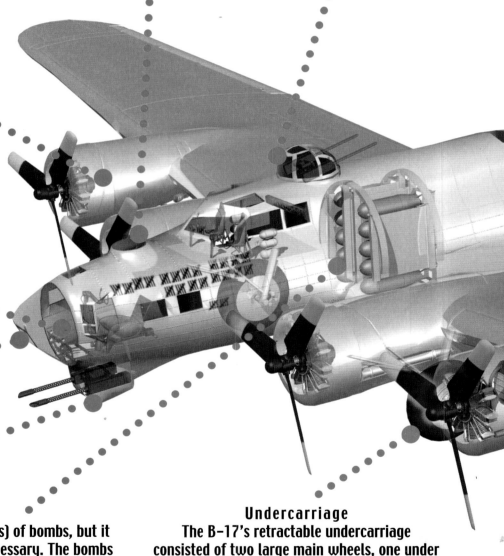

Bombs
The B-17 normally carried 2.7 tonnes (2.7 tons) of bombs, but it could manage up to 6.2 tonnes (6.1 tons) if necessary. The bombs were held in vertical racks in the bomb bay.

Undercarriage
The B-17's retractable undercarriage consisted of two large main wheels, one under each wing, and a smaller one near the tail.

BRISTLING WITH GUNS
World War II saw fighters and bombers develop by leaps and bounds to become fearsome military weapons. Huge formations of bombers caused massive destruction, and one of the most successful was the American Boeing B-17. Bombers were much slower than fighters and so were sitting targets for fast, agile enemy planes armed with machine guns and cannons. To counteract this threat, machine guns were mounted in almost every conceivable position on the B-17. In fact, the B-17 so bristled with armaments that one newspaper reporter called it a 'flying fortress' – and the name stuck!

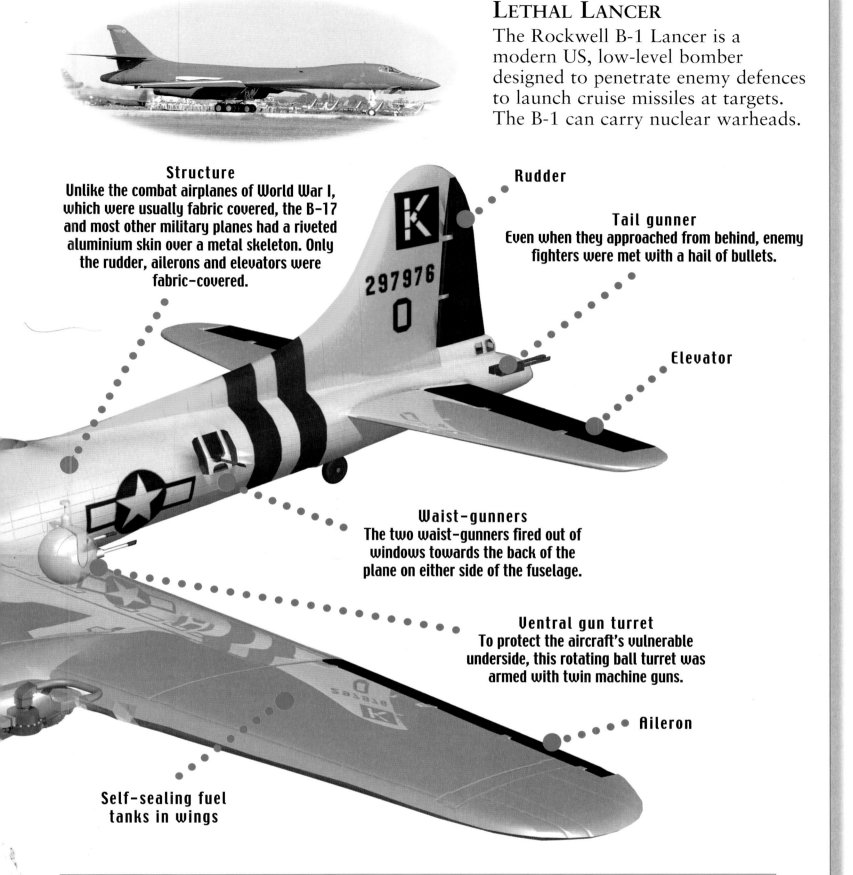

Structure
Unlike the combat airplanes of World War I, which were usually fabric covered, the B-17 and most other military planes had a riveted aluminium skin over a metal skeleton. Only the rudder, ailerons and elevators were fabric-covered.

Rudder

Tail gunner
Even when they approached from behind, enemy fighters were met with a hail of bullets.

Elevator

Waist-gunners
The two waist-gunners fired out of windows towards the back of the plane on either side of the fuselage.

Ventral gun turret
To protect the aircraft's vulnerable underside, this rotating ball turret was armed with twin machine guns.

Aileron

Self-sealing fuel tanks in wings

DAYLIGHT DANGER

Thousands of B-17s took part in daylight bombing raids over Europe, dropping more than 580,600 tonnes (571,450 tons) of high explosives on enemy targets. But daylight bombing made them vulnerable and initially many fell victim to German fighters. The B-17s' best defence was for large numbers of planes to fly in tight formation, so that fighters attacking from any direction faced a volley of fire from several aircraft. Flying like this, they managed to shoot down countless enemy planes.

The introduction of long-range escort fighters, such as the American P-51 Mustang, turned the tables. This allowed the B-17s to concentrate on their bombing missions while the escorts – their 'little friends', as the B-17 crews called them – dealt with enemy fighters.

BOEING 747-400 'JUMBO JET'

Class act
As in most airliners, there are different classes of seats, all priced differently and offering different levels of comfort and service. The cheapest seats are economy class, with business class being more spacious, and first class offering the best facilities – and costing the most!

Fuel tanks
Situated in the wings and the tail-planes, the tanks hold over 216,840 litres (15,400 gallons) of fuel.

Flight deck
Dials and gauges have been replaced by six computer screens displaying all the key data the flight crew need to fly the plane. For most of the journey the computer 'autopilot' flies the plane, with the flight crew assuming control for take-off and landing. A relief crew of two may accompany the pilot and co-pilot on long-haul trips.

Washrooms
Passengers can freshen up on long, exhausting journeys.

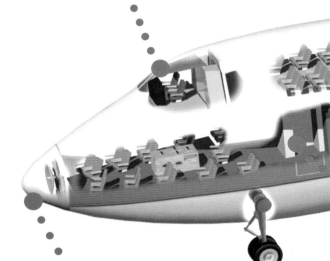

Engine pods
The four pods suspended from wing pylons each carry a Rolls-Royce RB-211-524H turbofan engine.

Nose cone
This houses the weather radar scanner.

Galley
Meals are prepared on the ground before take-off and heated up in the galley during the flight.

THE JET AGE

In 1952, Britain's De Havilland Comet, the world's first jet airliner, entered service. The jet engine has no pistons but burns a fuel-air mixture in a combustion chamber. A jet of hot exhaust gases rushes out from the rear of the engine, providing thrust to push the plane forward. The air is squeezed by a compressor as it enters the engine. The compressor is driven by a set of turbine blades, which is why it is normally called a turbojet engine. Most modern jet engines have a huge fan in front to suck more air into the engine and give extra power. These are known as turbofan engines. They are quieter and burn less fuel than turbojets.

ELEPHANTINE AIRPLANE

As more people could afford to travel by air, ever more aircraft were needed to cope with the rising levels of passengers. To prevent the airports and skies from being gridlocked with air traffic, wide-bodied, high-capacity jets were developed. Foremost among the wide-bodied jets is the Boeing 747, nicknamed the 'Jumbo' because of its huge size. When it entered service in 1970, it was twice as heavy and powerful as any other airliner, and could carry double the number of passengers. The 747-400, the most recent model, carries just over 420 passengers on long-haul international flights, not forgetting all their luggage, plus fuel for the plane and food for the journey, and the crew.

Passenger cabin
The cabin is pressurized so that the passengers can breathe air normally. Emergency oxygen masks automatically drop from above if the cabin pressure is lost. Passengers sit in rows of seats, which can recline to let people sleep. Small items of baggage can be stored in overhead lockers.

Fuselage
On the inside of the fuselage is a thick insulating blanket that keeps out the cold and cuts out most of the noise from the engines.

Airline livery
The tail fin usually carries the logo or colours of the airline that owns the plane. This is known as the livery.

Wings
The 747's hollow wings, with a skin of aluminium alloy, contain the fuel tanks. The wings must be not only extremely strong to take the strain of the plane's vast weight, but also flexible enough to bend in strong winds without breaking. They are swept back to give the plane a more streamlined shape.

Winglets
These small turn-ups at the ends of the wings, 1.8 metres (5 feet) high, reduce drag around the wing tips, saving fuel and increasing the 747's range.

Hold
Underneath the passenger cabin is the cargo hold, where the passengers' luggage is stored in large containers during the flight.

CONSTELLATION STAR

The 1940s saw a new generation of large passenger planes or 'airliners', which were propeller driven. The Lockheed Constellation was the first airliner with a pressurized cabin, enabling it to fly above bad weather and give passengers a more comfortable ride.

CONCORDE

Nose section
When taking off or landing, Concorde flies at a comparatively steep angle, with its nose in the air. To improve visibility from the cockpit, the hinged nose is lowered by 5 degrees for taxiing and take off, and 12.5 degrees when landing. For cruising, the nose is raised until it is straight.

Passenger cabin
Concorde's slender body can accommodate up to 128 passengers seated close together – far fewer than most modern long-distance airliners.

Radar located in the tip of the nose

AIR FRANCE

Flight deck
The pilot and co-pilot sit side by side, facing the control panel, with the flight engineer behind them.

Galleys
Concorde has two galleys, one at the front of the plane and one at the rear. Six stewards serve the passengers meals of the highest quality.

Undercarriage
Concorde takes off and lands on 10 wheels fitted with multi-ply high-pressure tyres. There are four wheels on the landing gear under each wing, and two on the fuselage landing gear behind the nose.

THE NEED FOR SPEED

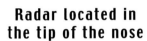

The fastest passenger plane in the world is Concorde, which can notch up an impressive 2,300 kph (1,430 mph). The fastest plane ever built, the North American X-15 rocket-powered research plane, flew more than three times faster than this!

SUPERSONIC MARVEL

Concorde is the world's fastest airliner. Jointly produced by Britain and France, Concorde is the only passenger plane that can fly faster than the speed of sound. Sound travels through the air at about 1,220 kph (755 mph) at sea level. But the speed of sound decreases with altitude as the air gets colder. A supersonic plane measures its speed with a Mach number, which is the plane's speed divided by the speed of sound at the height the plane is flying. Mach 1 is the speed of sound, Mach 2 is twice the speed of sound, and so on. Concorde's top speed is about Mach 2.2.

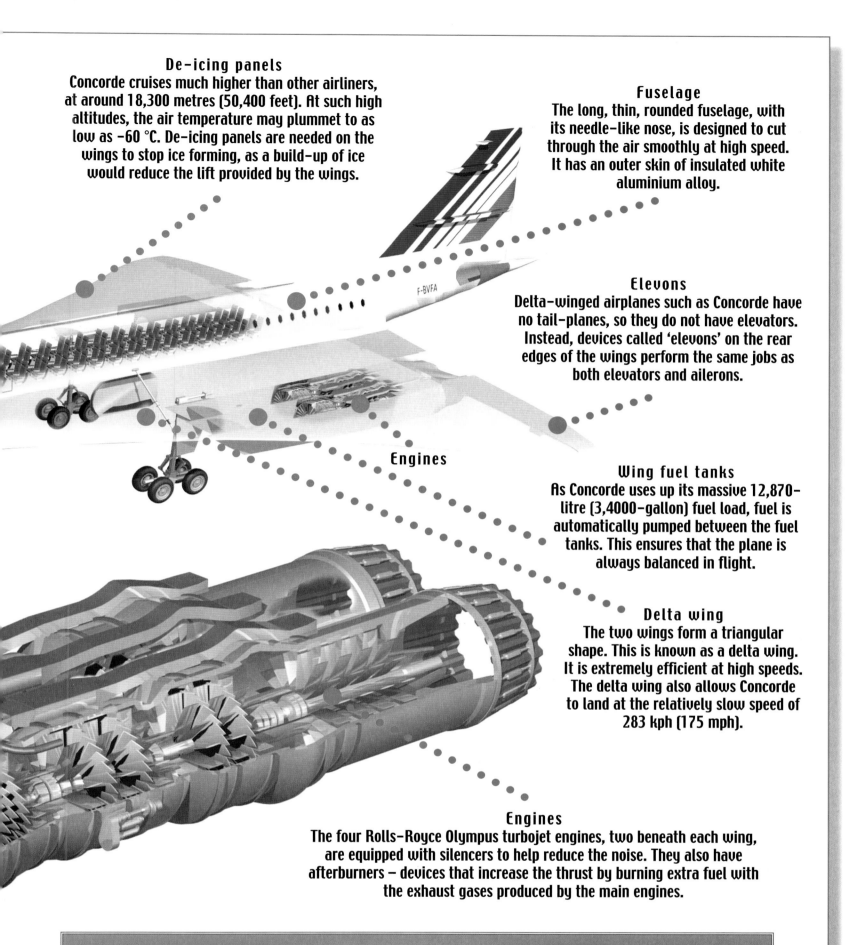

De-icing panels
Concorde cruises much higher than other airliners, at around 18,300 metres (50,400 feet). At such high altitudes, the air temperature may plummet to as low as −60 °C. De-icing panels are needed on the wings to stop ice forming, as a build-up of ice would reduce the lift provided by the wings.

Fuselage
The long, thin, rounded fuselage, with its needle-like nose, is designed to cut through the air smoothly at high speed. It has an outer skin of insulated white aluminium alloy.

Elevons
Delta-winged airplanes such as Concorde have no tail-planes, so they do not have elevators. Instead, devices called 'elevons' on the rear edges of the wings perform the same jobs as both elevators and ailerons.

Engines

Wing fuel tanks
As Concorde uses up its massive 12,870-litre (3,4000-gallon) fuel load, fuel is automatically pumped between the fuel tanks. This ensures that the plane is always balanced in flight.

Delta wing
The two wings form a triangular shape. This is known as a delta wing. It is extremely efficient at high speeds. The delta wing also allows Concorde to land at the relatively slow speed of 283 kph (175 mph).

Engines
The four Rolls-Royce Olympus turbojet engines, two beneath each wing, are equipped with silencers to help reduce the noise. They also have afterburners – devices that increase the thrust by burning extra fuel with the exhaust gases produced by the main engines.

UPS AND DOWNS OF SUPERSONIC FLIGHT

When an airplane travels faster than the speed of sound it creates a shock wave in the air that sounds like a tremendous echoing boom on the ground below. Because of this 'sonic boom', Concorde is not allowed to fly over some cities. The plane only attempts supersonic speeds over the ocean or when flying too high for the sound to be heard on the ground.

Everything in Concorde's design is geared towards making it as streamlined as possible to keep drag to a minimum at supersonic speeds. This is why the fuselage is so narrow, making seating in the passenger cabin cramped. But business people and VIPs are happy to pay Concorde's high prices for the convenience of travelling across the Atlantic in just 3.5 hours.

AIRBUS A300-600ST BELUGA

Cargo door
The Beluga's bulging 'forehead' is an upward-hinging door that is raised and lowered by hydraulic arms and secured by 24 latches. It is the largest door ever fitted to an aircraft.

Loading cargo
Large items of cargo, such as fuselage parts, are manoeuvred to the open nose of the plane on a raised, mobile gantry and transferred into the cargo bay by conveyor belt.

Guide rails
The guide rails on the cargo bay floor assist loading.

Cockpit
The cockpit has a strengthened roof to support the front end of the cargo bay floor. There are two fixed seats for the pilot and co-pilot, and two folding seats for extra crew members.

Radome
The hinged nose tip houses weather radar.

Cargo bay
The vast cargo bay measures 37.7 metres (123 feet) long and 7.6 metres (25 feet) wide. As all the crew travel in the cockpit, the cargo bay does not need to be pressurized.

Vital statistics
The Beluga is just over 56 metres (180 feet) long and more than 17 metres (47 feet) high. Unloaded, it weighs around 150 tonnes (148 tons).

CARGO CARRIERS

Planes designed to carry goods rather than passengers are called cargo or freight planes. The cargo can be anything from letters and parcels to emergency food supplies, military equipment such as tanks, and even parts of spacecraft. Some cargo planes are small light aircraft adapted to carry supplies to remote communities. Others are purpose-built workhorses of the air, such as America's Boeing C-130 Hercules, which has been ferrying cargo round the world since the 1950s. The record for the largest internal cargo bay belongs to the odd-looking Airbus A300-600ST Beluga, which has a capacity of around 1,400 cubic metres (1,100 cubic yards).

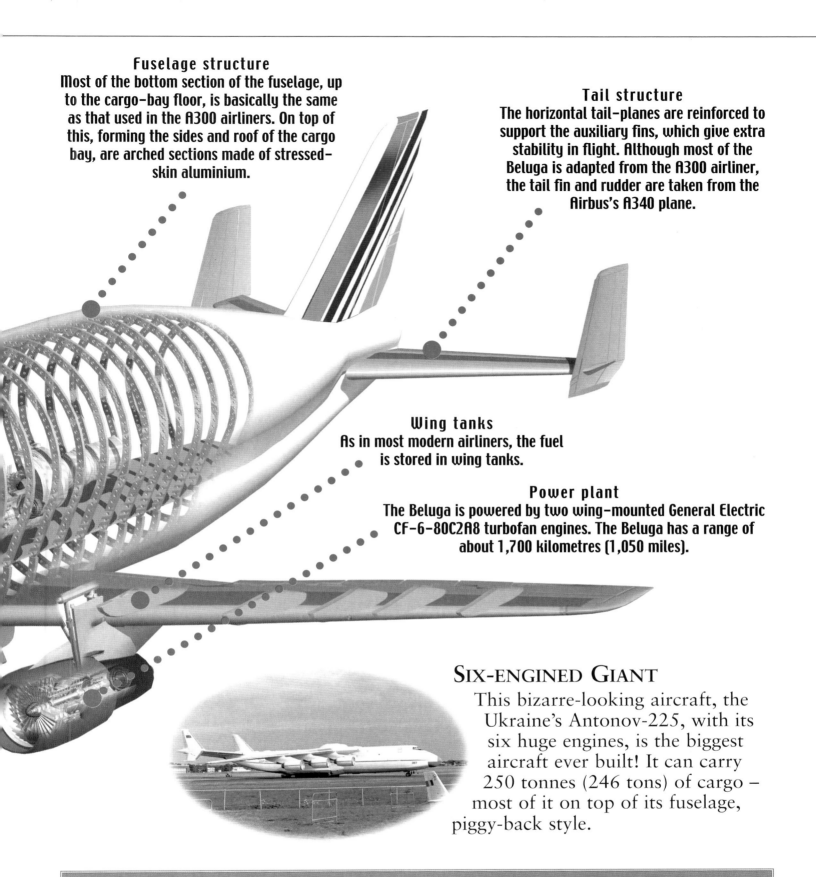

Fuselage structure
Most of the bottom section of the fuselage, up to the cargo-bay floor, is basically the same as that used in the A300 airliners. On top of this, forming the sides and roof of the cargo bay, are arched sections made of stressed-skin aluminium.

Tail structure
The horizontal tail-planes are reinforced to support the auxiliary fins, which give extra stability in flight. Although most of the Beluga is adapted from the A300 airliner, the tail fin and rudder are taken from the Airbus's A340 plane.

Wing tanks
As in most modern airliners, the fuel is stored in wing tanks.

Power plant
The Beluga is powered by two wing-mounted General Electric CF-6-80C2A8 turbofan engines. The Beluga has a range of about 1,700 kilometres (1,050 miles).

SIX-ENGINED GIANT
This bizarre-looking aircraft, the Ukraine's Antonov-225, with its six huge engines, is the biggest aircraft ever built! It can carry 250 tonnes (246 tons) of cargo – most of it on top of its fuselage, piggy-back style.

WHALE OF AN AIRCRAFT!
The Beluga, which entered service in 1996, is named after the white, bulbous-headed beluga whale. It was built by the European Airbus consortium as a 'super transporter' for carrying aircraft parts from their manufacturing sites around Europe to the assembly plant in Toulouse, France. The design for the Beluga was based on Airbus's successful A300 airliner. The cockpit was lowered and a new upper shell with a large front door was added. The tail fin was also changed to keep the plane stable when carrying heavy loads.
The Beluga is able to carry 45–50 tonnes (44–49 tons) in its cargo bay, which is big enough to transport large segments of fuselage for Airbus planes. Alternatively, it could hold a pair of wings for the A340 airliner or two pairs of A300 wings. The Beluga can also hold the complete first stage of the European Space Agency's Ariane 4 space rocket.

McDONNELL DOUGLAS AH-64 APACHE

Crew
The co-pilot/gunner sits in front of and below the pilot, in an armoured cockpit.

Power plant
Behind the rotor, and to either side of the fuselage, are the two 1,696 horsepower General Electric T700-GE-701C turbines. They give the Apache a top speed of around 300 kph (186 mph).

Main rotor
The four-blade rotor, with a diameter of 14.6 metres (40 feet), creates the helicopter's lift. The stainless steel and fibreglass blades have swept edges.

Controls
There are three main controls. The control column is operated to tilt the main rotor to go forwards, backwards or sideways. The collective pitch lever is operated to change the pitch of the rotor blades, making the helicopter go up, down, or hover. Control pedals in the floor adjust the pitch of the tail-blades to turn left or right.

Nose assembly
The all-weather, day and night weapon-sighting equipment is mounted in the nose, and includes a TV camera, laser tracker, and forward-looking infrared sensor.

Chin gun
Aimed by the co-pilot/gunner, the 30-millimetre M230 Chin Gun has 1,200 rounds of ammunition.

Weaponry
The stubby wings provide four 'hard points' to which weapons can be attached. The Apache's favoured armoury is Rockwell AGM-114 Hellfire anti-tank missiles and rocket launchers loaded with 70-millimetre FFAR rockets. Usually it carries a combination of both. Extra fuel tanks or alternative armaments could also be attached to the hard points.

AWESOME APACHE

The Apache is a two-seat, anti-tank attack helicopter whose armoury can include guns, missiles and rockets. The helicopter can be a devastating weapon on the battlefield, hovering out of sight behind trees or buildings and then popping up unexpectedly to send a hail of rockets on to an enemy tank. Sometimes helicopters work in pairs, with one helicopter highlighting the target with a laser beam and guiding the other's missiles on to their target. Equipped with sensitive electronic devices, it can fight in daytime, at night, and in poor weather.

ROTARY WINGS

Helicopters are the most versatile of all aircraft, able to hover, take off and land vertically, and fly backwards and sideways, as well as forwards. Their rotor blades are like spinning wings. The blades are aerofoil-shaped and slightly angled. The angle of the blades is known as the pitch. The whirring blades push the air downwards and generate lift. The steeper the pitch of the blades, the greater the lift they give. When the lift is greater than the helicopter's weight, the aircraft takes off. When lift and weight are equal, the helicopter hovers, and when weight is greater than lift, the helicopter descends.

Using the controls, the pilot tilts the entire set of rotor blades forwards, giving thrust that pushes the helicopter along. To move sideways or backwards, the pilot simply tilts the blades in the desired direction. Changing the pitch of the tail-rotor blades turns the helicopter left or right.

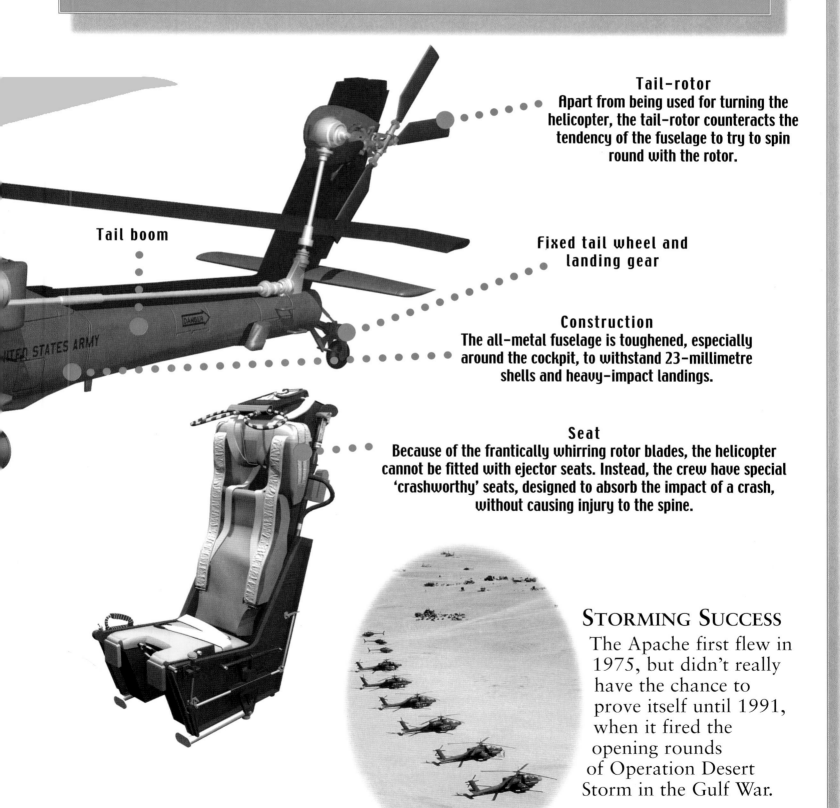

Tail-rotor
Apart from being used for turning the helicopter, the tail-rotor counteracts the tendency of the fuselage to try to spin round with the rotor.

Tail boom

Fixed tail wheel and landing gear

Construction
The all-metal fuselage is toughened, especially around the cockpit, to withstand 23-millimetre shells and heavy-impact landings.

Seat
Because of the frantically whirring rotor blades, the helicopter cannot be fitted with ejector seats. Instead, the crew have special 'crashworthy' seats, designed to absorb the impact of a crash, without causing injury to the spine.

STORMING SUCCESS
The Apache first flew in 1975, but didn't really have the chance to prove itself until 1991, when it fired the opening rounds of Operation Desert Storm in the Gulf War.

UNITED STATES ARMY

BOEING VERTOL CHINOOK CH-47

Capacity

The Chinook is extremely spacious inside, with a cabin measuring 2.3 metres (6 feet) wide, 2 metres (5 feet) high and over 9 metres (25 feet) long. It can carry 44 fully equipped troops or 24 injured soldiers on stretchers, along with medical attendants.

Turning technique

The fibreglass blades can spin at up to 225 times per minute. Because the Chinook doesn't have a tail-rotor, it needs another mechanism to turn the craft. Normally the speeds of the two rotors are the same so they balance each other out. But making one rotor spin faster or slower than the other turns the helicopter to the left or the right.

Cockpit

Two pilots and two crew sit in the cockpit. The cockpit seats have vibration absorbers to smooth the ride and reduce pilot fatigue. The flying controls are hydraulically powered.

Strong blast

The downrush of air from the Chinook's powerful rotors is equivalent to wind speeds of 90 kph (56 mph) – enough to blow a Cessna 172 on to its back!

Weapons

The Chinook rarely carries weapons, but it can if necessary. Armaments can include machine guns, and grenade and rocket launchers.

WORKHORSE OF THE SKY

When you need to get large numbers of troops, emergency supplies or heavy machinery into awkward places – call for the Chinook! The 15-tonne (about 15-ton) Boeing Vertol CH-47 Chinook is probably the most reliable and popular heavy-lifting helicopter in the world. First introduced in 1961, it has been constantly updated and is still in service with most modern armed forces.

Under its belly, the Chinook has three crane hooks for lifting heavy objects. The front and back hooks can lift up to 5 tonnes (5 tons), but the central crane hook can raise loads in excess of 9 tonnes (9 tons), though not over great distances. The cargo is usually armoured vehicles, field guns and battlefield supplies. Three loads can be moved at once by using cables of different lengths so that the loads do not collide in flight.

Drive shaft
This carries power from engines to front rotor.

Deadly blades
The Chinook's rotor span is 18.3 metres (50 feet). Approach from the front and you risk decapitation, as the blades. can skim to 1.2 metres (3 feet) off the ground! At the rear, clearance is 5.4 metres (15 feet).

Engines
The twin Lycoming T55-L712 turbines give a top speed of 306 kph (190 mph). A compressor first squeezes the intake air. The air is then mixed with fuel, and the mixture burned in a combustion chamber. The waste gases drive a set of turbine blades which, in turn, power the rotors.

Cargo ramp
The ramp descends at the rear of the helicopter for fast loading and unloading.

Undercarriage
Two pairs of landing wheels give stability when the Chinook is fully laden.

Floating Wokka
The fuselage is watertight in case the Chinook comes down in the ocean.

Fuel supply
The large tanks under the cabin floor hold enough fuel for up to 10 hours flying, depending on the load.

BLACK HAWK
The Sikorsky Black Hawk is a multi-role transport helicopter, used to carry troops and equipment to the battlefield.

MIGHTY WOKKA!

The Chinook does not have a tail-rotor, but it counteracts the fuselage's tendency to spin round by having two very large main rotors, each turning in a different direction. The sound they make – a deafening 'wokka wokka' – is the origin of the Chinook's nickname: the Mighty Wokka.

The rotors are over 15 metres (41 feet) in diameter and actually overlap in the middle. The rear one is higher than the front one, and the two are linked by a gearing arrangement that ensures that they do not strike each other – which would be disastrous. The rotors are powered by two powerful engines at the rear of the helicopter. The Chinook has also been used as a passenger helicopter to make short trips between cities, and to carry personnel to and from oil rigs far out at sea.

SIKORSKY SEA KING

Winch
Search and rescue helicopters have a motor-driven winch, which raises and lowers a line running over a pulley beside the main cabin door.

Tail-rotor
This is turned by a long drive shaft leading from the engines.

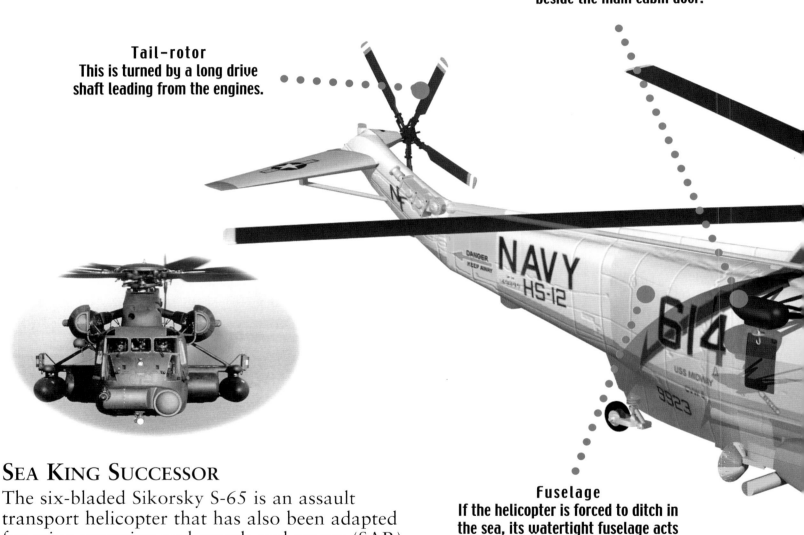

SEA KING SUCCESSOR
The six-bladed Sikorsky S-65 is an assault transport helicopter that has also been adapted for mine sweeping and search and rescue (SAR) work at sea. In some countries it has replaced the Sea King as the main SAR helicopter.

Fuselage
If the helicopter is forced to ditch in the sea, its watertight fuselage acts like the hull of a boat and keeps it afloat for a while, giving the crew time to escape into life rafts.

FIRST AND FOREMOST
As long ago as 1483, the Italian artist and inventor Leonardo Da Vinci made drawings of a muscle-powered helicopter. It had a large, screw-like wing made of starched linen. Although the machine was never built and could not have flown in reality, his idea was way ahead of his time. It was more than 400 years later, in 1907, that Frenchman Paul Cornu made a 20-second hop in a twin-rotor helicopter, but the fragile craft broke apart when it landed with a bump. Helicopters only became truly practical with Russian-born Igor Sikorsky's VS-300 single-rotor craft, which was first flown in 1939. It may have looked cumbersome but it worked, opening a whole new chapter in the history of aviation. Sikorsky went on to produce a host of important helicopters, including the Sea King, famous for picking up US astronauts after splash-down in the ocean.

SEARCH AND RESCUE

The Sea King can perform daring rescue missions beyond the range of lifeboats, such as hoisting people off burning vessels at sea. With the helicopter hovering over the water, a crew member can be lowered on a winch to pluck drowning sailors from the waves. The Sea King is fully equipped with emergency medical supplies to help the injured, who can be lifted up into the helicopter in a sling or harness. The Sea King then whisks them back to shore at speeds of up to 230 kph (140 mph).

The Sea King made its maiden flight in 1959, and has been regularly updated ever since. It was originally designed as an anti-submarine helicopter, and is still used in that role today. Its other uses include airborne early warning (AEW) missions, transporting troops or civilian passengers, and taking personnel and supplies to off-shore oil rigs.

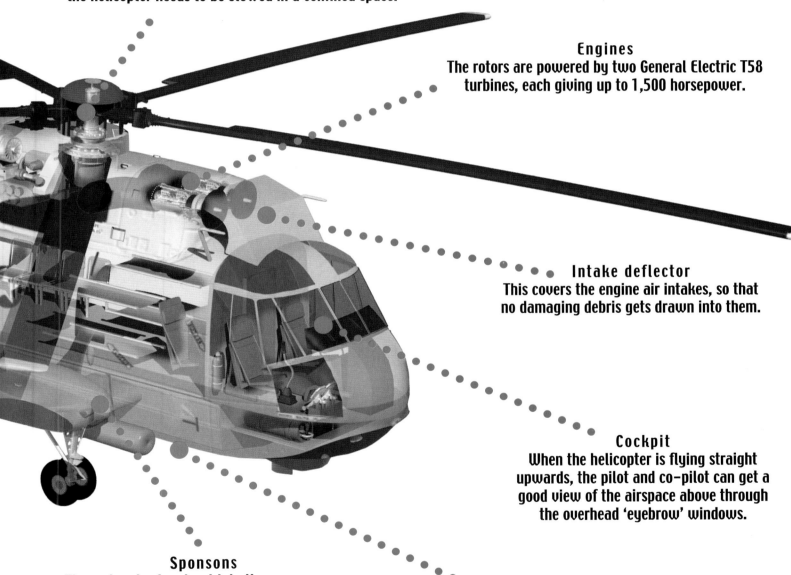

Main rotor
The main rotor has a span of 19 metres (52 feet). The five blades are hinged so that they can fold backwards if the helicopter needs to be stowed in a confined space.

Engines
The rotors are powered by two General Electric T58 turbines, each giving up to 1,500 horsepower.

Intake deflector
This covers the engine air intakes, so that no damaging debris gets drawn into them.

Cockpit
When the helicopter is flying straight upwards, the pilot and co-pilot can get a good view of the airspace above through the overhead 'eyebrow' windows.

Sponsons
The main wheels retract into the sponsons on either side of the fuselage. An emergency flotation bag in each sponson fills with air if the helicopter lands in water, to give it added buoyancy.

Fuel reserves
Five fuel cells located under the cabin floor hold 3,100 litres (820 gallons).

BELL BOEING V-22 OSPREY

Wings
For storage aboard ships, the entire wing rotates through 90°. When the wing is lined up with the fuselage and the rotors are folded inwards, the Osprey's width is reduced from nearly 26 metres (85 feet) to just over 5 metres (16 feet).

Rotors
The three-bladed rotors are 11.6 metres (32 feet) in diameter and made of fibreglass and graphite. They are specially designed so that if they break off, they will not strike the cockpit or the passenger cabin.

Cockpit
The large, low-cut cockpit windows give excellent visibility. There are no ejector seats for the two pilots, but the cockpit is specially strengthened to withstand the impact of a crash.

Fly-by-wire
As with most modern combat aircraft, the Osprey uses computer-generated signals carried by electrical wires from the cockpit to activate the control surfaces, such as the elevators and flaperons.

Cabin
Along each wall of the cabin are a dozen impact-resistant seats, which are designed to absorb the shock of a bumpy touchdown or crash-landing.

Sponsons
Two bulging floats called sponsons, on either side of the fuselage, allow the Osprey to float on water. They carry more than 4,500 litres (320 gallons) of fuel, in addition to nearly 3,000 litres (210 gallons) held in self-sealing wing tanks.

TILT-ROTOR AIRCRAFT

For many years, designers dreamed of producing an aircraft that would combine the speed of an airplane with the manoeuvrability of a helicopter. The result is the Bell Boeing V-22 Osprey, a 'tilt-rotor' aircraft that can take off and hover like a helicopter and fly like a normal plane. The Osprey's secret lies in its engines, which can be swivelled to point either upwards or forwards.

The Osprey takes off with its engines and rotors pointing upwards to generate lift. With the Osprey airborne and hovering, the rotors and engines swivel into a horizontal, forward-facing position. The lift now comes from the wings, rather than the rotors, which provide the thrust to drive the plane forwards. The Osprey's rotors are so long that it cannot land like a normal airplane, as the rotors would strike the ground.

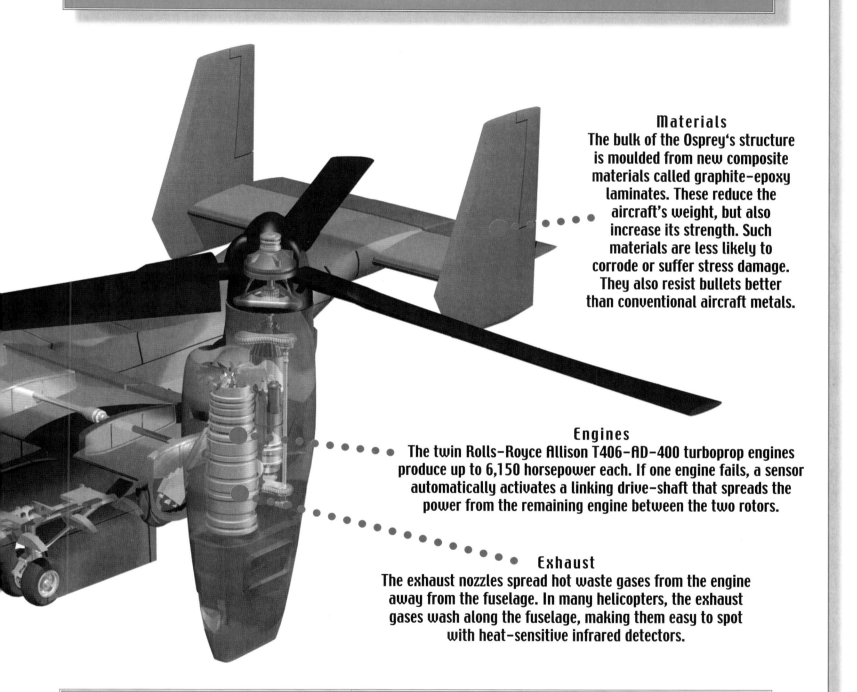

Materials
The bulk of the Osprey's structure is moulded from new composite materials called graphite-epoxy laminates. These reduce the aircraft's weight, but also increase its strength. Such materials are less likely to corrode or suffer stress damage. They also resist bullets better than conventional aircraft metals.

Engines
The twin Rolls-Royce Allison T406-AD-400 turboprop engines produce up to 6,150 horsepower each. If one engine fails, a sensor automatically activates a linking drive-shaft that spreads the power from the remaining engine between the two rotors.

Exhaust
The exhaust nozzles spread hot waste gases from the engine away from the fuselage. In many helicopters, the exhaust gases wash along the fuselage, making them easy to spot with heat-sensitive infrared detectors.

OSPREY IN ACTION

The Osprey was designed as a troop transporter, to launch quick assaults from ships against land-based targets. It can reach combat zones much faster than other helicopter transporters, carrying 24 fully equipped troops or 9,000 kilograms (4,090 pounds) of cargo. It can also be armed with a variety of weapons – from machine guns to anti-tank missiles, cannons and bombs – to operate as a 'gunship'. It can carry depth-charges and torpedoes to hunt and destroy enemy submarines. The Osprey could also be used by Coast Guard services for search and rescue missions at sea, as a reconnaissance aircraft, or even as an air ambulance.

CANADAIR CL-215

Windows
The large cockpit windows give all-round visibility, helping the pilot to aim the water drops accurately.

Power
The CL-215's powerhouses are two Pratt & Witney Canada 18-cylinder R2800 engines, which each produce 2,100 horsepower to drive the three-bladed propellers.

Chemical tanks
The CL-215 carries a special fire-fighting foam, which is stored in concentrated form in the plane's two chemical tanks.

Mooring pendant
To keep the plane steady when it rests on the water with its engines off, it can be moored to a jetty by a rope or cable attached to the pendant.

Nose undercarriage
Strong waterproof doors protect the steerable front wheels when they are withdrawn into the fuselage.

Drop doors
The water is dropped on to the fire by opening doors in the base of the water tanks.

Water tanks
The CL-215 can carry up to 5,346 litres (1,100 gallons) of water in its two storage tanks. The tanks can be filled by a hose before take-off.

WATER BOMBER

The Canadair CL-215 is designed specifically to reach forest fires quickly and get them under control. It quenches the flames by sweeping low over the blaze and 'bombing' them with huge quantities of water released from its water tanks. The plane refills by scooping up water from rivers and lakes. Flying at 130 kph (80 mph), with the fuselage skimming the water's surface, it can take just 10 seconds to fill the CL-215's tanks.

The CL-215 can fight fires for up to four hours before needing to refuel, making as many as 100 water drops and hurling nearly half a million litres (132,000 gallons) of water on to the blaze in a day.

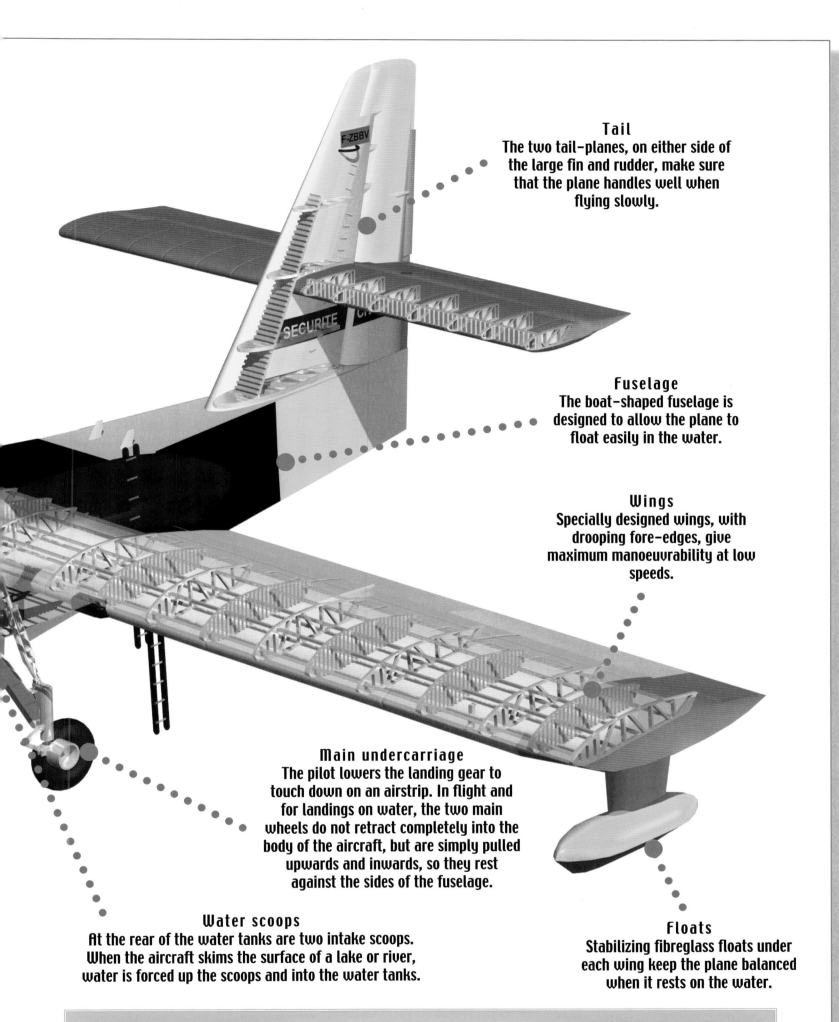

Tail
The two tail-planes, on either side of the large fin and rudder, make sure that the plane handles well when flying slowly.

Fuselage
The boat-shaped fuselage is designed to allow the plane to float easily in the water.

Wings
Specially designed wings, with drooping fore-edges, give maximum manoeuvrability at low speeds.

Main undercarriage
The pilot lowers the landing gear to touch down on an airstrip. In flight and for landings on water, the two main wheels do not retract completely into the body of the aircraft, but are simply pulled upwards and inwards, so they rest against the sides of the fuselage.

Water scoops
At the rear of the water tanks are two intake scoops. When the aircraft skims the surface of a lake or river, water is forced up the scoops and into the water tanks.

Floats
Stabilizing fibreglass floats under each wing keep the plane balanced when it rests on the water.

AERIAL FIRE-FIGHTING

Although the CL-215 can fight a fire with water alone, the best effects are produced using a fire-fighting foam. A small amount of a special chemical is added to the water as it is released from the tanks, forming a foam that expands as it falls. The foam blankets a large area of the fire, starving it of oxygen and extinguishing the flames. Foam is also dropped on to unburned trees around the blaze to prevent the fire from spreading.

BRITISH AEROSPACE /BOEING HARRIER

JUMP JET

In a tight dog-fight with enemy fighters, manoeuvrability is more valuable than speed. The Harrier is a V/STOL (Vertical/Short Take-Off and Landing) fighter and strike airplane. It can take off and fly straight upwards, and land by coming straight back down. If it has a heavy load, the Harrier takes a short run-up to help it 'jump' into the air.

Wings
The short, backward-sloping wings have a span of just 9.25 metres (25 feet). They are 'shoulder wings', which means that they are joined to the plane at the top of the fuselage.

Engine air-intake
There are two semicircular air-intakes, one on either side of the fuselage. A large fan at the front sucks air into the engine.

Engine
The Harrier is powered by a single Rolls-Royce Pegasus vectored-thrust turbofan engine located in the centre of the plane. Hatches just behind the cockpit give easy access for repairs and maintenance.

Nose cone
This contains sensors that can lock laser- and TV-guided weapons on to their targets.

Cockpit
The cockpit is equipped with a head-up display, video-screen information displays, a digital moving map, and night-vision goggles for the pilot.

Ejector seat
The pilot sits in a rocket-powered ejector seat unit, which has an oxygen mask, a parachute for descent to the ground and a rubber dinghy in case of a watery landing.

Cannon pods
The Harrier has two 30-millimetre cannon pods, one on each side of the plane's belly.

Front engine nozzles
These expel cold air drawn in by the front fan.

Main landing wheels
These descend from the centre of the fuselage.

Rear engine nozzles
These expel hot gases fro burning fuel in the engin

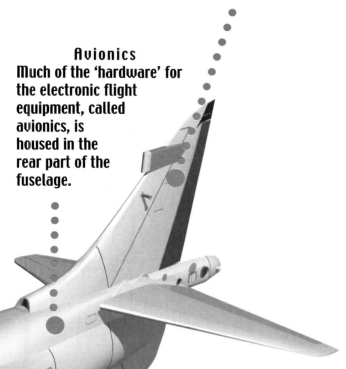

Materials
The Harrier's fuselage and wings are built from light, strong aluminium alloys and 'composite' materials such as carbon-fibre.

Avionics
Much of the 'hardware' for the electronic flight equipment, called avionics, is housed in the rear part of the fuselage.

NOT FAST BUT DEADLY
The Harrier is not a fast airplane, with a top speed of about 1,200 kph (745 mph), but it is very agile. It can fly backwards, or from side to side, and it can even hover. It can also slow down from 1,000 kph (620 mph) to a virtual standstill in about 12 seconds.

Reaction jets
The main engine is too powerful for fine manoeuvres at low speeds, so the plane has small compressed-air 'puffers', called reaction jets. Located in the nose, wing-tips, and tail, the reaction jets are fed pressurized air from the compressor in the main engine.

Control surfaces
The control surfaces – such as the rudder, ailerons and flaps – work only during normal flight. At all other times, the plane is controlled by the engine nozzles and the reaction jets.

Wing wheels
Towards each wing-tip, away from the exhaust jets from the engine nozzles, the Harrier has a small wheel. Mounted on shock-absorbing legs, these wheels steady the plane during take-off and landing. The wheels fold back when the plane is flying.

Hard point/pylon
Missiles, bombs and extra fuel tanks are carried on the hard points (also called pylons). The Harrier can be fitted with up to nine hard points on the wings and fuselage.

VECTORED THRUST
The secret of the Harrier's success is its 'vectored thrust'. This is the ability to control and direct gases leaving the engine. The single jet engine has four rotating (vectoring) exhaust nozzles, just under where the wings meet the fuselage. For a vertical take-off, the nozzles point towards the ground, directing the gases downwards so that the plane is pushed up into the air. As the Harrier gains height, the nozzles swivel to point diagonally downwards, so that the gases push the plane both up and forwards. For normal flight the nozzles are directed backwards, and as the Harrier is propelled forwards the flow of air over the wings provides lift to keep the plane airborne. To fly backwards, the nozzles point down and slightly forwards.

A-10 THUNDERBOLT

Fuel tanks
The fuel is kept in special foam chambers that prevent fumes from forming. This lessens the risk of fire if the fuel tanks are damaged. The tanks are hidden right in the centre of the plane and protected by fire-detectors and extinguishers.

Canopy
The large bubble-shaped canopy gives good all-round vision. Its toughened glass can withstand small-arms fire.

Cockpit
The single pilot sits in a protective 'bathtub' made of ultra-strong titanium-alloy. The cockpit is filled with a host of switches, gauges and dials. During training, every pilot must pass a blindfold test in which they have to find and activate controls by touch alone.

Head-up display (HUD)
Modern combat aircraft often have a see-through screen that displays important flight information in front of the pilot's face. The pilot can read the details without having to look down at the flight instruments. HUDs can also be used for aiming guns or missiles at targets. Some pilot helmets have a special visor that does the same job as the HUD.

Boarding ladder

Ammunition belt and drum
Shells are fed to the cannon by the ammunition belt. The drum in the plane's belly carries 1,174 rounds of ammunition. It also collects the used shell-cases to prevent them flying into the engine's fans.

Rotary cannon
Slung beneath the cockpit is the single Avenger cannon, whose seven rotating barrels shoot bursts of high-velocity 30-millimetre high-explosive or armour-piercing shells. A short burst is all that is needed to put a tank out of action. The noise of the firing cannon gave it its nickname – the 'burp gun'.

ROVING DESTROYER
The A-10's role is to support ground forces. The A-10 entered service in 1976 and proved its worth to devastating effect in the Gulf War of 1990 and during the Kosovo conflict of 1999. The A-10 is slow compared to most combat airplanes, with poor acceleration, but the straight wings give tremendous lift and make it very agile at low speeds and low altitudes. They also allow it to take off and land on short runways built close to the combat zone. It can still fly with an entire engine shot off its mounting, one rudder missing, or a large chunk of a wing blown away in combat!

LINGERING THREAT

The A-10 lingers over the battlefield making low-level jinking runs, often at tree-top height, to attack tanks and other armoured vehicles.

Tail
The twin tail fins are designed to improve low-speed manoeuvrability. They also help to conceal the engine's hot exhaust gases from heat-seeking infrared missiles, making the A-10 a harder target for the missiles to lock on to.

Engines
The A-10 has two General Electric TF34-GE-100 turbofan engines mounted high on the rear of the fuselage so that the pilot has an unhindered view of the terrain below. The engines give the A-10 a top speed when fully loaded of 725 kph (450 mph) and a cruising speed of 555 kph (345 mph).

Ailerons
The special split ailerons help to stabilize the plane in flight as it blasts enemy tanks with its powerful cannon.

Undercarriage
In flight, the wheels only partly retract. In the event of a crash-landing, they may help to lessen the impact, limiting damage to plane and pilot.

Weapons payload
The 11 pylons, three under the fuselage and four under each wing, can carry over 7,250 kilograms (3,300 pounds) of weapons or equipment. Weaponry can include rockets, air-to-air and air-to-ground guided missiles, and free-fall and guided bombs. The A-10 can also carry electronic countermeasures (ECM) pods, which contain transmitters that jam enemy radar.

FLYING PIG

The pilots who fly the strange-looking A-10 nickname it the 'Warthog', after the fierce, ugly African wild pig. Like its animal namesake, the Warthog is not to be messed with. The A-10 was designed around its gun – a fearsome 6-metre (18-foot) long cannon that can spit out shells at a rate of up to 4,200 per minute. The cannon shoots straight ahead. This means that pilots have to fly directly towards targets, often facing flak (anti-aircraft fire) full on, so the A-10 needs to be tough – and it is! Titanium armour plating, up to 38 millimetres (1.5 inches) thick, surrounds the cockpit, and also helps to protect the engines and some of the flight control systems. The A-10 can survive direct hits from armour-piercing shells and high-explosive projectiles.

DAEDALUS PEDAL- POWERED PLANE

Wing-span
The huge wing-span allowed *Daedalus* to take off at speeds as low as 6.4 kph (4 mph), but meant it was likely to be thrown about by the gentlest winds. Kanellopoulos and his team waited in Crete for a month until the weather was calm enough to risk the flight.

Wing materials
The wings were made of styrofoam and balsa wood, with a main spar of carbon-fibre. They were strengthened by bracing wires and coated with mylar.

Vital statistics
During the flight, the 8.6-metre (24-foot) long *Daedalus* travelled about 5 metres (14 feet) above the water at an average speed of 30 kph (19 mph).

PIONEER OF PEDAL POWER

In April 1998, Greek cycling champion Kanellos Kanellopoulos pedalled a lightweight airplane across the Aegean Sea between the Greek islands of Crete and Santorini. The 119-kilometre (75-mile) flight, which took nearly four hours of non-stop pedalling, set a world record for human-powered flight. The airplane was named *Daedalus*, after the mythical Greek engineer who made wings of wax and feathers for himself and his son to escape from King Minos of Crete. *Daedalus* was built by a team of engineers at Massachusetts Institute of Technology (MIT), USA.

PEDAL-POWER PROBLEMS

The main problem with airplanes such as *Daedalus* is the lack of power. Pedalling constantly, Kanellopoulos averaged an output of just 0.27 horsepower – even the Wright brothers' *Flyer* produced 12 horsepower. The amazing flight was only possible because the plane had a wing-span as wide as a Boeing 727 airliner and weighed just 32 kilograms (70 pounds). The 34-metre (94-foot) wings gave tremendous lift, while modern, ultra-light materials kept the weight down. However, the huge wing-span made *Daedalus* unstable even in gentle winds, and Kanellopoulos fell into the sea just 10 metres (28 feet) short of his destination, when a gust of wind snapped the tail boom.

Fresh-air intake
A scoop beneath the wing collected fresh air and fed it into the cockpit, to keep the pilot cool.

Flight instruments
The small electronic airspeed and altitude monitors were fixed to the pedal column.

Propeller
The 3.4-metre- (9-foot-) diameter propeller turned 108 times per minute. The pilot could alter the pitch of the blades to maintain the optimum pedalling rate.

Airspeed gauge
Daedalus's movement through the air made a tiny balsa propeller behind the main propeller spin round, generating electrical signals that displayed the airspeed on the cockpit monitor.

Carbon-fibre tail boom

Cockpit
Kanellopoulos sat in the cockpit with both his feet clipped to the pedals. The cockpit was smooth and streamlined to reduce drag.

Slide stick
This lever controlled the rudder and elevators, via cables and pulleys.

Vital fluids
On either side of the pilot's seat were bottles of salt-glucose solution for the pilot to drink to avoid dehydrating.

GRUMMAN HAWKEYE

Rotodome
Measuring about 8 metres (22 feet) in diameter, the motor-driven radar disc, or 'rotodome', revolves five times per minute. Hydraulic jacks raise the rotodome for AEW patrols and lower it when the plane is out of action.

Fins and rudders
While the fuselage and wings are metal, the fins and rudders are largely fibreglass, to reduce radar reflection.

Chemical toilet
Even the best trained aircrew need to use the bathroom from time to time!

Control centre
The three systems operators – radar operator, air control officer and combat information officer – sit facing electronic display panels along the fuselage wall. The seats swivel to face forwards when taking off and landing.

Catapult tow-bar
Airplanes are launched from carriers by catapults, which hurl the planes from a standing start to speeds of around 320 kph (200 mph). For take-off, the tow-bar is attached to the catapult, which runs along a track in the deck.

SPY IN THE SKY

The Grumman Hawkeye is an airborne early warning (AEW) airplane. It may look as though it's carrying its own parasol, but the huge disc on top of the plane is actually a rotating radar antenna that scours the skies and seas for unfriendly intruders. Bristling with sophisticated electronic equipment, the Hawkeye can track over 2,000 aircraft, missiles, and ships simultaneously. It can detect and identify bomber-sized targets as far as 530 kilometres (330 miles) away – not bad for an airplane that made its maiden flight about 40 years ago! The E-2C II is the latest upgrade of the basic Hawkeye structure, and the Hawkeye 2000, currently under development, will continue to be the airborne eyes and ears of the US Navy for many years to come.

RADAR RECONNAISSANCE

The Hawkeyes travel with a fleet of naval ships on board an aircraft carrier. Once airborne, they can fly beyond the range of the carrier's own radar, giving a vast coverage of sky and sea. In a combat situation, they can give fighter pilots an idea of the 'big picture' of what's going on in an air battle, and alert them to threats and targets coming their way. The plane has a crew of five: two pilots, and three systems operators who analyse the data collected by the plane's monitoring equipment and communicate with the carrier and other aircraft.

Vital statistics
The Hawkeye is nearly 17.6 metres (48 feet) long, 5.6 metres (15 feet) high and has a wing-span of about 24.6 metres (8 feet).

Wings
When not in use, hydraulic jacks fold the wings back so that the Hawkeye does not take up too much space on the crowded carrier deck, and can fit on to the lifts that descend to the hangers below deck.

Engines
Two Allison T56-A-427 turboprop engines, mounted either side of the fuselage on the high, straight wings, drive the four-bladed composite propellers.

Cooling system
This intake duct houses the vapour-cycle radiator, which controls the temperature inside the plane. An efficient cooling system is needed, because the mass of electronic equipment on board the Hawkeye generates a lot of heat.

Hardware
The electronic hardware for all the Hawkeye's systems is packed into the area behind the pilot's cockpit.

Cockpit
The side windows bulge outwards so the pilots can get a good downward view. The windscreen is electrically heated, to prevent ice formation. Parachutes are located behind the pilots' seats.

GUIDE IN THE SKY
Hawkeyes are always the first planes to take off from an aircraft carrier and the last to land. They act as 'flying control towers' for other aircraft launched from the carrier, such as this Northrop Grumman F-14 Tomcat. The Hawkeyes guide their flight to and from the ship.

NORTH AMERICAN X-15

Wing jets
Like the nose jets, these helped to make minor adjustments to the X-15's flight. They controlled rolling.

Helium sphere
Helium gas from this sphere, at the rear of the aircraft, was used to keep the fuel tanks pressurized.

Heat dispersal
Friction with the air generated temperatures of almost 650 °C. The whole plane was coated with a special pink material (MA-25S) which 'boiled' away in flight, taking heat with it. Beneath this covering, the X-15 was spray-painted jet-black with a special silicone-based paint that helped to disperse heat.

Skin
The outer skin of the X-15 was made of special nickel–chromium alloy, called Inconel X, while most of the underlying structure was titanium alloy.

Rocket engine

X-PLANES

Many unusual-looking experimental aircraft, often called X-planes, have been built for research into high speed flight. One of the most famous X-planes was the Bell X-1. Flown by Captain Charles 'Chuck' Yeager, it became the first plane to fly faster than the speed of sound in October 1947, when it reached 1,078 kph (668 mph). Perhaps the most amazing X-plane of all was the dart-shaped North American X-15. This rocket-powered plane was used in the 1960s to investigate flight at hypersonic speeds (at least five times faster than the speed of sound).

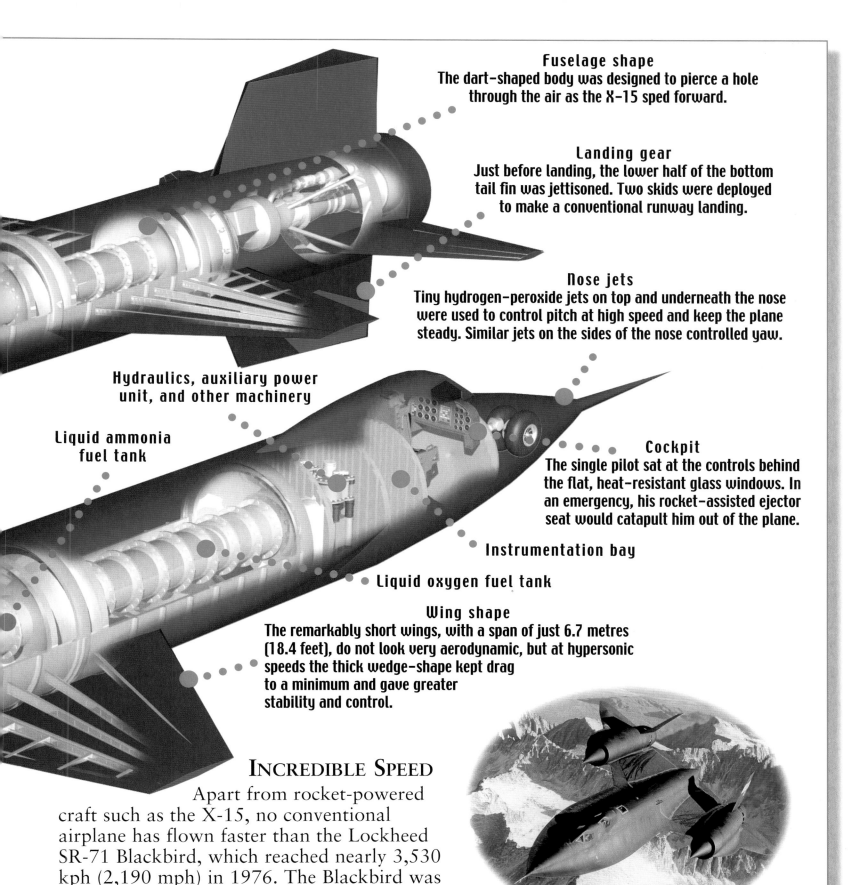

Fuselage shape
The dart-shaped body was designed to pierce a hole through the air as the X-15 sped forward.

Landing gear
Just before landing, the lower half of the bottom tail fin was jettisoned. Two skids were deployed to make a conventional runway landing.

Nose jets
Tiny hydrogen-peroxide jets on top and underneath the nose were used to control pitch at high speed and keep the plane steady. Similar jets on the sides of the nose controlled yaw.

Hydraulics, auxiliary power unit, and other machinery

Liquid ammonia fuel tank

Cockpit
The single pilot sat at the controls behind the flat, heat-resistant glass windows. In an emergency, his rocket-assisted ejector seat would catapult him out of the plane.

Instrumentation bay

Liquid oxygen fuel tank

Wing shape
The remarkably short wings, with a span of just 6.7 metres (18.4 feet), do not look very aerodynamic, but at hypersonic speeds the thick wedge-shape kept drag to a minimum and gave greater stability and control.

INCREDIBLE SPEED

Apart from rocket-powered craft such as the X-15, no conventional airplane has flown faster than the Lockheed SR-71 Blackbird, which reached nearly 3,530 kph (2,190 mph) in 1976. The Blackbird was used for secret reconnaissance missions by the US air force, but has now been withdrawn from service.

THE EDGE OF SPACE

The X-15 was carried into the air by a modified B-52 Stratofortress bomber and released at a high altitude. Once the X-15 was clear of the 'parent' plane, the pilot fired the rocket engine, which burned liquid ammonia fuel with liquid oxygen. With the rocket blazing, the X-15 climbed to the edge of the atmosphere, on the very fringes of space, where small jets in the nose and wings helped to keep it steady and on course. The X-15 made so many flights near to the edge of space that six of the 12 pilots qualified for astronaut's wings. Much of the technology that later went into making the Space Shuttle was tested on the X-15.

APOLLO 11 SATURN V ROCKET

Escape tower

Stage three
The third stage put the spacecraft into orbit and sent it heading towards the Moon. Its fuel tanks contained liquid hydrogen and liquid oxygen for its single engine.

Command and service modules
Having reached the Moon, the command and service modules remained in orbit, with Michael Collins aboard, while the LEM took Armstrong and Aldrin down to the lunar surface.

LEM

Docking manoeuvres
After separating from the third stage of the Saturn V rocket, the command and service modules had to turn round and dock with the LEM before continuing on to the Moon.

Main engine nozzle

Service module
This contained life–support systems for the crew, such as oxygen for the astronauts to breathe and fuel cells that generated electricity to power Apollo 11's equipment. The fuel cells also converted hydrogen and oxygen into water for the astronauts to drink. The service module housed the engine for sending Apollo 11 back from the Moon.

Command module
The cramped command module was where the three astronauts lived and worked for most of the mission. It was the only part of the Saturn V rocket to return to Earth.

THE SPACE RACE

In April 1961, Yuri Gagarin astonished the world by becoming the first person in space on board Vostok 1, the Soviet Union's rocket-launched spacecraft. Spurred on by the success of its arch-rivals, the US National Aeronautics and Space Administration (NASA) at once began work on the Saturn V moon rocket to put the first astronauts on the Moon.

This vast liquid-fuelled rocket was 111 metres (305 feet) high and weighed over 2,900 tonnes (2,850 tons). Early Apollo space missions tried out the Saturn V rocket, and on 16 July 1969, Saturn V launched Apollo 11 from Cape Canaveral, Florida, and headed for the Moon with astronauts Neil Armstrong, Buzz Aldrin, and Michael Collins on board...

MOON VOYAGE

The Saturn V rocket had three stages, each of which carried Apollo 11 further into space. As each stage used up its fuel, it was jettisoned. Only the command, service and lunar excursion modules continued on to the Moon. Once in orbit around the Moon, the lunar excursion module (LEM) separated and descended to the surface. Wearing protective suits, Armstrong and Aldrin explored the lunar landscape, gathering rock samples and setting up experiments.

After 22 hours, the top part of the LEM blasted off from the Moon's surface and rejoined the command and service modules in orbit. Armstrong and Aldrin were reunited with Collins, the LEM was jettisoned and Apollo 11 headed back to Earth. The command module separated from the service module before re-entering the atmosphere, and finally parachuting into the Pacific Ocean.

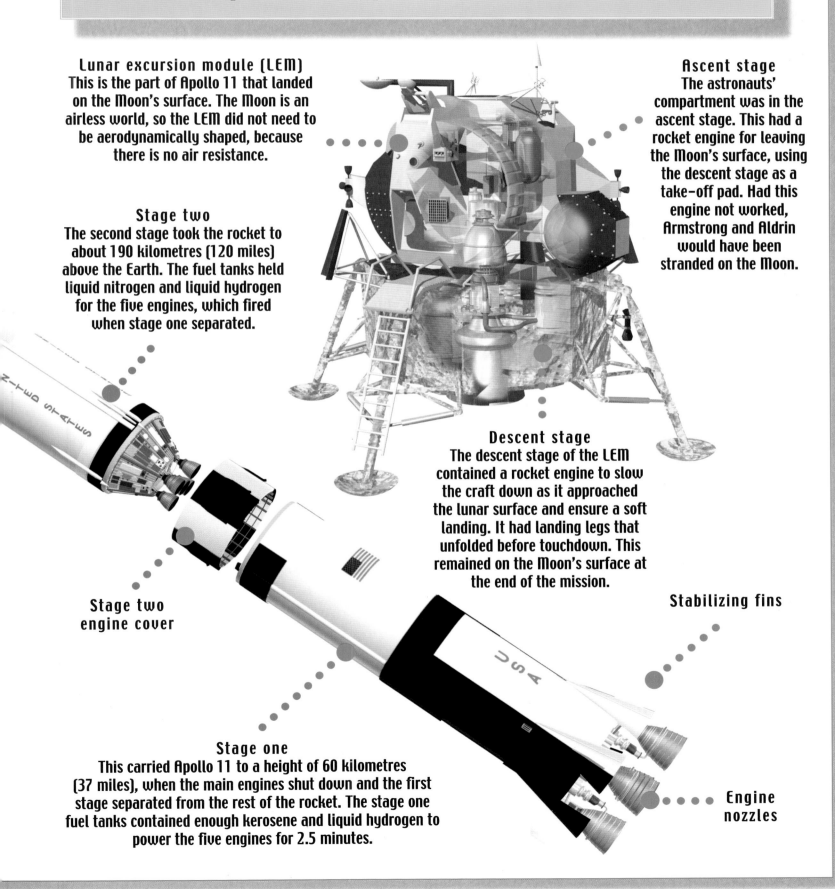

Lunar excursion module (LEM)
This is the part of Apollo 11 that landed on the Moon's surface. The Moon is an airless world, so the LEM did not need to be aerodynamically shaped, because there is no air resistance.

Stage two
The second stage took the rocket to about 190 kilometres (120 miles) above the Earth. The fuel tanks held liquid nitrogen and liquid hydrogen for the five engines, which fired when stage one separated.

Ascent stage
The astronauts' compartment was in the ascent stage. This had a rocket engine for leaving the Moon's surface, using the descent stage as a take-off pad. Had this engine not worked, Armstrong and Aldrin would have been stranded on the Moon.

Descent stage
The descent stage of the LEM contained a rocket engine to slow the craft down as it approached the lunar surface and ensure a soft landing. It had landing legs that unfolded before touchdown. This remained on the Moon's surface at the end of the mission.

Stage two engine cover

Stabilizing fins

Stage one
This carried Apollo 11 to a height of 60 kilometres (37 miles), when the main engines shut down and the first stage separated from the rest of the rocket. The stage one fuel tanks contained enough kerosene and liquid hydrogen to power the five engines for 2.5 minutes.

Engine nozzles

SPACE SHUTTLE

Tiled surface
On re-entry, friction between the orbiter and the Earth's atmosphere heats the outside of the craft to as much as 1,500 °C. Much of the orbiter's surface is covered by a protective layer of silica-fibre tiles, which fit together like the pieces of a jigsaw. The tiles absorb heat and prevent the orbiter from melting. The tip of the nose and the wings' leading edges get hottest, so they are also coated with a special type of carbon for extra heat insulation.

Flight deck
The pilot and mission commander sit on the flight deck. There are also two seats for specialist astronauts who may need to be on the flight deck during the mission.

Structure
The 37-metre- (100-foot-) long orbiter has a construction similar to a normal airplane, with a framework made of light aluminium alloy.

Space laboratory

Robot arm
Controlled from inside the orbiter, this long jointed arm can lift satellites out of the payload bay and recapture them in orbit.

Mid-deck
During the mission, which may last up to 16 days, the living area for the seven astronaut crew is the mid-deck. Some sleeping berths are horizontal and others are vertical, but it doesn't really matter in a weightless environment. There is also a washroom, a galley and an airlock allowing access into the unpressurized payload bay.

Windows
The heat-resistant, triple-glazed windows are 65 millimetres (2.5 inches) thick.

Discovery

Thrusters
Small adjustments to the craft's orbit can be made by firing different combinations of the 44 jet thrusters.

Lower deck
The crew's life-support systems are housed in the orbiter's lower deck. Air-filters remove carbon dioxide and water vapour breathed out by the astronauts, keeping the air breathable.

LAUNCHING THE SHUTTLE

The speed needed to get into orbit around the Earth is an astonishing 28,080 kph (17,410 mph). To achieve this, the Shuttle's three main engines need the help of two solid-fuel boosters. These five engines produce as much power as more than 140 Boeing 747 jumbo jets! At an altitude of 45–50 kilometres (around 30 miles), the boosters shut down and fall back to Earth, slowed by parachutes. They drop into the ocean, to be recovered and used again.

A fuel tank attached to the bottom of the orbiter carries liquid hydrogen and liquid oxygen for the main engines to burn. After eight minutes, and a height of about 110 kilometres (68 miles), the fuel tank is jettisoned and burns up in the atmosphere. Less than 10 minutes after blast-off, the craft is in orbit.

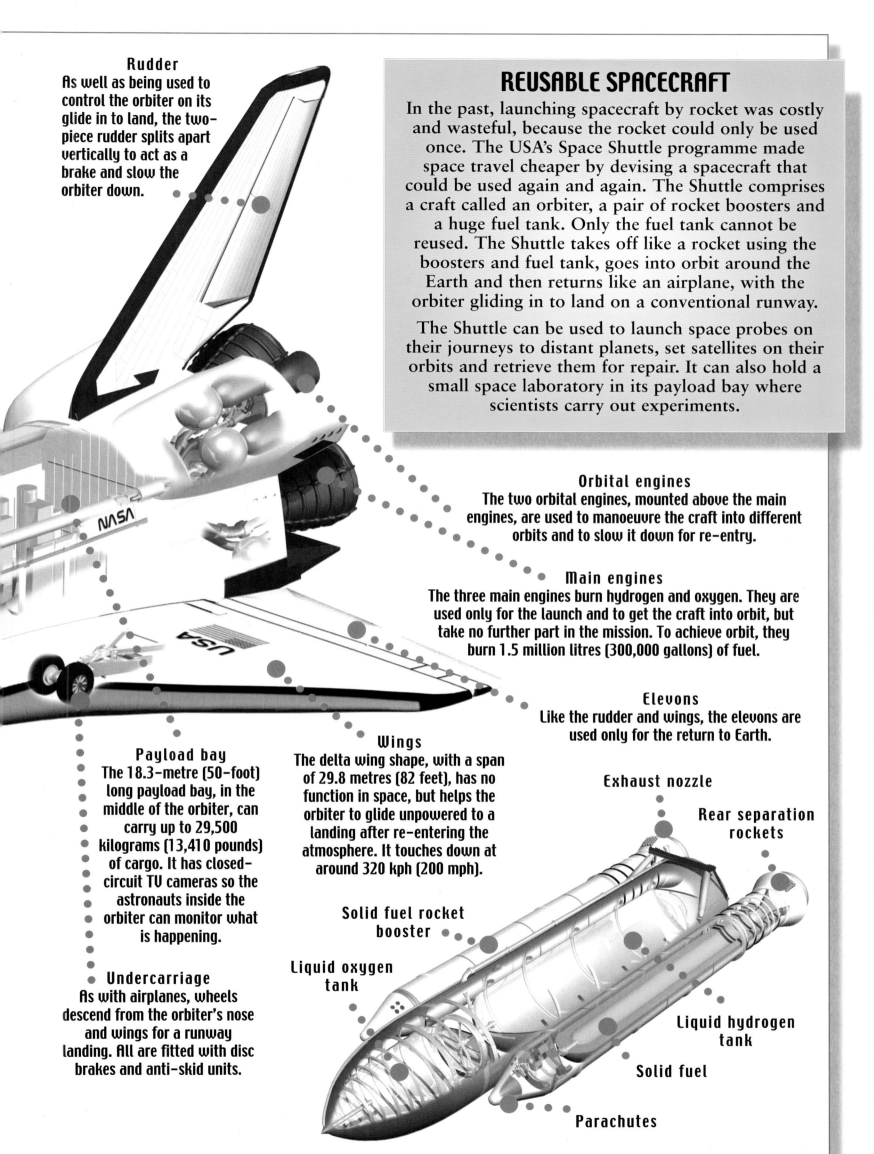

Rudder
As well as being used to control the orbiter on its glide in to land, the two-piece rudder splits apart vertically to act as a brake and slow the orbiter down.

REUSABLE SPACECRAFT

In the past, launching spacecraft by rocket was costly and wasteful, because the rocket could only be used once. The USA's Space Shuttle programme made space travel cheaper by devising a spacecraft that could be used again and again. The Shuttle comprises a craft called an orbiter, a pair of rocket boosters and a huge fuel tank. Only the fuel tank cannot be reused. The Shuttle takes off like a rocket using the boosters and fuel tank, goes into orbit around the Earth and then returns like an airplane, with the orbiter gliding in to land on a conventional runway.

The Shuttle can be used to launch space probes on their journeys to distant planets, set satellites on their orbits and retrieve them for repair. It can also hold a small space laboratory in its payload bay where scientists carry out experiments.

Orbital engines
The two orbital engines, mounted above the main engines, are used to manoeuvre the craft into different orbits and to slow it down for re-entry.

Main engines
The three main engines burn hydrogen and oxygen. They are used only for the launch and to get the craft into orbit, but take no further part in the mission. To achieve orbit, they burn 1.5 million litres (300,000 gallons) of fuel.

Elevons
Like the rudder and wings, the elevons are used only for the return to Earth.

Exhaust nozzle

Rear separation rockets

Payload bay
The 18.3-metre (50-foot) long payload bay, in the middle of the orbiter, can carry up to 29,500 kilograms (13,410 pounds) of cargo. It has closed-circuit TV cameras so the astronauts inside the orbiter can monitor what is happening.

Wings
The delta wing shape, with a span of 29.8 metres (82 feet), has no function in space, but helps the orbiter to glide unpowered to a landing after re-entering the atmosphere. It touches down at around 320 kph (200 mph).

Solid fuel rocket booster

Liquid oxygen tank

Liquid hydrogen tank

Undercarriage
As with airplanes, wheels descend from the orbiter's nose and wings for a runway landing. All are fitted with disc brakes and anti-skid units.

Solid fuel

Parachutes

CASSINI/ HUYGENS SPACE PROBE

Radio antenna dish
When Cassini is orbiting Saturn, it will be between about 760–950 million kilometres (470–590 million miles) from Earth. Radio signals will take up to 84 minutes to travel between Earth and Cassini. So if anything unexpected happens to the probe, it will be three hours before mission controllers on Earth are aware of it.

Equipment pallet
Huygens has two 'pallets', one on either side of the craft, laden with equipment for scientific experiments. It will map surface features by radar, analyse cosmic dust, take pictures in visible, ultraviolet and infrared light, and study the gravity of Saturn and its moons.

Nuclear power source
Cassini's equipment and systems are powered by its own nuclear generators. Some probes use solar panels, which harness the energy of the Sun, as their power source. This would not be practical for Cassini, as Saturn is too far from the Sun.

Engines
Two powerful 445-N engines give propulsion for major changes to Cassini's course. Sixteen small jet-thrusters make minor alterations to the probe's flight path.

SPECTACULAR SCIENCE

In November 2004, Huygens will detach from Cassini. Three weeks later it will land on Titan, the largest of Saturn's 18 moons. A heat shield will prevent the probe burning up as it enters Titan's atmosphere, then Huygens will parachute to the surface through the thick orange clouds.

On-board instruments will photograph and sample the surface and atmosphere, measure winds and relay data to the Cassini orbiter, which will transmit it back to Earth. Because Titan's atmosphere is mostly nitrogen gas, like the Earth's, scientists hope that Huygens' experiments will help them to understand more about how life began on Earth.

Magnetometer boom
This can detect and measure the strength of a planet's magnetic field.

Heat shield
The heat shield, 2.7 metres (7.4 feet) in diameter, will have to withstand temperatures of up to 2,000 °C as the probe enters Titan's atmosphere. The delicate scientific equipment underneath will be damaged if Huygens' internal temperature exceeds 180 °C.

PROBING THE SOLAR SYSTEM

Using on-board cameras and scientific instruments, space probes send back pictures and data that teach us about our Solar System. Launched by a rocket or the Space Shuttle, a space probe can use a technique called 'gravity assist' to help it reach its target. This involves flying close to another planet so that its gravitational field accelerates the probe and changes its direction. Like a slingshot, the planet's gravity hurls the probe out into space again on a new course.

NASA's Cassini orbiter probe was launched in 1997. It carries a smaller lander probe, called Huygens, built by the European Space Agency (ESA). After four gravity assist flybys – two at Venus, and one each at Earth and Jupiter – Cassini will reach Saturn in 2004 and will spend four years studying the planet.

Descent module
Beneath Huygens' heat shield is the descent module, which consists of two platforms within an aluminium shell. The upper platform holds communications antennae and parachutes. The lower platform holds all the scientific equipment for testing Titan's atmosphere.

Huygens probe
Huygens is secured to Cassini in a ring-like harness by exploding bolts. Approaching Titan, the bolts will be fired, freeing Huygens from the harness. Springs and rollers will then eject Huygens and send it spinning towards Titan.

FANTASTIC FUTURE

It is only about 100 years since the age of powered flight began with the Wright brothers' Flyer. Yet in that time, aircraft have revolutionized the way we live and taken us to new parts of the Solar System. It is difficult to predict what the flying machine of the future will be like, but one thing is for sure: there will be ever increasing numbers of people wanting to travel, and wanting to get to where they're going more quickly and more cheaply.

RETURN OF THE AIRSHIP

Airships were the wonders of the skies in the past, and they could be again in the future. A new generation of airships is now being designed, some of which will be huge cargo-lifters, rather like flying cranes, with the load suspended beneath the airship. Others will be moored over major cities and act as airborne telecommunications stations. There are even plans to produce passenger airships to take tourists on sky cruises.

Airliners
We may see a new range of 'jumbo' Jumbo jets, such as the planned Airbus A3XX, which could carry an incredible 658 passengers, or perhaps a new generation of supersonic airliners – although the development costs of Concorde and the noise problems it creates have put off many aircraft developers.

Robot planes
The fighters and strike planes of the future may be pilot-less robot vehicles. Directed by computer operators in a mission control station – either on the ground, in a ship or in another aircraft – these small, light planes could undertake daring raids with no risk to air crew. They could perform all the current roles of combat aircraft and carry out much more extreme aerial manoeuvres, without worrying about the stresses and strains they put on the pilot's body.

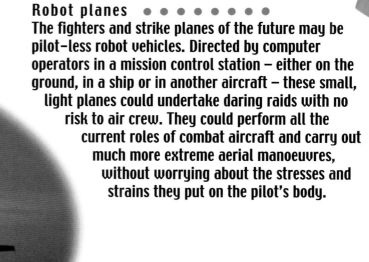

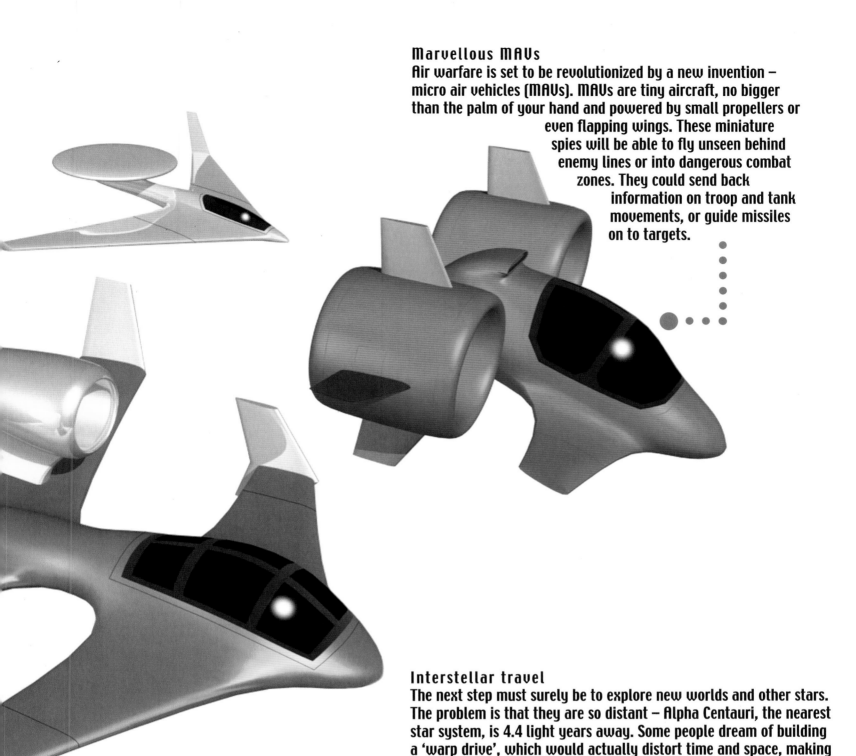

Marvellous MAVs

Air warfare is set to be revolutionized by a new invention – micro air vehicles (MAVs). MAVs are tiny aircraft, no bigger than the palm of your hand and powered by small propellers or even flapping wings. These miniature spies will be able to fly unseen behind enemy lines or into dangerous combat zones. They could send back information on troop and tank movements, or guide missiles on to targets.

Interstellar travel

The next step must surely be to explore new worlds and other stars. The problem is that they are so distant – Alpha Centauri, the nearest star system, is 4.4 light years away. Some people dream of building a 'warp drive', which would actually distort time and space, making it expand behind the craft and contract in front, so propelling the spacecraft to new parts of the Universe.

SPACE PLANES

One of the most exciting concepts on the horizon is the space plane, which would take off and land like a normal jet airliner, but fly round the Earth in space at more than Mach 26. With virtually no friction above the atmosphere to slow it down, it could cut journey times to the other side of the globe to less than two hours!

There are plans for space planes that could cut journey times to other parts of the world dramatically, a new breed of airship, robot fighters, and tiny micro-surveillance planes. There are also many possibilities that might become reality one day, such as gravity modulation – the idea of shielding an aircraft from gravity so that it weighs virtually nothing and can easily be launched into space. Whatever the future holds, it's bound to be astonishing!

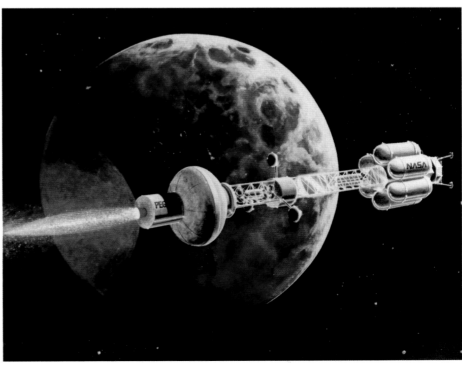

GROOVY
GADGETS

Gadget Crazy	128	CD Player	158
Mobile Phone	130	Widescreen TV	160
Personal Stereo	132	Personal Computer (PC)	162
Synthesizer	134	Image Scanner	164
Microwave Oven	136	Fax Machine	166
Power Drill	138	Videophone	168
Go-Ped	140	Hi-Tech Office	170
Scuba	142	Medical Scanner	172
Hologram	144	Light Show	174
Video Cassette Recorder (VCR)	146	Telecom System	176
Camera	148	Satellite TV	178
Camcorder	150	Internet	180
Hi-fi System	152	Satellite Navigation System	182
Games Console	154	Future Gadgets	184
VR Headset	156		

GADGET CRAZY

The twenty-first century is the Age of the Gadget. Never before have we had so many small machines, devices, bits of kit and equipment for use in daily life. Imagine a row of gadgets that includes TV and hi-fi remote controls, a miniature television, a mobile phone, a palmtop or notebook computer, a personal stereo, a satellite navigation receiver, a small computer games console, the latest mini-camcorder and a voice recorder (dictaphone). They are all small plastic cases with displays and buttons and easily slip into the pocket. At first glance you could hardly tell the difference between them. But they are very different. Some are taken apart in this book to explain how they work and what they do.

DEPENDING ON GADGETS

These gadgets and larger ones such as the video cassette player, widescreen TV, microwave oven and hi-fi music system, also shown on the following pages, are designed to make our daily life easier, quicker and more convenient. But we may come to depend on them so much that they cause more problems than they solve! Losing the remote control for the TV or being unable to log on to the Internet might seem like the end of the world. However we somehow manage to get by, usually by getting another gadget.

PROFESSIONAL GADGETS

Some potentially life-saving devices and pieces of machinery are also featured in this book. They include medical scanners for diagnosing diseases and the satellite navigation system, which helps people at sea or in remote areas of land to reach safety. There are also many office gadgets that speed along business, such as the computer, fax machine, image scanner and videophone. The power drill is an example of a gadget that makes physical work easier, more controlled and more precise.

Telecom system
Tele-communications means sending knowledge and information over long distances. It could be two people chatting on the phone, or several networked computers sending vast lists of numbers about bank accounts and business finances. The telecom system is immensely complex and involves huge amounts of old and new technology, from metal wires strung along poles to the latest fibre-optic cables, satellites, microwave links and computerized line exchanges.

It seems real

Virtual reality is becoming more real each year. The headsets, earphones, sensors and other systems get faster and more accurate. VR is not just an electronic toy for the games arcade. It is used in many professions for simulations that train experts such as pilots, surgeons and racing drivers.

GADGETS FOR FUN

Another group of gadgets includes those used mainly for fun, pleasure, creative pastimes and art. Examples are the music synthesizer, the virtual reality headset and the Go-Ped engine-powered scooter. They allow people to use their skills and talents to entertain and amaze us. Without all these gadgets, from the smallest in-ear radio, mobile phone or TV spectacles to massive computer networks and the global telecom system, the world would be less safe, less convenient, less accessible, less interesting – and less fun!

Compact disc revolution

We still have huge libraries filled with books. We still have large rolls of cinema film in bucket-sized cans for the latest feature movie. We still have cupboards full of games, from chess to fight-the-alien. But we can put all of these, and more, on to a compact disc that is read by a laser beam.

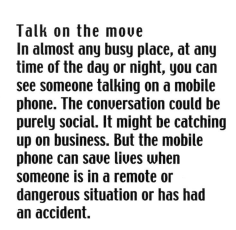

Talk on the move

In almost any busy place, at any time of the day or night, you can see someone talking on a mobile phone. The conversation could be purely social. It might be catching up on business. But the mobile phone can save lives when someone is in a remote or dangerous situation or has had an accident.

MOBILE PHONE

Recall and redial
Recall brings names, phone numbers, addresses and notes from the memory and displays them on the screen. Redial calls the last number used.

ON-OFF buttons
The mobile is switched on and powered up by the ON button. It can receive incoming calls in this condition, but with the display light and other unnecessary circuits switched off to save battery power. When switched off it is unable to send or receive calls, but tiny amounts of electricity still keep the memory active so it remembers its stored information.

Number (digit) buttons
These buttons are pressed to call a certain telephone number or to choose numbered options from the lists and menus on the screen.

Case
The mobile phone is protected inside a strong plastic case moulded to fit easily in the hand. It may have another cover over the top to cushion the phone from knocks, protect it from splashes and lessen the risk of the phone being switched on or buttons pressed by accident.

Mouthpiece
This is a miniature simplified microphone, the same as in a normal telephone handset.

Hash and star buttons
The hash (#) and star (*) are used for automated calls when communicating with a recorded voice and computer, where a number button might cause confusion. For example, the hash button may be pressed to show the end of a sequence of digits, such as a credit card number.

Powerpack
Rechargeable batteries give many hours of call time and more than a week of standby time (switched on and able to receive calls). They supply only a few volts of electricity. They are recharged by plugging the phone into its power supply recharger which is connected to the mains.

MORE AND MORE MOBILES
No gadget in history has sold so well and advanced so fast as the mobile phone. In 1998 Finland became the first country to have more mobile phones than fixed phones. By the year 2000 in many countries, more people had mobile phones than those who did not. Some mobiles can be linked to the Internet and have miniature screens on them for truly mobile global communications.

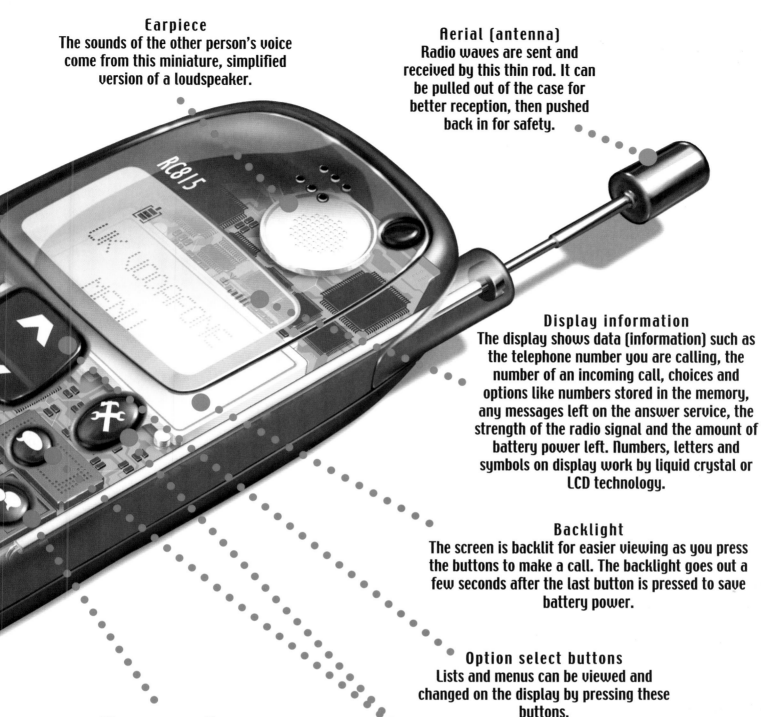

Earpiece
The sounds of the other person's voice come from this miniature, simplified version of a loudspeaker.

Aerial (antenna)
Radio waves are sent and received by this thin rod. It can be pulled out of the case for better reception, then pushed back in for safety.

RC815

Display information
The display shows data (information) such as the telephone number you are calling, the number of an incoming call, choices and options like numbers stored in the memory, any messages left on the answer service, the strength of the radio signal and the amount of battery power left. Numbers, letters and symbols on display work by liquid crystal or LCD technology.

Backlight
The screen is backlit for easier viewing as you press the buttons to make a call. The backlight goes out a few seconds after the last button is pressed to save battery power.

Option select buttons
Lists and menus can be viewed and changed on the display by pressing these buttons.

Three-way call
The user can call and speak to one person and then call another person so that all three may talk to each other, in a three-way conference call.

Special function buttons
The function buttons carry out short-cut tasks such as calling up the list of names and phone numbers stored in the memory or checking on redial or alarm calls.

HOW MOBILES WORK

A mobile phone is really a low-power radio transmitter and receiver. When switched on it sends out radio signals that are detected by nearby cellular transmitter-receivers. Each of these sends and receives by radio over a local area or 'cell'. Several receivers may send their identity signals back to the phone. The phone then selects the most suitable receiver and establishes connection through it to the network.

The size of a cell varies but is usually a few kilometres across. Cities where more people are packed together have small cells, because each cell can cope with only a limited number of calls. Also tall buildings or hills might disrupt signals and cause dead spots.

If you use a mobile on the move, it detects the fading signal as it moves farther away from the cell's transmitter-receiver. As soon as possible it automatically switches to the stronger signal in the next cell along.

PERSONAL STEREO

Audio mini-cassette
The cassette is a small case of magnetic tape used for sound only (audio). It has two spools. When the tape play direction reverses, the supply spool becomes the take-up spool.

Playback head
This detects the varying pattern of magnetic patches on the tape as it slides past and converts them into a similar pattern of electrical signals for the earpieces.

Tape guide
Revolving pulleys of smooth plastic guide the tape around corners.

Play button
This large button switches on the tape play motor and works a lever that presses the pinch wheel against the motor capstan to make the tape move along.

Tape reverse switch
The direction of the tape drive motor and capstan can be reversed so that the tape slides in the opposite direction, when the supply spool becomes the take-up spool. This means you do not have to take out the cassette and turn it over to play the other side.

Tape select
Various types of tapes have different particles in the magnetic coating. For better sound quality, these are usually ferric or Fe (iron), CrO_2 (chromium dioxide) or metal (a combination of various magnetic metals).

Fast rewind button
RW (FR or REW) makes the motor turn the supply tape spool at high speed to wind back the tape.

Fast forward button
FF (FWD) makes the motor turn the take-up tape spool at high speed to wind on the tape.

Pinch wheel
The rubber pinch wheel pushes or pinches the tape against the motor capstan when the play button is pressed, to make the tape move along.

Earpiece
This is an in-the-ear design that fits snugly into the middle part of the ear. The two earpieces are not identical. The plastic cases are shaped differently and marked L and R for left and right ears.

Motor capstan
This metal or plastic post is part of the shaft of the electric motor. It whizzes around and makes the tape, pressed against it by the pinch wheel, move along at a constant speed – no matter how much of the tape is on the take-up spool.

Radio/tape switch
In the radio position the electricity supply to the tape motors and playback head circuits is switched off.

CASSETTE TAPE

Mini-cassette audio tape is about 4 millimetres (one-twelfth of an inch) wide and some 260 metres (715 feet) long for a playing time of 90 minutes (C90). It is made of a flexible plastic strip coated with a layer of tiny magnetic particles, and on top of this is another layer for protection and smooth running past the playback head.

INSIDE THE EAR

Headphones or earpieces work in a similar way to loudspeakers. In the 1970s earpieces became much smaller while still giving clear, loud sounds, especially to low or bass notes. This improvement was due to new and very powerful combinations of magnetic materials, such as samarium-cobalt. There are various earpiece designs:

- In-the-ear as shown here.

- Around-the-ear with a flexible plastic loop that hooks around the back of the ear flap.

- Side-entry where the earpiece is shaped like a button but fits sideways into the ear leaving an air gap around it. This type is worn on a headband.

- Headphones also have a headband over the top of the head. A foam-edged, cup-shaped cushion fits over the whole ear to help cut out sounds from the surroundings.

- Some headphones have fluid-filled cushions that mould themselves exactly to the shape of the person's ear.

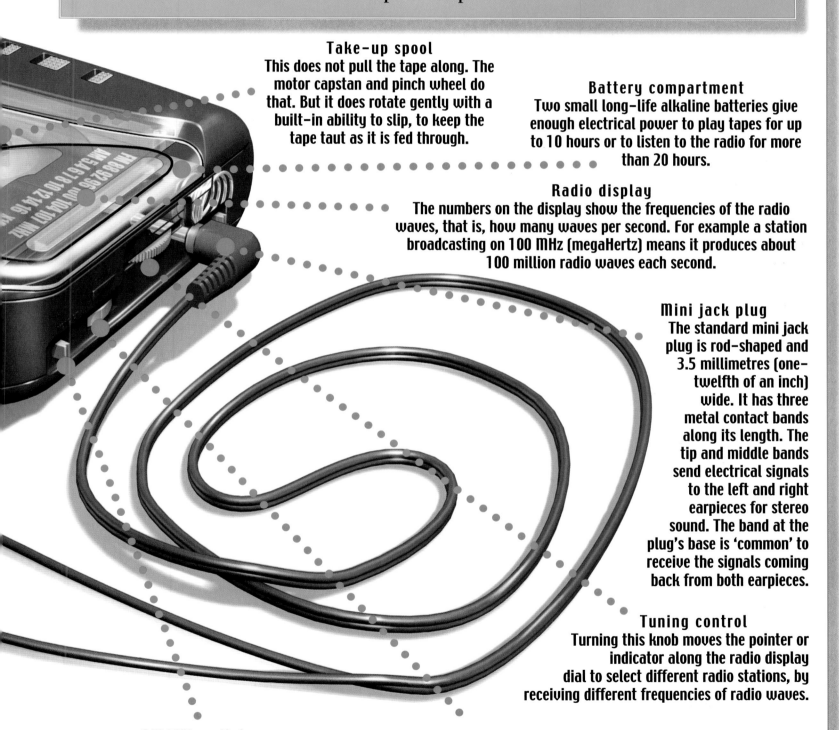

Take-up spool
This does not pull the tape along. The motor capstan and pinch wheel do that. But it does rotate gently with a built-in ability to slip, to keep the tape taut as it is fed through.

Battery compartment
Two small long-life alkaline batteries give enough electrical power to play tapes for up to 10 hours or to listen to the radio for more than 20 hours.

Radio display
The numbers on the display show the frequencies of the radio waves, that is, how many waves per second. For example a station broadcasting on 100 MHz (megaHertz) means it produces about 100 million radio waves each second.

Mini jack plug
The standard mini jack plug is rod-shaped and 3.5 millimetres (one-twelfth of an inch) wide. It has three metal contact bands along its length. The tip and middle bands send electrical signals to the left and right earpieces for stereo sound. The band at the plug's base is 'common' to receive the signals coming back from both earpieces.

Tuning control
Turning this knob moves the pointer or indicator along the radio display dial to select different radio stations, by receiving different frequencies of radio waves.

AM/FM switch
There are two radio bands called AM (amplitude modulation) and FM (frequency modulation).

Volume control
The volume or loudness of the sounds from the earpieces is controlled by this rotating knob.

SYNTHESIZER

Built-in speaker
The sounds generated by the synthesizer can be played through its own small stereo loudspeakers, with left and right channels, especially when putting sounds together to check how they are coming along. The signals are sent to a bigger and more powerful sound system when performing in front of many people.

Mode switch
The synthesizer can be used to deal with and manipulate individual sounds or groups of sounds, one after the other, and then combine together or arrange all of the individual sounds and groups into one musical piece.

Sampler effect
External sounds can be recorded in the digital memory for sampling, changing or manipulation later. A snatch or sample of recorded sound can be altered by changing it from a low to high pitch, by making it faster or slower or by filtering out some of the pitches or frequencies.

Pressure switch
The keys don't make hammers strike strings as in a piano. They turn on electrical switches. But the keys are touch-sensitive. Pressing harder on the key makes it produce stronger electrical signals which end up as a louder sound, as on a real piano.

Keyboard
The keyboard notes are laid out in the traditional manner of a piano or organ. The white notes are A, B, C and so on through to F, and then A, B, C and so on again. This is the traditional 'doe-ray-mee' musical scale. The black keys are in-between notes called sharps or flats. The note shown here is C.

Tone/style pad
The synthesizer has various types and styles of music already built into its memory, such as different drum rhythms for rock, house, hip-hop, techno, reggae and so on. These can be used unaltered and 'straight' or changed in the manipulator.

Sampler player
This plays or slots the different samples of sound from the memory into the whole arranged piece of music.

SAMPLING
A sample is a short snatch or piece of sound, taken out or isolated from another sound recording. It may be a single drum beat, a few seconds of massed violins, a word or two in a song or the screaming wail of an electric guitar. In the form of electrical signals it can then be altered and added into another recording.

MUSIC FROM NOWHERE

Acoustic instruments such as drums, trumpets and violins make their sounds in a physical way. They have fast to-and-fro vibrations that cause sound waves in the air. Electronic instruments such as the synthesizer don't begin with sound waves. They make up different patterns of electrical signals which are then put together or synthesized and converted into sound waves by loudspeakers or headphones.

Real sound waves can be altered or manipulated slightly. A cup-like mute placed over the end of a trumpet makes its notes sound thin and weak. But electrical signals can be manipulated in many more different ways. They can be cut up and pasted together, made faster or slower, bigger or smaller, and with smoother or sharper wave shapes. You can see what you are doing as the signals are shown as waves, spikes or bars on a display.

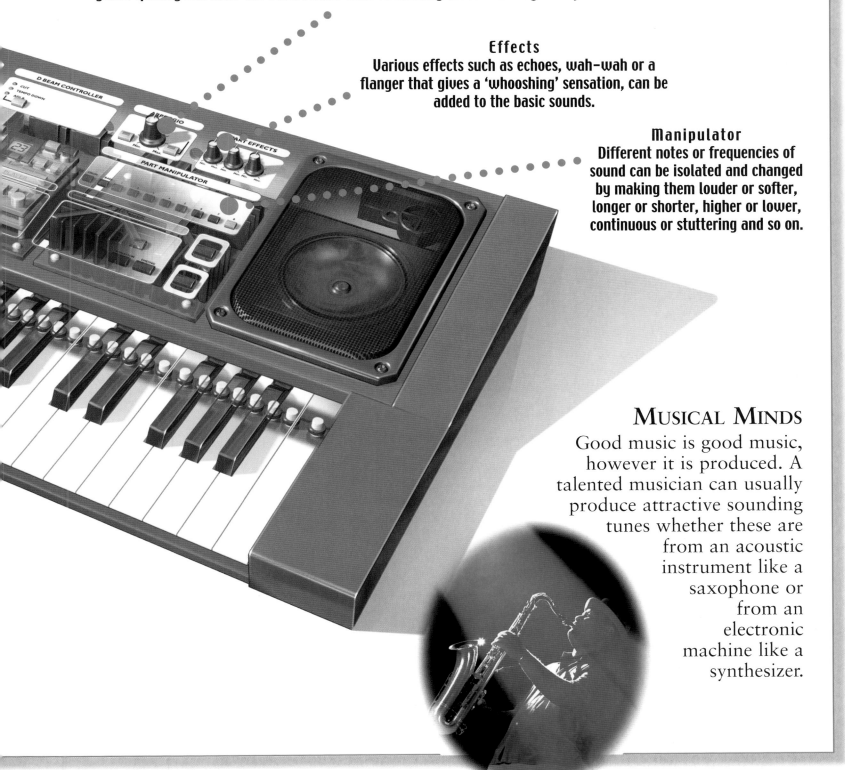

Arpeggio
An arpeggio is a set of notes that go together to make up a chord, but which are played rapidly one after the other instead of all together. (It's like picking out the strings of a guitar quickly one after the other rather than strumming all of them together.)

Effects
Various effects such as echoes, wah-wah or a flanger that gives a 'whooshing' sensation, can be added to the basic sounds.

Manipulator
Different notes or frequencies of sound can be isolated and changed by making them louder or softer, longer or shorter, higher or lower, continuous or stuttering and so on.

MUSICAL MINDS
Good music is good music, however it is produced. A talented musician can usually produce attractive sounding tunes whether these are from an acoustic instrument like a saxophone or from an electronic machine like a synthesizer.

MICROWAVE OVEN

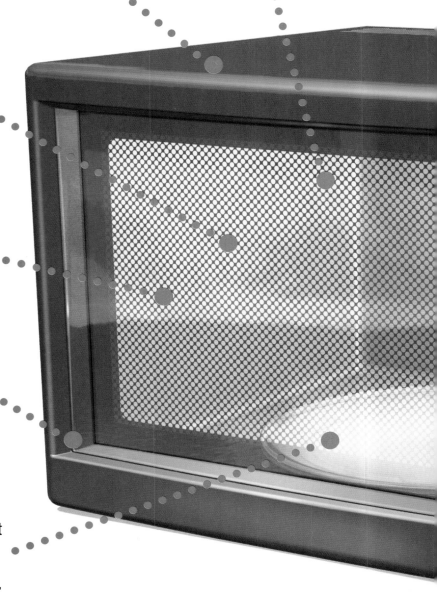

Microwave-proof case
The metal casing prevents microwaves from escaping and possibly causing harm to people or animals near by.

Internal light
The light comes on automatically, both to show that the microwave oven is working and so that you can see the cooking food inside.

Lining
The lining of the oven reflects microwaves so that they bounce about inside and their energy is used, and so that they do not leak through the walls and cause problems outside.

Protective grill door
The grill allows you to see what is happening inside the oven, to check whether the food is cooked, but it does not let microwaves out.

Door seal
The most likely place for microwaves to escape is around the door seal when this gets worn, loose or broken. Safety checks involve looking carefully at the condition of the seal. A microwave meter held nearby can detect if there is any leakage.

Revolving platter
The food turns round on this large plate so that it cooks more evenly and thoroughly. In some versions the platter stops and revolves in the opposite direction after a certain amount of time.

WHAT ARE MICROWAVES?

Microwaves are a form of what is known as EM (electromagnetic) energy. They are invisible up-and-down waves of both magnetism and electricity. There is a whole range of these waves, known as the EM spectrum. The longest, with individual waves many metres or even kilometres long, are called radio waves. Microwaves are each about 1–100 centimetres (half an inch to 39 inches) long.

Much, much shorter, with waves only millionths of a metre long, are visible light rays. These are the only electromagnetic waves we can see. Next shortest are ultraviolet waves and then X-rays and gamma rays. All these waves travel at the speed of light, about 300,000 kilometres (186,000 miles) per second.

HOW MICROWAVES HEAT

Microwaves work mainly by agitating or shaking the molecules of water within the food. A molecule that shakes or vibrates more has more heat energy, that is, it gets hotter. The heat energy is transferred from each water molecule to the other molecules around it. The food cooks inside, rather than from the outside inwards as in a normal oven. The process also continues for a time after the microwaves are switched off. So food from a microwave oven is left to 'stand' for a time afterwards to finish cooking.

Paddles
Some microwave ovens have revolving paddles, like a fan in the roof. These help to scatter the microwaves around inside the oven for more even, thorough cooking.

Waveguide
Microwaves made by the magnetron are led along the hollow waveguide and into the general oven compartment.

Magnetron
This works in a similar way to a TV 'tube' (cathode ray tube). A high-voltage electric current heats a part called a cathode. This gives off energy, which is converted into microwaves. The waves are made at the rate of about 2,500 million every second.

Step-up transformer
The mains electricity is increased in voltage for the magnetron.

Control buttons
The buttons program the cooking time, cooking power and other information for the oven. Preset buttons make it easier to cook fairly standard items such as a chicken.

Step-down transformer
The mains electricity is reduced in voltage for the electronic control circuits.

Pause button
The cooking can be paused for a short period by stopping the magnetron and revolving platter. Information such as the cooking time and power are kept in the memory for when cooking resumes.

Door lock button
The door is locked shut and can't be opened while the oven is working so that microwaves cannot escape.

Start button
This switches on the magnetron, timing and power circuits, oven light and revolving platter.

POWER DRILL

Reverse switch
Normally a twist drill rotates clockwise. This switch makes it turn the other way, anti-clockwise. It can be useful when the twist drill has 'screwed' itself rapidly into a soft substance and can't be pulled out easily.

Reduction gears
At full speed the motor spins far too fast to be useful for turning a twist drill. The reduction gears slow down the speed of rotation, and at the same time, by the principle of mechanics, make the turning force more powerful.

Hammer switch
In the hammer position the drill bit not only turns around but also punches forwards many times each second. It is used for drilling into very hard substances, such as rock, mortar and concrete.

Electric motor
The powerful electric motor has many sets of coils or windings so it rotates smoothly.

Speed control circuit
These circuits feed the electric current controlled by the variable speed dial and trigger up to the electric motor.

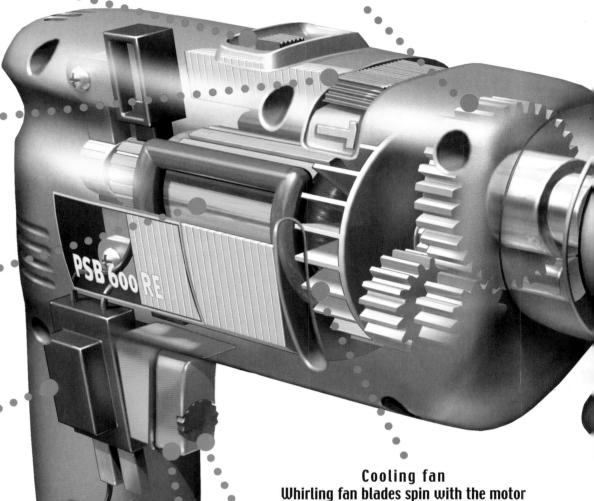

Cooling fan
Whirling fan blades spin with the motor to push air past it so that it does not overheat. They also blow loose material from the hole away from the motor so that it does not clog.

Variable speed dial
The knob is turned to control the maximum speed of the drill, that is, the fastest rate it turns when the trigger is pushed in fully.

Handle grip
This is the main handle for holding and gripping the tool. Pushing it forwards provides the force to drive the drill bit into the object. However, too much force will cause the drill bit to overheat or stick, or the motor to burn out. The pistol grip handle at the front of the drill steadies and positions the front of the drill for two-handed operations, to make sure the drill tip does not slip sideways on a hard, shiny surface and begin a hole in the wrong place.

Variable speed trigger
The more the trigger is pushed in, the faster the drill bit rotates, up to a maximum speed set by the variable speed dial.

138

Depth gauge
This sliding rod can be pulled forwards by a measured amount and then secured in position with a screw. As you drill into an object the end of the rod moves towards it. When the end of the rod touches the surface of the object the hole is the correct depth.

MORE POWER
A modern workshop is packed with electrical power tools, including circular saws, jigsaws with narrow blades that go up and down very fast, orbital sanders, belt sanders and grinders with rotating discs.

Chuck
The chuck is turned by a special key so that its three jaws come together and grip the near end or shank of the drill.

Drill tip
The tip of the drill is specially shaped, angled and sharpened to bite into and slice away a tiny bit of material with each turn. Drill bits for brick, rock and concrete have a wedge of very hard tungsten-based metal at the tip.

Drill bit
The drill has helical (corkscrew-like) slots along its sides. These gather the loose material that the drill bit has cut away and push it back out of the hole so it does not collect and clog.

GEARING UP
Many machines and gadgets use gears, from power drills and concrete mixers to bicycles and racing cars. There are two main features of gearing. First is turning rate, usually measured in revolutions per minute or second. If two gear wheels have same number of same-sized teeth, one will drive the other at the same speed. If one is large with twice as many teeth as the other, the larger one will make the smaller one turn at twice the speed. So gears can be used to change the speed of rotation for different tasks. However there is a price to pay...

GEARING DOWN
The second feature of gearing is turning power, known as torque. In the above example, when the large gear wheel drives the small one it will make the small one spin twice as fast – but with only half the turning force or torque of the large one. This is because, in mechanics, you cannot get something for nothing. In the power drill shown here, the reduction gears mean that the motor may spin 20 times faster than the drill bit. But this gives the drill bit much greater torque to bore into an object.

GO-PED

Handlebars
The rider holds both handlebars and turns them to steer the Go-Ped just like a bicycle.

Throttle trigger
The trigger is linked to the engine throttle by a cable. The throttle supplies more fuel and air to the engine to increase its speed and so make the vehicle go faster, up to 32 kph (20 mph).

Engine kill
An easily accessible switch cuts off and stops the engine in case of problems or an emergency.

Handlebar stem
A safety spring on the stem allows the handlebars to move down so that they are less likely to harm the rider in case of an accident. The handlebars and stem fold flat along the foot deck for carrying and storage.

Brake lever
Pulling on the lever works the front caliper brakes by a long cable, as on a bicycle.

SPECIAL ENGINE

The two-stroke petrol engine is similar to those used in some power tools, and also in certain off-road or track motorcycles. In some Go-Peds it drives the rear tyre via a roller. In others it is linked by a transmission unit that only makes the rear wheel turn as the engine gains speed and power. This allows the vehicle to stay still with the engine running.

Frame
The main frame is made of strong but lightweight metal tubing.

Front fork
The fork holds the front wheel and tyre, which turn to one side or the other and steer the vehicle.

Brake
Caliper brakes make the brake blocks press against the tyre to slow down the vehicle.

Wheel and tyre
The tyre is not air-filled (pneumatic) but solid natural rubber. It cannot suffer punctures, yet it still smoothes out lumps and bumps in the road.

140

PPT

Personal powered transport is a very busy area for engineers and inventors. The small vehicles use fewer raw materials and much less fuel than a car, reducing demand for natural resources and cutting pollution.

• The Go-Ped 'motorized skateboard' is small, convenient and lightweight, and can be transported easily when not in use. It carries up to 180 kilograms (almost 400 pounds) so it can be used for shopping. However, it is not suited to wet and slippery surfaces.

• Similar two-wheeled scooter or cycle-type designs driven by electric motors are also being developed. They carry rechargeable powerpacks of batteries that are plugged into the mains electricity overnight.

• The mini-bubble car has three wheels like those on a tricycle and is powered by an engine. The wrap-around clear plastic bubble protects the driver from rain and danger.

UP AND AWAY

Whenever a new vehicle or craft is invented, people begin to hold races and competitions and to test each other's skills. Motorcycles soon evolved into special 'dirt bikes' on which riders negotiate mud, hills, water jumps and fallen logs.

Fuel tank
The tank holds the usual mixture of petrol and two-stroke oil designed for two-stroke petrol engines.

Foot deck
The rider stands and balances on the deck as the vehicle moves along. He or she leans slightly to the side to go around curves, but not so much as on a motorcycle because the Go-Ped's wheels are so much smaller.

Engine
The two-stroke petrol engine drives the rear wheel directly. Whenever it is running the rear wheel turns.

Centre stand
Levered on to this stand the Go-Ped stays upright and the rear wheel is off the ground, for starting or for staying still with the engine running and the rear wheel turning.

Pull start
With the rear wheel off the ground, the start cord is pulled out sharply to turn over the engine and get it working. Once the engine has been warmed up, it can be started again after being stopped by 'scooting' the Go-Ped along.

SCUBA

Tank
Air or a special mixture of breathing gases is pumped into here. It's at a very high pressure, so a large volume becomes extremely squeezed or compressed into a small space.

Water pressure
The surrounding water presses on the high-pressure diaphragm to make the valve open when necessary and to keep up the intermediate pressure in the first stage regulator chamber and the air hose.

On-Off valve
This tap seals or closes the tank so air cannot come out into the first stage regulator. It's used to turn the tank 'off' when not in use and also when refilling it.

First stage regulator
The first regulator reduces the very high pressure of the air in the tank to an in-between or intermediate pressure in the air hose, about 80–150 pounds per square inch.

Valve
The valve keeps the high-pressure air in the tank unless the pressure in the air hose drops, then it lets some air from the tank into the first stage regulator chamber and hose.

Air hose
The first stage regulator chamber leads to the flexible air hose that carries the air to the second stage regulator.

OUT OF BREATH

There are many ways of seeing the underwater world, watching fish swim, admiring the incredible variety and colour of life on the coral reef or even hunting for shipwrecks and buried treasure. Most forms of diving require some equipment. But in free diving the diver has no gadgets, equipment or artificial aids at all. With plenty of care, practise and expert help on standby, some divers can stay under for more than 20 minutes or descend below 150 metres. But such feats are extremely specialized and very dangerous. Most people struggle to stay under for more than a minute or descend to below about 4–5 metres.

WHAT IS SCUBA?

The letters stand for Self-Contained Underwater Breathing Apparatus. It's a piece of equipment that lets you swim freely underwater for long periods of time, without having to come up for air. Before scuba gear, divers had to hold their breath or they were attached by tubes or hoses which carried air down to them from the surface. They also had to undergo hours of special training and be physically fit and healthy. Scuba gear, after a period of training, can be used by almost anyone. It has opened up the exciting underwater world to millions of people. The early and well-known type of scuba called the aqua lung appeared in the early 1940s. It was developed by Emil Gagnan and the famous French diver, film-maker, writer, conservationist and ocean expert Jacques-Yves Cousteau.

Depth gauge
The depth gauge contains a pressure sensor so the divers know how deep they are. Most divers are advised not to go below about 40 metres. The water pressure increases with depth and by this depth it becomes dangerous. When the divers return to the surface the release of pressure on the body may cause the dangerous, even deadly condition called 'the bends'.

Ambient-pressure diaphragm
As the diver breathes in the air, pressure in the second stage regulator chamber falls. The outside water pressure pushes on the flexible diaphragm which curves or bows inwards and works a lever to open the valve and let in intermediate air from the air hose.

Second stage regulator
This device lowers the intermediate pressure of the air in the air hose, to the ambient pressure in the second stage regulator chamber. The ambient pressure is the pressure of the surroundings where the diver happens to be – that is, the water pressure all around. The regulator self-adjusts so that as the diver goes down and the water pressure on the body increases, the pressure of the breathed-in air also increases. This ensures the pressures are balanced and the diver's chest can expand against the surrounding water pressure, so breathing is comfortable.

Exhaust
Breathed out air leaves the mouthpiece by pushing open flap-like valves into the exhaust manifolds, and then out into the water. It produces a stream of bubbles with each breath.

Mouthpiece
Air flows from the second stage regulator chamber through the mouthpiece, into the diver's mouth and own breathing system.

Valve
The valve opens when worked by the ambient-pressure diaphragm and lever, to let air from the air hose pass into the second stage regulator chamber. This air can then be breathed in.

DEPTH/AVT TIME 56 MIN   MAX DEPTH 198 FT   SURFACE TIME 3 HR
0 58 MIN   NORMAL CONDITION

HOLOGRAM

Coherent light waves
Every light wave from a laser has the same length. (In ordinary light the waves have different lengths, which give them different colours.) Also all the waves are in step or in phase so they rise and fall together, with their peaks lined up. (In ordinary light the waves are not in step or in phase and rise and fall at random.)

Holographic image
The holographic image recorded on the film does not look like an ordinary photographic image, which is a realistic picture of the object with dark and light areas of different colours. The holographic image is recorded as an interference pattern or interferogram.

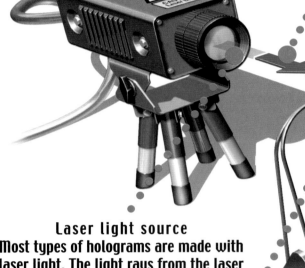

Laser light source
Most types of holograms are made with laser light. The light rays from the laser differ from ordinary light rays in that they are coherent. The feature of coherence is vital to make a hologram.

Beam splitter
This focuses and splits or separates the laser beam into two parts, the object beam and reference beam.

Reference beam
The reference part of the original laser light beam shines directly on to the photographic film where the holographic picture or image is recorded.

Viewing the Hologram
To view a holographic image, light must shine on it in a certain way. There are two main kinds of holograms with different ways of doing this. In a transmission hologram the same type of laser light used in the original reference beam is shone on to the image to illuminate it. A reflection hologram uses ordinary daylight which has been altered or filtered to illuminate it. The reflection hologram is more convenient to look at since you don't need to shine a laser beam on it. But it usually gives a smaller, less clear image.

Reflected object beam
The object beam bounces or reflects off the object being photographed and then shines onto the photographic film.

WHAT ARE HOLOGRAMS USED FOR?
Holograms have many different uses. They can be found on small pictures on identity cards, licences, credit-cash cards, security passes and similar personal documents. Architects and planners may use them for 3-D plans of the insides of big buildings, underground railway networks or the maze of pipes, drains, tunnels and wires under a city. Scientists might have 3-D holographic maps of the atoms in a tiny molecule. Holograms are also used as 3-D memory in computers. And they are often used for publicity stunts, advertising, exhibitions and works of art in their own right.

DOTS AND CIRCLES

The holographic image recorded on photographic film is not a realistic picture or view like an ordinary photograph. If you could see a microscopic view it would have millions of dark spots surrounded by alternating dark and light curved lines, like ripples on a pond when a stone is thrown in. This is an interferogram. Imagine that as two light rays hit the same spot on the film they are in phase with their wave peaks lined up. This forms a light area. But in other places two light rays are out of phase. For example one wave is at its high point or peak and the other is at its low point or trough. So the waves 'interfere' and cancel each other out to form a dark area. A holographic image is this pattern of light wave interference – an interferogram. To create a normal life-like picture it must be viewed in a special way.

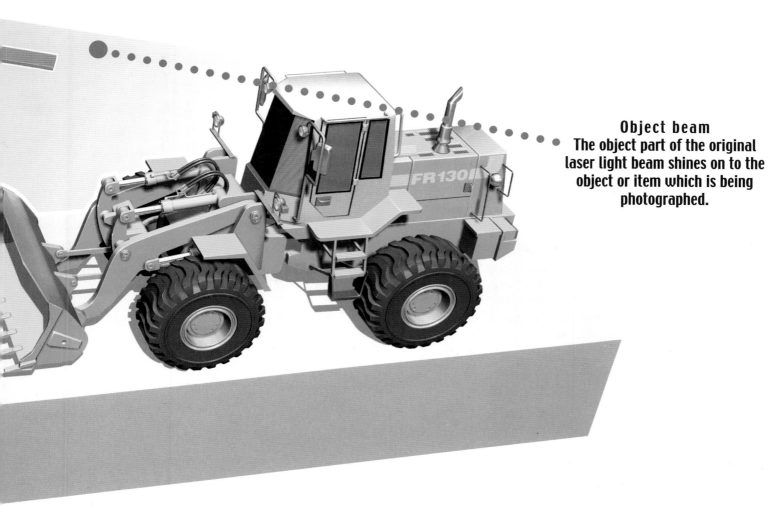

Photographic film
Like ordinary film for a normal camera, this has billions of spots of light–sensitive chemicals in it. They change when the film is exposed, that is, when the object and reference laser beams shine on to it. The changed chemicals record the pattern of laser light waves which hit it to make up the holographic image.

Object beam
The object part of the original laser light beam shines on to the object or item which is being photographed.

HOLOGRAMS ARE 3-D PICTURES

Normal photographs and pictures are two-dimensional, 2-D. They have width and height. But they do not have depth. You can see items at different distances, but you cannot look around them to see what is behind. Only the parts of the scene directly facing the camera are in the picture. A hologram (which means 'whole picture') is three-dimensional, 3-D. It shows all parts of the scene, including the sides and back of objects and what is behind them. If you move to the side you can see around objects and look at things that were 'hidden' behind them. This 3-D quality makes holograms very life-like and sometimes startling and eerie.

VIDEO CASSETTE RECORDER (VCR)

Record-playback video head
This drum-shaped device spins around to store more information on the tape.

Protective flap
Inside the VCR, one long side of the cassette flips up to reveal the tape. This is hooked out by sliding posts which wrap it around the record-playback head.

Guide slide frame
As the cassette loads automatically, the guide posts on this frame slide up behind the tape and then along to pull it away from the case, towards the video and audio heads .

SP and LP
The longest tape time on SP or standard play is about 4 hours. It can be increased to 8 hours if the VCR is switched to LP or long play. This makes the tape move at half the speed past the video head. LP gives slightly less high-quality pictures and sound.

Standby
A VCR on standby has some of its circuits and displays activated so they can switch on the rest of the machine for a pre-programmed recording.

Eject
The cassette is automatically fed into the machine when you push it through the slot for loading. Pressing the eject button makes it pop out again. The automatic mechanism for loading makes sure the tape is pulled out of the cassette and looped around the guides and heads correctly.

Video cassette
Video tape is almost 13 millimetres (half an inch) wide. It has various layers like an audio tape. The thinner the base layer of the tape, the more tape can be fitted into the cassette, usually up to about 300 metres (984 feet).

Display
Numbers and symbols on the display show information such as the time, the TV channel or programme selected, the amount of tape time that has passed or is left, and whether the tape is playing, recording or fast-winding.

SPINNING HELICAL HEAD

A TV does not show moving pictures. It displays 25–30 still pictures each second. These come and go so quickly that they blur together to give an illusion of continuous movement. Also, each picture on the screen is not made of areas of continuous colour. It is a mosaic of hundreds of thousands of tiny units, which again are blurred by the eye to look like continuous colours.

To record and play back so much information the VCR has a helical spinning video head. This turns in the opposite direction to the tape that slides past it. So the speed of the tape moving past the head is effectively increased, and this allows more information to be packed in. The information is recorded as a series of helical strips, like a diagonal corkscrew pattern, which again allows more information to be stored.

Connectors
At the rear of the VCR are sockets and connectors for electrical signals coming in from the terrestrial aerial or satellite system, out to the television or monitor screens and out to a surround sound or full hi-fi system.

Record-playback audio head
The audio head deals with the electrical signals for sounds, which are separate from those for the pictures.

Drive capstan
As in an audio cassette player, the capstan has the tape pressed against it by the pinch wheel and rotates to make the tape move along past it at a constant speed.

Power supply transformer
The transformer reduces the high voltage from mains electricity to much lower voltages for the electronic circuits in the VCR.

Tuner
Most VCRs now have automatic set-up. When this is activated the tuning circuits scan all the incoming TV signal channels, identify those which are strong enough to give a good-quality picture and sound, and lock these into the memory.

Cassette tray
The cassette feeds through the loading slot on to this tray, which carries it down and back into position for the tape to be exposed.

OTR
One-touch recording or OTR is a simple one-press button that starts the VCR recording whichever channel is selected at the time.

Main control button
The four major tape controls – play, stop, fast forward wind and fast rewind – are activated by pressing the sides of one large button. These and more controls are also on the remote control handset.

CAMERA

Shutter release
Pressing this button makes the swinging mirror tilt up out of the way and then opens the shutter for a brief time so light rays can shine past and reach the photographic film.

Shutter speed control
The dial or button manually adjusts the amount of time that the shutter is open so light can shine on to the film. In normal use this could be as little as 1/1000th of a second or as long as 1/60th of a second. Many modern cameras have automatic shutter speed control too.

Aperture control
This ring makes the hole in the iris bigger or smaller, to let more or less light through to the film. Many modern cameras have automatic aperture control, too.

Case
The case must be strong and light-proof because any stray light rays that enter will affect or fog the photographic film.

Manual focus
The main lenses can be moved manually by turning this ring, to focus the scene instead of using autofocus.

Main lenses
There are several objective lenses that gather and bend or focus the light so that blurring, haloes, coloured fringes and other distortions are as small as possible.

Pentaprism
This five-sided glass block turns the scene or image, reflected from the mirror below, the right way round and right way up. It then shines it through the viewfinder. So what you see is what will be in the photograph.

PICTURES OF THE PAST

Cameras from years ago were often heavy, bulky and awkward to handle. They were very sensitive to changes in light levels and also to any shaking that could make the photo look blurred.

Iris
A ring of spiral flaps twists to make the hole at its centre, the aperture, larger or smaller. This lets more or less light through to the film. Because of the way lenses work, it does not make the scene larger or smaller. But a smaller aperture does make the whole scene more clearly in focus.

Autofocus drive
In some cameras an electric motor adjusts the main lenses so that the scene is sharp and clear (in focus).

TYPES OF CAMERAS

- Movie (cine) camera: The roll of photographic film goes past the shutter quickly and lots of still or stationary photos are taken very rapidly one after the other, many every second. When played back the images blur together and give the impression of movement, as on a TV screen.

- Camcorder: A camera that records movie-style 'moving pictures' but on video-type magnetic tape.

Hotshoe
A flash unit slides into this. The button in the middle of the shoe touches a contact on the base of the flash unit so that when the shutter release button is pressed, the light flashes at precisely the correct time to make the scene brighter.

Viewfinder
When you look through here you see exactly the view that will appear in the photograph, through the main lens. So you can check that the scene is clear and sharp (in focus), and that it is precisely the area you want to see (it is framed properly). In some cameras the viewfinder has a separate lens and is not an accurate representation of what will be in the eventual photograph.

Viewfinder meters
In the viewfinder there are display readouts, meters or scales around the edges of the scene. You can check the exposure or light level, the shutter speed (how long the film will be exposed), the battery strength and so on.

Rewind button
When all of the film is used up and the roll is on the take-up spool, this button makes a motor turn the supply spool so that the film winds backwards on to it. The spool can then be removed and a new film fitted.

Swinging mirror
Normally the mirror reflects light rays that come in through the main lenses, up through the pentaprism and into your eyes. When you take a photo the mirror swings up out of the way so that the light rays can shine briefly on to the photographic film.

Motor drive wind-on
When a photo is taken, an electric motor turns sprockets which pull or wind on the film on to the take-up spool by the right amount. Then a fresh blank area is ready for the next photo.

Film
The photographic film has light-sensitive chemicals on a flexible plastic base. It is in a long ribbon or roll and gear teeth (sprocket teeth) fit into holes along each edge to wind the film along for the next photograph.

SMILE FOR THE CAMERA!
More types of cameras include:

- SLR camera: SLR means single lens reflex (as shown in the diagram here).

- Compact: A simpler type of camera where the viewfinder is separate from the main lenses. It usually has fewer controls or automatic gadgets than an SLR camera.

- Disposable: An even simpler compact camera with built-in battery and film. When the roll of film is finished you hand in the whole camera for the film to be processed.

- Instant camera: A sheet of photographic film slides out of the camera after you take the photo. Chemicals built into it make the photo appear or develop in seconds.

CAMCORDER

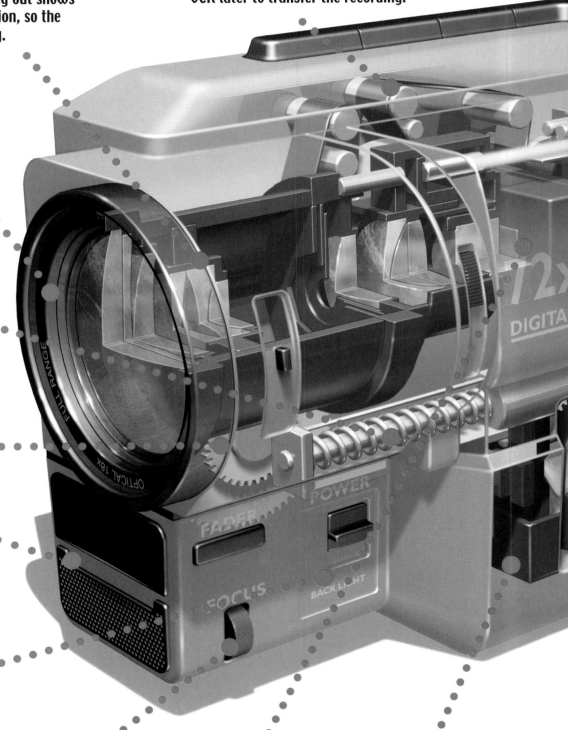

Zoom lens system
There are many lenses in groups along this lens system. Zooming means they move in and out to change the field or area of view. Zooming in is like looking through a telescope – it shows a small area greatly enlarged. Zooming out shows a broader view at less magnification, so the scene looks further away.

Objective
The large lenses at the front are called the objective because they point at the object – the item or scene that is being recorded. They gather light rays from the scene and begin to bend or focus them as they pass through the lens system inside the camera.

Zoom return
A spring on a sliding rod makes sure that the lens system slides smoothly for zooming in and out.

Zoom gearing
This moves the main lens system forwards and backwards to zoom the image in and out.

Microphone
Two small microphones angled to each side behind the protective grill detect stereo sound, which is recorded on the tape.

Screen backlight
This switches on the backlight for the screen so that it can be viewed in dull conditions. It can be switched off in bright conditions to save power, when the LCD screen works by reflected light.

Focus
The focus knob moves the lenses in relation to each other to make the picture clear and sharp.

Video tape
The electronic signals from the CCD circuits (representing the picture) and microphones (the sound) are recorded on a video tape in the same way as for a VCR. In some designs the cassette is removed. In others the camcorder is plugged into a VCR later to transfer the recording.

CCD
The charge coupled device (CCD) is like a miniature screen that senses light rays and turns their positions and brightnesses into patterns of digital electronic signals.

Powerpack
A pack of rechargeable batteries provides power for the motors of the tape recorder and lens movements and for the electronic circuits and display screen.

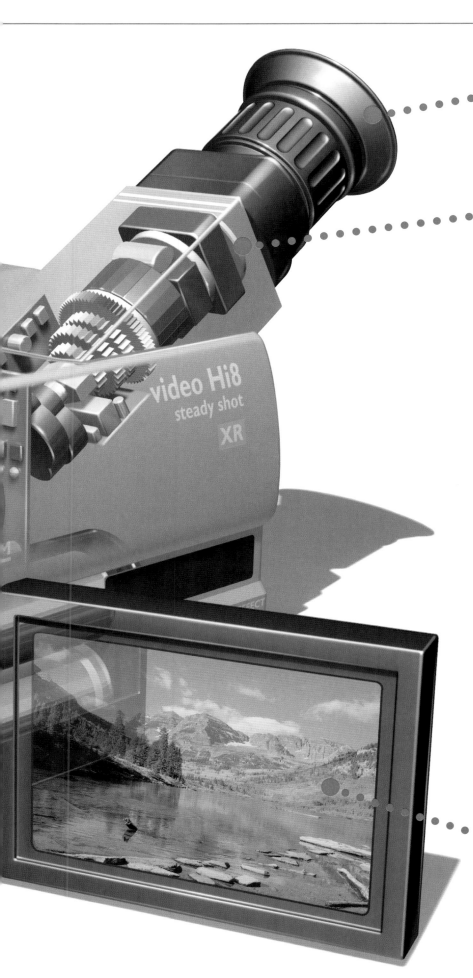

Eyepiece
The user looks through this to see the viewfinder, which shows the pictures that the camcorder is taking.

Viewfinder
Unlike the photographic camera, light rays don't come all the way through the camcorder, so the user cannot see the scene. Instead, a miniature TV screen in the viewfinder shows the user what is being filmed.

CAMERA-RECORDER
A camcorder is a combination of a video camera and video recorder. The video camera is designed to take many still pictures or images (usually 25) each second. When they are played back they give the impression of continuous movement as on a TV screen. There is no photographic film in a camcorder as there is in a movie camera. The patterns of light rays that form the images are converted into corresponding patterns of electronic signals by components called CCDs, charge coupled devices. The signals are then recorded as tiny patches of magnetism on to a video tape.

Display screen
Pictures recorded on the tape can be played back for several viewers on the LCD screen. They can either be saved, or stored for later use to save tape time, or wiped and recorded over if they are not wanted.

THE SHRINKING CAMCORDER
Early camcorders were so heavy that they had to be held steady with two hands. They were complicated to use and worked only in bright light. Today's versions fit into the palm of the hand. They have simple controls with auto-focus and auto-exposure to adjust the camcorder to suit the changing brightness of the light. They work even in light levels that are almost too dim for the human eye.

HI-FI SYSTEM

Crossover circuit
The electronic crossover separates the electrical signals from the amplifier into high and low frequencies and feeds each set to the correct loudspeakers in the speaker enclosure or 'box'.

Tuner and preamp unit
The tuner tunes into and receives radio broadcasts. It has a built-in rod aerial to receive AM programmes and a socket or length of wire at the rear as an aerial for FM stations. The preamplifier (preamp) alters the electric signals from any input or source such as the tuner, tape or CD player, for example making them louder and with more bass or low notes, before feeding them into the main amplifier.

Digital display
This shows information as numbers, such as the track number and time from the CD-MD player, or the radio station being received by the tuner.

Program presets
Different radio stations or programmes can be locked into the memory so that you don't have to re-tune the radio tuner each time when changing stations.

Graphic display
A graphic display shows information in visual form but without numbers. The coloured bars represent signals being sent from the preamplifier to the amplifier or from the amplifier to the speakers. Low or deep notes (LF, low frequency) are on the left and they get higher or shriller (HF, high frequency) towards the right.

Amplifier unit
The amplifier has the simple job of making the electrical signals it receives from the preamplifier much stronger so that they can power the loudspeakers.

Input (source) selector
These buttons select which unit feeds or inputs its signals to the preamplifier – that is, the source of the sound. It may be the system's CD-MD, the tape or tuner, or an external source (EXT) such as a microphone, vinyl record player or VCR attached by wires to the back of the system.

Skip and search
The user can jump or skip straight to the next or previous track on the CD, or move quickly forwards or backwards through the current track while still listening to the 'high-speed' version, to search for a particular part.

WHAT IS 'HI-FI'?
It means high fidelity, which is a certain standard of high quality, clear, undistorted sound. But the term 'hi-fi' has entered everyday language and is often used to mean almost any equipment on which music is played.

152

FM AND AM

FM or frequency modulation, and AM or amplitude modulation, are ways in which information is carried by radio signals in the form of waves. In FM the number or frequency of waves per second is altered or varied (modulated) slightly in an ongoing pattern. In AM the height or amplitude of the waves is modulated. The pattern of modulation is a code to carry the information.

AM sound may be muffled and distorted and is not in stereo, but it is usually easy to pick up. FM produces much clearer sounds in stereo but may not be easy to receive in certain areas.

CD-MD unit
The compact disc player accepts audio compact discs, CDs, which can contain up to about 75 minutes of full-quality music or other sounds. Some CD players also accept mini discs, MDs. These work in the same way but are smaller than CDs. They are used more for recording since they are digital and so of higher quality than audio cassettes.

Speaker cabinet
The cabinet is usually made of heavy, dense material to hold the loudspeakers firmly and produce the clearest sounds, especially of low notes. Its size and air space are carefully calculated so that it does not buzz or vibrate (resonate) and make certain frequencies unnaturally loud.

HF speaker (tweeter)
The small loudspeaker is designed to produce high-pitched or HF (high frequency) notes, such as the upper range of the human voice, trumpets, acoustic guitars, flutes, cymbals and birdsong.

LF speaker (woofer)
The large loudspeaker is for low-pitched or LF (low frequency) notes, such as the deeper range of the human voice, bass guitars, drums, tubas and trumpeting elephants.

Tape controls
These play, pause, stop, fast-forward wind and fast rewind the audio cassette. When recording, the tape can be set to begin as soon as the input or source starts feeding through its signals.

Tape deck
The audio cassette is played in this unit. When the tape finishes at one end it automatically moves in reverse to play the other 'side'.

GAMES CONSOLE

Memory card
This small plug-in memory device receives and stores information fed into it, or written to it, from the console. It might be a game or the current scores of each player and where they got to in the game during one play session. The card can then be unplugged. At a later date it is plugged in again and the information read back into the console, so the players can continue where they left off last time.

Select and start
Once the cursor or highlighted part of the screen is on the desired option, the selector chooses it and gets it ready to start. The start button begins the game.

Cursor movers
These buttons move a cursor, highlighted area or special symbol around the screen – up, down, left or right.

Special function buttons
These have special jobs or tasks according to the individual game. They may fire a weapon or allow you to jump from one place to another.

Thumb joystick
The joystick can move about in the ball-and-socket joint at its base, worked by the thumb on the top pad. It is used for aiming weapons, steering spaceships and other movements up–down and left–right.

Hand grip
The palm of the hand wraps around this pistol-type grip so the thumb and fingers are free to operate the joystick and buttons.

Handset connector
The handset plugs into the console. One or two players can play each other or work as a team against the machine.

GAMES FOR REAL
Computer games are fun and they can also have a useful and more serious side. Sims (simulations) are games that mimic or copy real-life activities such as playing golf, running a business, organizing a hospital, managing a sports team or surviving on a desert island. Playing the game can be good practice and help you to prepare for the real thing later – should you ever be stuck on a desert island!

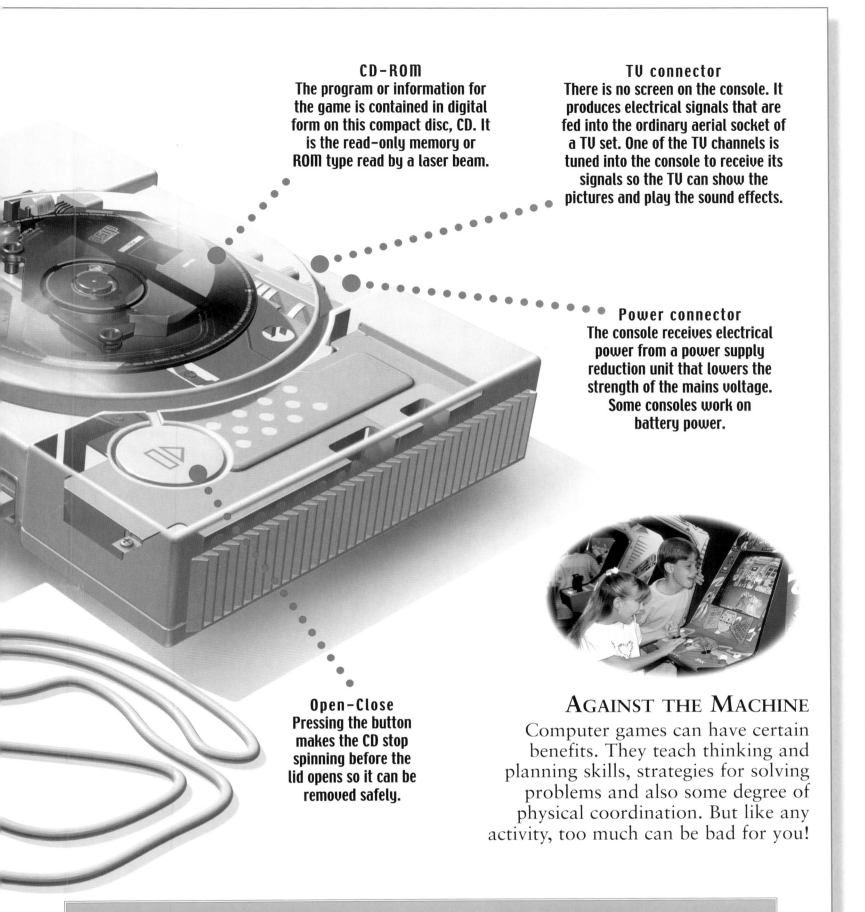

CD-ROM
The program or information for the game is contained in digital form on this compact disc, CD. It is the read-only memory or ROM type read by a laser beam.

TU connector
There is no screen on the console. It produces electrical signals that are fed into the ordinary aerial socket of a TU set. One of the TU channels is tuned into the console to receive its signals so the TU can show the pictures and play the sound effects.

Power connector
The console receives electrical power from a power supply reduction unit that lowers the strength of the mains voltage. Some consoles work on battery power.

Open-Close
Pressing the button makes the CD stop spinning before the lid opens so it can be removed safely.

AGAINST THE MACHINE

Computer games can have certain benefits. They teach thinking and planning skills, strategies for solving problems and also some degree of physical coordination. But like any activity, too much can be bad for you!

FASTER AND BETTER

Games consoles from just a few years ago already look very old-fashioned. They work slowly and have simple graphics. In a few years' time, we will look back at today's most modern versions and think exactly the same. This shows the speed of progress in electronic and computerized gadgets, which has been happening since the 1960s.

A general guideline is that microchips and electronic circuits double in speed and/or memory every 18 months, and become cheaper to manufacture, too. This allows the colours and shapes on the games console screen to be clearer, sharper, more colourful and more realistic. People, animals, aliens and vehicles can move around the screen in more complicated ways. It also allows the games themselves to have more options, levels and possibilities.

VR HEADSET

Headset
The computer sends electrical signals to the headset screens which convert these into light rays. The user sees the patterns of rays with his or her eyes and understands them as a scene in his or her brain.

3-D vision
In the vision centres at the back of the user's brain, the two slightly different views from the two eyes are merged to give a single view in the 'mind's eye'. This has width, height and also depth or the illusion of distance. It is three-dimensional or 3-D stereoscopic vision.

Video controls
These knobs control the screen colour, brightness and contrast, as on a normal TV set.

Speaker
A speaker plays sounds directly into the ear on that side. Some headsets have earpieces or built-in headphones, which help to cut out unwanted sounds from around the user.

Strap adjuster
The straps are adjusted to suit the head size and shape of the individual user.

PCB
The main electronic components are fitted into a PCB, printed circuit board. This is made with metal strips already built or 'printed' into it. The components are then fitted on to the board so that the metal strips act as wires to connect them.

Topstrap
A wide strap passes over the top of the head to join the backstrap at the rear, so that the headset is comfortable.

Screens
The screens show the images or pictures for the eyes. They show slightly different images for each eye. In real life the two eyes see slightly different views since they look at the scene from slightly different places and directions.

Audio controls
The audio knobs control the volume of the stereo sound, its balance (whether it is too loud in the left or right ear), and its tone of high and low notes.

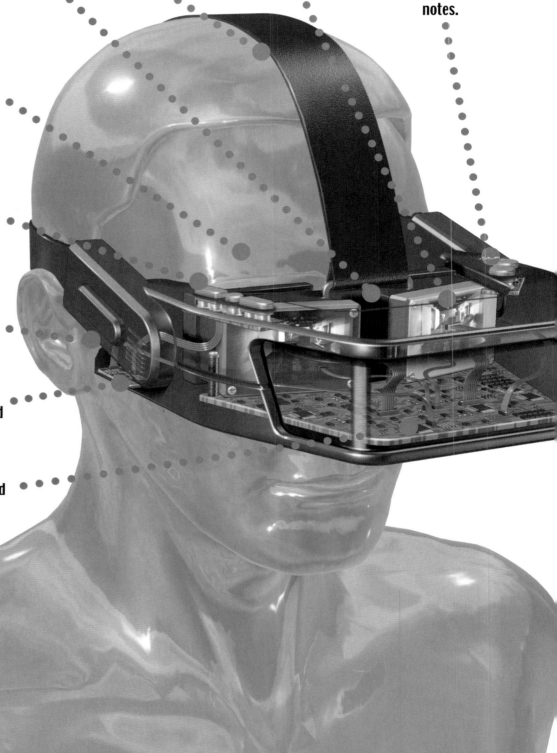

SERIOUS VR

VR systems vary from simple slip-on headsets to full helmets and body suits that look like deep-sea diving suits. These not only provide sight and sound but also physical pressure for the skin's sense of touch and perhaps scents for the nose, too. They also have feedback. They detect the user's movements, so that the computer can alter what he or she sees, hears and feels. The user seems to be moving about in a complete virtual world.

VR can be great fun for flying jet planes, shooting aliens and playing other games. But it also has many serious uses. It helps to train people such as pilots, surgeons, firefighters and rescue workers, where a mistake in the virtual world harms no one.

TAKING OFF TO NOWHERE

A form of VR has been used for many years in flight simulators where pilots train. The simulator is a whole room and the computer controls large motors or pistons that make it tilt and rock like a real aircraft.

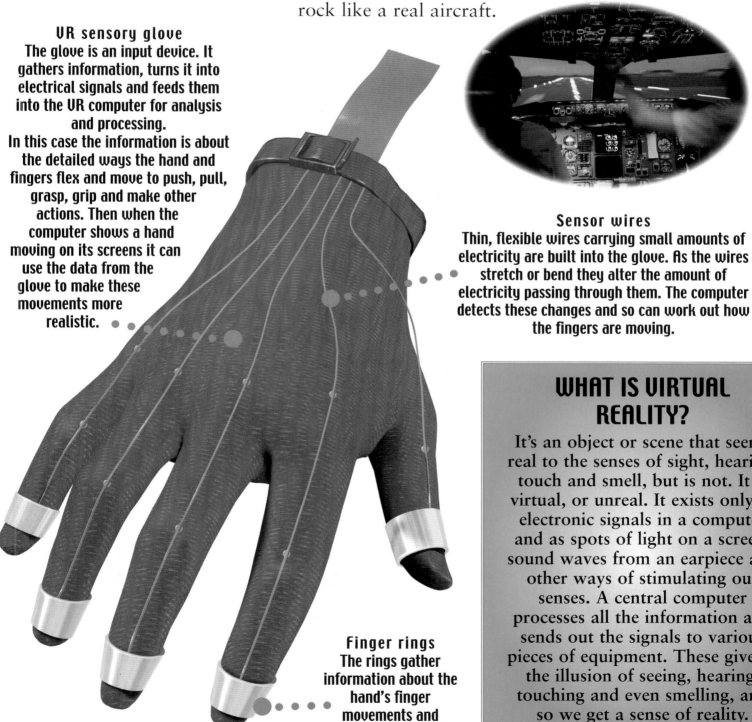

VR sensory glove
The glove is an input device. It gathers information, turns it into electrical signals and feeds them into the VR computer for analysis and processing.
In this case the information is about the detailed ways the hand and fingers flex and move to push, pull, grasp, grip and make other actions. Then when the computer shows a hand moving on its screens it can use the data from the glove to make these movements more realistic.

Sensor wires
Thin, flexible wires carrying small amounts of electricity are built into the glove. As the wires stretch or bend they alter the amount of electricity passing through them. The computer detects these changes and so can work out how the fingers are moving.

Finger rings
The rings gather information about the hand's finger movements and gripping pressure.

WHAT IS VIRTUAL REALITY?

It's an object or scene that seems real to the senses of sight, hearing, touch and smell, but is not. It is virtual, or unreal. It exists only as electronic signals in a computer and as spots of light on a screen, sound waves from an earpiece and other ways of stimulating our senses. A central computer processes all the information and sends out the signals to various pieces of equipment. These give us the illusion of seeing, hearing, touching and even smelling, and so we get a sense of reality.

CD PLAYER

Reflection
A micro-pit on the CD scatters rather than reflects the light that shines up from the laser beam below. The shiny metal between the micro-pits does reflect the beam, which travels back down again.

Focusing lens
This lens focuses the laser beam to a tiny spot on the disc.

Reflected laser beam
The reflected laser beam passes down the optical tube towards the light sensors.

Semi-silvered mirror
The laser beam from the laser is reflected upwards here towards the disc. If the beam is reflected by a shiny flat metal portion between the micro-pits, it passes back down through this mirror to the light sensors below.

Optical tube
This contains the mirrors, lenses and sensors for the laser beam. It slides along as the screw thread turns to read different parts of the disc.

Cylindrical lens
A lens makes the reflected laser beam narrower or more focused before it shines on the light sensors.

STORING INFORMATION
Since its introduction on to the open market in the early 1980s, the CD has proved itself as a small, light, tough, convenient way to store information. An audio CD can store up to 75 minutes of high-quality sound or over 100 million words of text. A CD-ROM (read-only memory) for a computer or similar machine holds about 640 MB (megabytes) of data, programs and other information. Blank CDs are inexpensive and can have the pits 'burned' or 'toasted' into them by a CD burner. They are used for storing computer information.

Light sensors
A pad of sensors produces a tiny pulse of electricity when illuminated by the reflected laser beam. This is an 'on' or 1 signal of the digital code. A micro-pit on the disc means no reflection, which gives an 'off' or 0 signal.

Compact disc
The disc is made mainly of plastic and is 12 centimetres (5 inches) across. The working part is its underside, which is coated with a thin layer of shiny aluminium-based metal.

CD drive motor
Under the CD is a variable speed motor that makes the disc spin around. A vinyl record spins at a constant speed, such as 33.3 turns or revolutions per minute (rpm) for a long player (LP). The CD turns at a varying speed according to whether the inside or outside part of the track is being read, so that the pits and flats always pass the laser beam at a constant rate.

CD track (underside)
As on a vinyl record, the CD track spirals out from the centre, round and round towards the edge. It is more than 5 kilometres (3 miles) long and contains more than 3 billion micro-pits. The sequence of micro-pits is a code for information.

Micro-pits (underside)
The micro-pits are microscopic holes or gaps in the CD track. The pits and the flat areas between them are read at the rate of 1.3 million per second.

Semiconductor laser
A small solid-state laser produces the reddish coloured laser beam for reading the sequences of micro-pits on the disc.

Ribbon connector
These flexible multi-wire connectors are used to link parts which move in relation to each other, such as the optical tube and the main circuit board in this CD player.

Optical drive screw
A screw thread turned by an electric motor moves the whole optical tube so that it follows the spiralling track of micro-pits as the disc spins. Unlike a vinyl record, the CD starts playing nearest the middle and finishes out at the edge.

DIGITAL AND ANALOGUE
The CD is digital. This means it stores information as a sequence or code of numbers or digits. In fact it has only two digits, 0 and 1. The 0 can be thought of as no reflection from the disc where there is a micro-pit. The 1 is a reflection where there isn't a micro-pit. Using two numbers is called binary code. Computers work using binary code, too, making CDs very useful for them.

Analogue systems do not use numbers or on-offs. They use continually varying quantities like a 'wave' of electrical voltage. Although the wave is meant to vary, much smaller natural variations occur within it and mean that it is not an exact way to carry information. As it is played or copied many times, the variations and errors can build up. Copying digital information means copying out lists of 0s and 1s, which is not prone to errors.

WIDESCREEN TV

Stereo sound
Two sets of loudspeakers play different sounds for the left and right channels. These reach our left and right ears and give the effect of sounds spread out in front of us across the breadth of the screen. This is known as stereophonic sound.

Wide sound
Extra loudspeakers positioned to the sides or rear help to spread out the sound. Sometimes a car or plane can be heard approaching from the side before it appears on the screen.

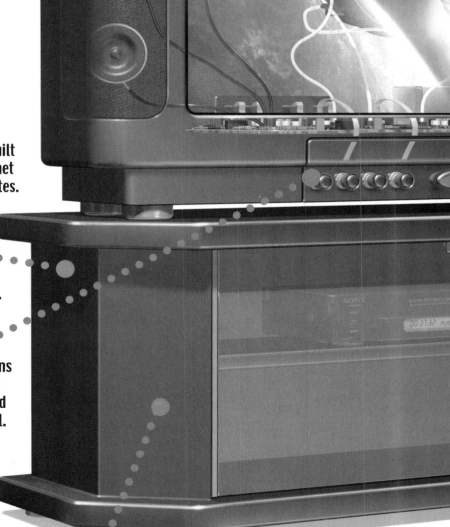

Subsound
A large loudspeaker built into the TV stand cabinet produces very deep notes. These are not so much heard as felt – for example, the rumble of an earthquake or the boom of a thunderclap.

Zoom control
The size and proportions of the picture on the screen can be changed with the zoom control.

Stand
The widescreen TV is very heavy. It has a strong, stable cabinet as a stand. This also stores a VCR and its videotape cassettes, a DVD player and its discs, and perhaps the week's television broadcast guide.

Pixels

A pixel or picture element is a tiny unit of the screen whose brightness and colour can be controlled. It consists of tiny dots that glow in different colours, red and green and blue. Pixels are built up like spots of colour in a mosaic to make the whole screen picture.

Picture quality

The quality of a TV picture depends on many features such as the quality of the original electrical signals and the number of lines on the screen. Standard TV screens have pictures made up of some 100,000 pixels arranged in 625 horizontal lines across the screen. The lines are scanned or made to glow from top to bottom.

TU SCREEN PROPORTIONS

The proportion or ratio of the screen is the length from side to side compared with the height from top to bottom. A typical TV is about 4:3 – that is, one-third again as wide as it is high. However, a full-sized movie screen in a cinema has the ratio 16:9, almost twice as wide as it is high. This was designed to fit comfortably into our field of vision or view, which is the area in front of us that our eyes can see and take in easily. It allows us to watch much broader, more spectacular scenes. Widescreen TV has similar proportions to a movie screen for the same spectacular effect.

HDTV

Picture quality improves with HD or high definition TV. The screen has more and closer-together horizontal lines, over 1,000, compared to the normal 625.

Wide screen

The screen is much wider than that of a conventional TV screen. Its proportions suit the natural field of view of our eyes better.

Words on-screen

Teletext may have over 1,000 pages of writing giving all kinds of information such as news headlines, sports results, weather forecasts and adverts for holidays, money loans and many other items.

TU SCREEN SIZES

The size of a TV or monitor screen is usually measured diagonally, from one top corner to the bottom opposite corner. However, the edges of the screen may be covered by the frame of the plastic case for the set, so the amount of screen that actually shows the picture is slightly less. A typical smallish 'portable' TV set screen is 35 centimetres (14 inches). A standard domestic TV may be 63 centimetres (25 inches). A widescreen TV may be 100 centimetres (40 inches) or more. The screen is the front of a glass part called a 'tube' (CRT, cathode ray tube or vacuum tube). It looks like a mushroom lying on its side with the 'stalk' projecting backwards. FST is a flatter, squarer tube. The screen surface is flat rather than slightly domed and has more angular rather than rounded corners.

UCR/DUD

If there are no suitable programmes on terrestrial, satellite or cable TV, the VCR (video cassette recorder-player) and DVD (digital versatile disk player) can show pre-recorded programmes.

PERSONAL COMPUTER (PC)

Computer tower
Most of the computer's circuits and drives are housed in a tower unit. This can be placed on a shelf or nearby table if there is not enough room on the desktop.

Hard disc drive
The hard disc is really a stack of magnetic discs in a case. It is kept in the computer and holds all the computer's programs and data.

Magnetic disc drive
Removable discs can be placed in this drive. Information is fed from the computer, or written, to the disc and recorded as tiny patches of magnetism on the disc surface. Later the information may be read, or fed back into the computer. This means the discs are read-write rather than read-only.

Motherboard
The large printed circuit board contains most of the main microchips and components. They include the CPU or central processing unit, which is the computer's 'central brain', and the RAM or random access memory chips, which are its working memory.

Optical disc drive
Compact discs (CDs) are placed in this drive. They store information as patterns of microscopic pits on their surface and are read optically by laser light. Many computers have read-only optical drives. This means the information stored on them like a memory can only be taken from the disc into the computer. New information cannot be taken from the computer and stored on the disc. So the drive and discs are called CD-ROM, compact disc read-only memory.

Rear panel
On panels at the back of the computer are sockets and connectors to link it by wires and cables to the monitor screen, keyboard, mouse and extra devices or peripherals.

Loudspeaker
The computer may be able to play music from its discs or programs. It also makes various beeps, pings and other sounds. These show that it is working properly, has completed a task or is unable to carry out some process.

Mouse
Moving the mouse moves a pointer or cursor on the screen on to various choices, options, lists and menus. Clicking a button on the mouse selects that choice or option. In image-based programs the mouse can be used like a pen to draw and alter pictures.

High capacity magnetic drive
Larger magnetic discs that hold more information are slotted in here.

Mouse mat
This gives a flat but grippy surface for the mouse to roll on. A rubber ball inside the mouse must roll for the mouse to work.

ADD-ONS

A basic computer usually has a main unit with the circuits and drives, a keyboard, a mouse and a monitor screen. The main unit and screen may be in the same case. But there are dozens of add-ons, plug-ins or peripherals that can be connected to the computer. A common one is the printer to produce 'hard copy' – writing or pictures on paper rather than on the screen. Others that input or send signals to the computer include an image scanner, microphone, digital camera, joystick and music keyboard. Then there are outputs, which receive signals from the computer. These include a hi-fi system, a large and accurate printer called a plotter, image projector and a moving robot arm.

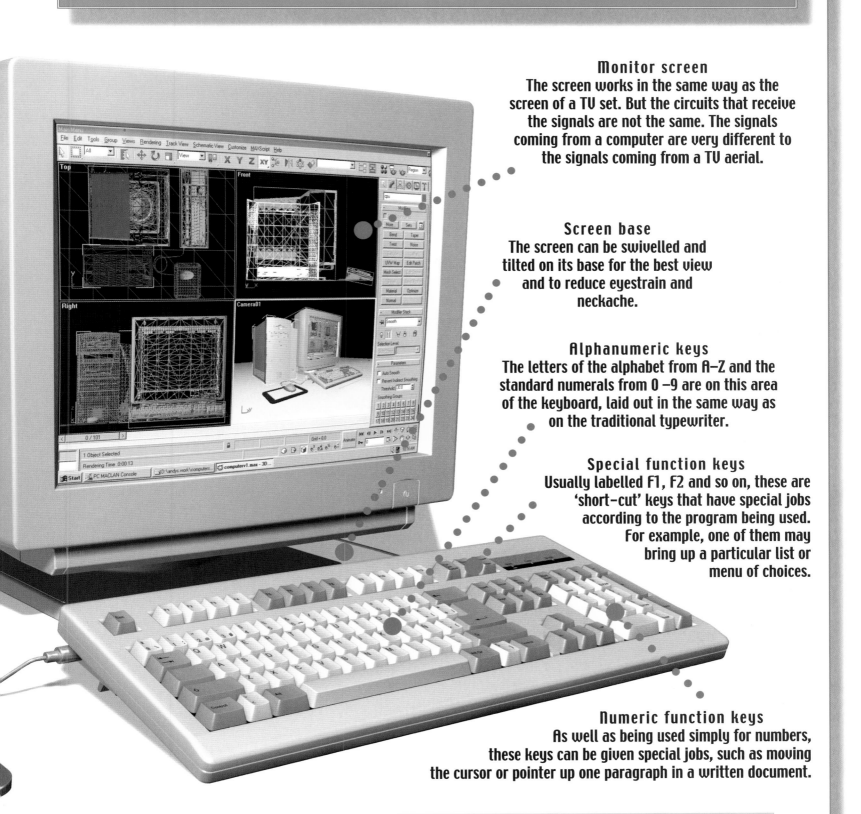

Monitor screen
The screen works in the same way as the screen of a TV set. But the circuits that receive the signals are not the same. The signals coming from a computer are very different to the signals coming from a TV aerial.

Screen base
The screen can be swivelled and tilted on its base for the best view and to reduce eyestrain and neckache.

Alphanumeric keys
The letters of the alphabet from A–Z and the standard numerals from 0 –9 are on this area of the keyboard, laid out in the same way as on the traditional typewriter.

Special function keys
Usually labelled F1, F2 and so on, these are 'short–cut' keys that have special jobs according to the program being used. For example, one of them may bring up a particular list or menu of choices.

Numeric function keys
As well as being used simply for numbers, these keys can be given special jobs, such as moving the cursor or pointer up one paragraph in a written document.

COMPUTER TERMINALS
The computer shown here is a complete working unit and can be used on its own. A computer terminal may look similar. But it is usually just a screen, keyboard and mouse. These are connected by longer wires or a network to a main computer. Many other terminals are connected too. Lots of people can use the same computer at the same time, sharing the information and programs.

IMAGE SCANNER

Scan head drive
This toothed cog or gear wheel pulls on the belt and makes the scan head move along. It must work to very exact measurements since the scan head may slide along by only a tiny amount between each scanned line.

Hinged lid
The lid protects the glass platen beneath to keep it clean, and presses down the paper or card carrying images to be scanned on to the glass so that they are sharp and in focus.

Connectors
The rear of the machine has various sockets and connectors for the power supply and the cable to the computer.

Scan drive motor
The motor turns by minute, precise amounts. It moves the scan head along fractionally, stops while the line is scanned, and then does the same again, moving many thousands of times to scan one page.

Slide groove
The end of the scan head slides along in this groove. It must be extremely smooth and free from dirt or dust, or the scan head will twist or jump.

Scan head
The scanning beam lights and sensors are contained in the scan head, which slides along the machine from back to front while scanning.

SCANNING AND OCR

Image scanners scan any images or pictures such as drawings, sketches, diagrams, paintings and photographs. They convert them into a series of digital electronic pulses that can be fed into a computer. This is called digitizing the image.

Scanners can scan writing, too, and feed it into the computer. But normally the computer would not understand the shape of, for example, the letter A as the actual letter A, the first letter of the alphabet. The A from a scanner is just a series of lines – a shape. It is not the same code as the letter A typed in from the keyboard.

However, some scanners and computers have OCR programs, optical character recognition. The program looks for certain patterns of lines, recognizes them as a letter such as A, and converts the digital code of the shape into the digital code for that letter. In this way the computer can almost 'read'.

HOW SCANNERS SCANS

A scanner records its first very straight, thin line across the top of the image. It measures the image's colour and brightness at points along this line. It then moves itself or the image slightly and records another straight line right next to the first. It repeats these actions to build up a point by point, line by line representation of the image.

The distance between the points and lines is called the resolution. The smaller the distance, the higher the resolution, and the clearer the picture. Low resolution gives a spotty, coarse, mosaic-like appearance.

Scan sensor
The sensor is programmed to detect the brightness or intensity of the light reflected by the image, at each of the main colours or wavelengths of light – red, green and blue.

RGB scans
The image is scanned by three coloured beams in turn – red, green and blue. Between them these detect all parts of all colours. They are the same colours as used for the tiny glowing dots on a TV screen.

Scan beams
The coloured beams shine at the image, which is on a sheet of paper or card on the platen. The amount and colour of the beam's light that reflects back is detected by the scan sensor.

Ribbon connector
Many wires side by side carry electrical signals between the moving scan head and the main circuits in the machine.

Indicator lights
The lights blink in certain combinations to show what the machine is doing, such as scanning, or returning the scan head to its resting position at one end of the machine.

Glass platen
The platen is made of specially clear, smooth optical glass. The sheet of paper, card, book or other item to be scanned is placed face down on it.

Toothed return pulley
The gear-type teeth on the pulley fit into the teeth on the rubber belt. This pulley is not driven round but simply holds the belt out taut and moves as the belt turns it.

Scan drive toothed belt
This flexible rubber belt is moved by the scan drive. The teeth moulded into the belt make sure that it moves very precisely and does not slip.

EPSON GT-8000

165

FAX MACHINE

Digital display
Various numbers are shown on the display, such as the telephone number of the fax machine you are sending to or the telephone number of the fax machine sending you a document.

Program buttons
These buttons program instructions and information into the machine's memory, such as the number of times the phone rings before the fax machine or answerphone cuts in to answer it.

INSTANT PICTURES

Fax machines are especially useful for sending pictures, diagrams and sketches. Almost as the paper feeds through the sending machine, the receiving machine prints out the same thing at the other end of the phone line.

Number pad
Telephone numbers are dialled by pressing the numbers on this pad. The buttons are also used to put instructions into the machine.

Handset
You can use this handset to make a telephone call and speak to the person at the other end in the normal way. But you can't do this while a fax is being sent.

Paper roller
The paper is for faxes which the machine receives and feeds out at the top.

Feed slot
The sheet of paper with the writing, drawing or other marks on it, that you want to send as a fax, is fed into this slot.

WHY 'FAX'?

The name is a shortened version of 'facsimile' which means an exact copy or duplicate. A document fed into a fax machine doesn't get rolled up and squeezed down the telephone line! The machine scans the document for dark marks, converts them into a series of electrical signals and sends them along the phone line to another fax machine. That machine prints the marks on to a clean sheet of paper. As the document passes through the sending machine its copy emerges from the receiving machine with only a split second delay. The sender still has the original document and the receiver has the copy or fax.

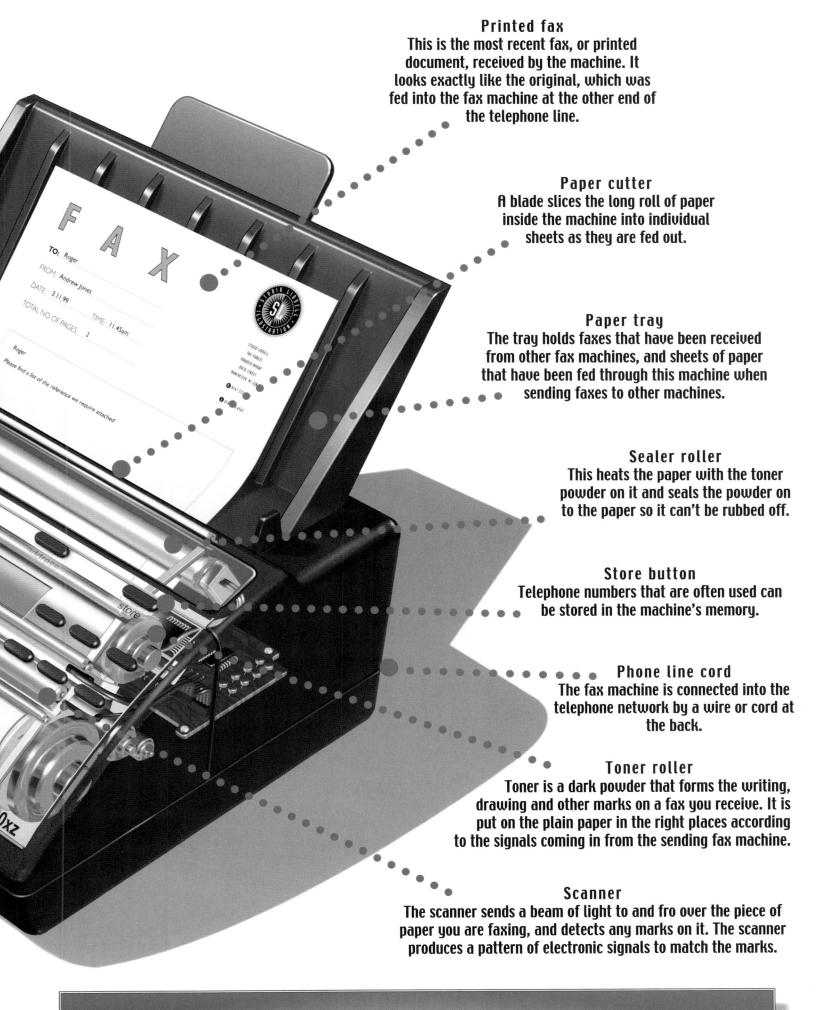

Printed fax
This is the most recent fax, or printed document, received by the machine. It looks exactly like the original, which was fed into the fax machine at the other end of the telephone line.

Paper cutter
A blade slices the long roll of paper inside the machine into individual sheets as they are fed out.

Paper tray
The tray holds faxes that have been received from other fax machines, and sheets of paper that have been fed through this machine when sending faxes to other machines.

Sealer roller
This heats the paper with the toner powder on it and seals the powder on to the paper so it can't be rubbed off.

Store button
Telephone numbers that are often used can be stored in the machine's memory.

Phone line cord
The fax machine is connected into the telephone network by a wire or cord at the back.

Toner roller
Toner is a dark powder that forms the writing, drawing and other marks on a fax you receive. It is put on the plain paper in the right places according to the signals coming in from the sending fax machine.

Scanner
The scanner sends a beam of light to and fro over the piece of paper you are faxing, and detects any marks on it. The scanner produces a pattern of electronic signals to match the marks.

WHAT CAN I SEND BY FAX?

Any marks or dark patches on paper can be faxed. This includes handwriting, typewriting, printed pages from books and magazines, photocopies, drawings, illustrations, sketches, photographs, patterns and diagrams. Some faxes send and receive in black and white only. Others can do so in colour, but only if the machine at the other end also works in colour.

VIDEOPHONE

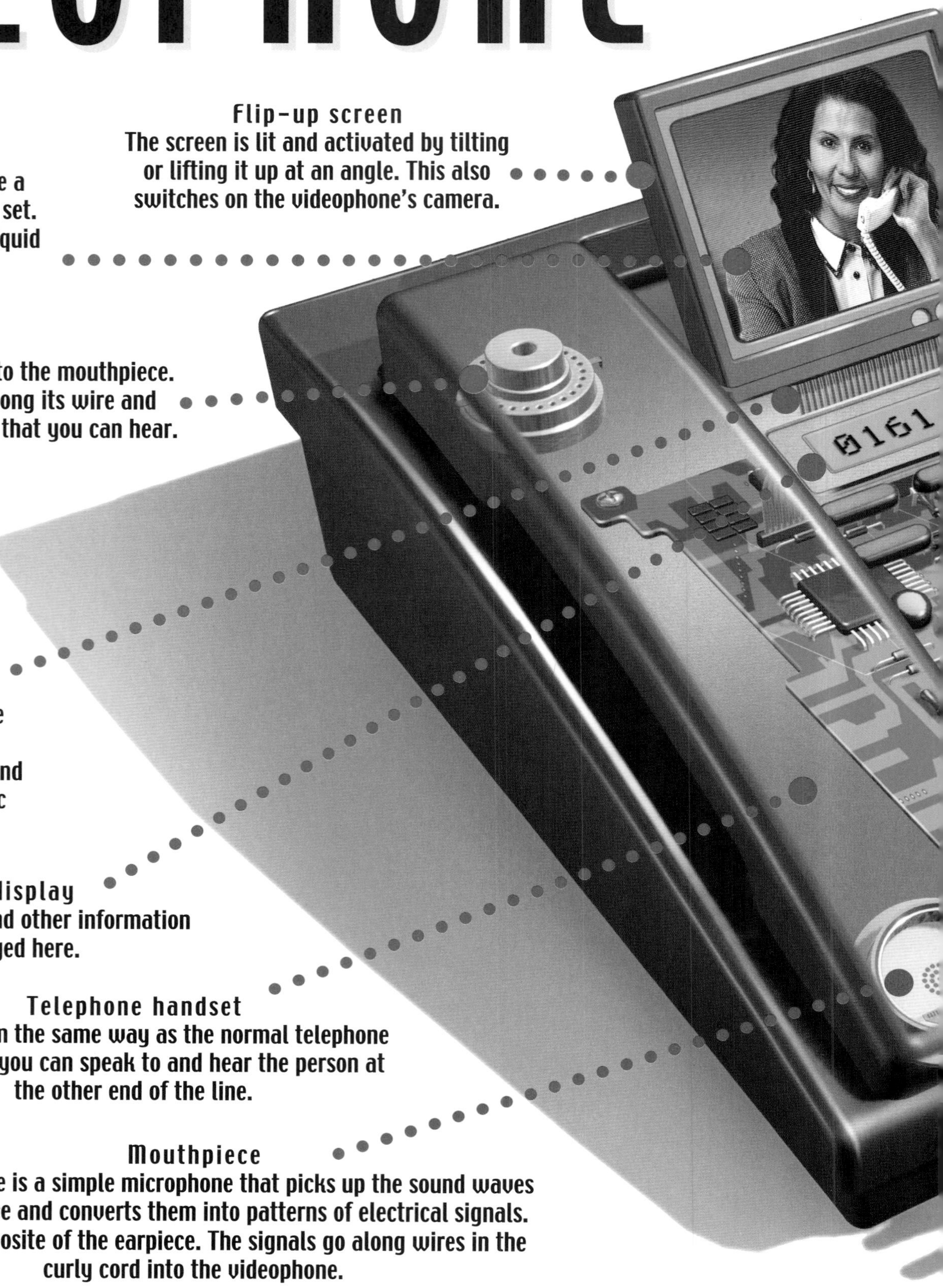

LCD
The small screen does not use a 'tube' like a normal television set. It has a much flatter, lighter liquid crystal display (LCD).

Flip-up screen
The screen is lit and activated by tilting or lifting it up at an angle. This also switches on the videophone's camera.

Earpiece
This works in the opposite way to the mouthpiece. It receives electrical signals along its wire and converts them into sound waves that you can hear.

Loudspeaker
The loudspeaker produces the sound of the other person's voice if the handset is not being used. It has to give out only a limited range of sound pitches or frequencies, those produced by the voice, compared to the music of a full orchestra. So it can be small and simple compared to a proper music system loudspeaker.

Digital display
Telephone numbers and other information are displayed here.

Telephone handset
This works in the same way as the normal telephone handset, so you can speak to and hear the person at the other end of the line.

Mouthpiece
The mouthpiece is a simple microphone that picks up the sound waves from your voice and converts them into patterns of electrical signals. This is the opposite of the earpiece. The signals go along wires in the curly cord into the videophone.

LCD TECHNOLOGY

A liquid crystal display (LCD) is much smaller, flatter and lighter than the 'tube' for a normal television screen. However, its picture isn't quite as sharp and clear. In an LCD tiny spots of coloured crystalline substances, like coloured jelly, let through or stop light by a certain amount according to how much electricity is passed through them. In the backlit display the light comes from the lowest or base layer of screen behind the crystals, passes through them and shines into the eyes. This is brighter than the non-backlit version, where light from the surroundings is reflected off the back of the screen. Most digital watches have non-backlit LCD displays. Backlit are used in laptop and palmtop computers, in miniature and wristwatch TVs, and in some giant screens at sports stadia, music concerts and similar big events.

Camera
The camera uses CCD technology to take several photographs of your face every second as you sit in front of the videophone. These are converted into patterns of electrical signals and sent along the phone line with the voice signals, to be displayed on the screen at the other end.

Screen controls
These small knobs adjust the screen's brightness, colours and contrast as for a normal television.

Numerical pad
You press the buttons to call another telephone number in the usual way. You also use the numbers in combination with other buttons to programme various functions into the machine.

Function buttons
The videophone can be programmed in various ways using these buttons, such as to recall a phone number at a certain time or call it every so many minutes.

Circuits
Most of the electronic components are fixed to a single PCB – printed circuit board – inside the videophone.

Mains or battery
Ordinary voice-only phones are powered by the electrical signals coming along the telephone wire. The videophone needs extra electricity for its screen so it has the option of batteries or plug-in mains power.

A JUMPY PICTURE

When a full colour picture is converted into electrical signals, even at the small size of the videophone screen shown here, the result is many thousands of signals. If the picture is designed to show movement, this becomes millions of signals per second. Most phone lines are unable to carry this much information. They are designed for the relatively limited number of signals representing the sound of the voice. Because of this limited capacity, only a small colour picture can be sent and this can change only a few times a second, producing a jumping or flickering image.

HI-TECH OFFICE

Ceiling fan-filter
The fan circulates scented air around the office and filters out bits of dust and nasty smells. It also changes the weak amounts of static electricity on the tiny specks floating in air. This 'ionizing' helps some people to feel more energetic and lively, work better and avoid headaches and stress.

Scented wall light
The wall lamp automatically brightens or dims as the outside light levels change. It also gives out scents such as pine, rose, lemon, mint, fresh-baked bread or fresh-ground coffee. These help to put the people in the right type of mood for whatever work they are doing.

Voice control sound system
The music system can be used to play the radio, audio cassettes and audio CDs in the usual way. It is also linked to a voice control programme so you can turn it up or down, switch programmes or link it into the computer network with just a word or two of command.

Flat wall screen
This looks like a flat painting on the wall. But it is a televison screen linked to the music system. It can also become a computer monitor screen. It is hung or propped up almost anywhere, linked into the computers and video systems by the cable-less IR network.

Videophone terminal
When you make a telephone call, you can both hear and see the person at the other end of the line. This screen also shows people outside the door waiting to come in, for security.

Secure door
The door stays locked unless it recognizes your exact voice, fingerprints and eye scan.

Massage seats
The cushioning in the seats gradually ripples, and the angles of the seat base and back slowly change, to gently move the body and massage away aches and pains.

Multi-screen
These two screens are both connected to the same computer. They can show different versions of the same image, one of the broad picture and one in close-up.

CAN YOU EVER KEEP UP?

The speed of development in computers, scanners, printers and other electronic equipment is staggering, even frightening. It's often said that as soon as you take a new computer out of its box, it is out of date. Keeping up with the latest technology can be a costly business.

True, progress is astonishing. But many computers and other machines are 'update-able' or 'forwardly compatible' or 'upgrade-able'. For a few years at least they can have new chips or circuits slotted into them. This will make them work faster, hold more memory and run the newest programs. In this way you do not have to buy a whole new device, just a part for it.

Projection screen
A large screen pulls down from the top of the window so that images from a television or monitor screen can be shone on to it, for everyone in the office to see.

Automatic sun and shade
The window blinds are computer controlled to rise or open when it's cloudy or the sun is not too bright, and to lower or close when the sunshine is too fierce or at night. Coupled with the lighting controls, this maintains the best light levels in the office.

Laptop
This small computer is taken out of the office for meetings elsewhere and for work while travelling or on business trips.

Mood wall
The walls are yellow – at the moment. They are huge light panels that can glow very softly and change colour to match the mood and type of work.

Picture window
The window is clear glass so that you can see outside. But it can also change to show a range of pictures, such as snow-capped mountains, cliffs, fields and hedges or the beach, for a change of scene.

Scanner-printer
This gadget is a combined image scanner and colour printer. It can also be used as a back-up fax-copier if the main one fails. It can print out photographs, too.

Fax-copier
This gadget is a combined colour fax machine and colour photocopier. It can also be used as a back-up scanner-printer if the main one fails. It can print out the day's newspapers, too, after these have been sent in electronic form along the telecom network.

IR cable-less networking
All of the equipment and gadgets in the office are linked by a system of invisible infra-red beams. Also they are all powered by battery packs which plug into the mains once each week for recharging. So any item of equipment can be picked up and moved around without trailing wires and cables.

BOB-WER (BOBW)
This office has BOBW – the 'best of both worlds'. It can be quiet and peaceful with restful colours, dimmed lighting, countryside surroundings and few gadgets and equipment on show. Yet in a few seconds it can be a hive of activity and energy, full of colour and brightness, movement, lively sounds and numerous machines all working away at top speed. This might seem like an extreme example, but it could be the workplace of the future!

MEDICAL SCANNER

Rotating drum
The drum inside the casing twists so that the magnets and detectors can rotate around the body and scan it from different angles.

Superconducting magnets
Very powerful magnets 'magnetize' the body for a short period and affect the way the billions of hydrogen atoms in its parts and tissues line up and spin around. (Hydrogen, H, is one of the most common chemical elements in the body, making up part of each water molecule, H_2O – and the body is almost two-thirds water.)

Patient
The patient lies still on a bed-like table. He or she may be given a sedative to relax the body and mind and ease any worries. A particular substance or chemical may also be injected into the patient to make certain kinds of scan clearer.

Scanner casing
The working parts of the scanner are contained inside a strong metal case, to protect the people on the outside and the delicate circuits and components inside.

Sliding table
The table slides to move the patient along so that successive horizontal levels or sections of the body can be scanned, one at a time. This builds up a 3-D image.

Connecting cables
Thick cables containing many individual wires link the scanner and control console.

A WORRYING EXPERIENCE

Having a scan can be a worrying process. But it is painless and usually over very quickly. Modern scanning machines are as harmless as they can be made, and there are virtually no risks.

Radio units
Radio waves are beamed through the magnetized body and affect the way the hydrogen atoms line up and spin. As they alter their alignment and spin, the atoms send out their own tiny pulses of radio waves, which are detected by the radio sensors. They form electrical signals, which are sent to the computer along with signals about the angle, strength and timing of the beams.

Viewing window
Operators can watch through the window to check all is well with the patient and equipment. The glass is specially strengthened and treated for protection.

Monitor screen
The scan images are shown on the TV-style computer monitor screens. Different body parts such as nerves, bones and blood have different amounts of brightness or intensity. These can be colour-coded by the computer to make the differences clearer.

Protective screen
A protective wall surrounds the operators and other people and shields them from any harmful effects of the scanning equipment. For an individual patient who is in the room for a short time the risks are almost zero. But they increase for the operators and other staff who are there hour after hour, week after week.

Computer
Huge amounts of computer power are needed to decode the signals coming in from the radio sensors and other equipment, analyse them and gradually build up the scan pictures section by section.

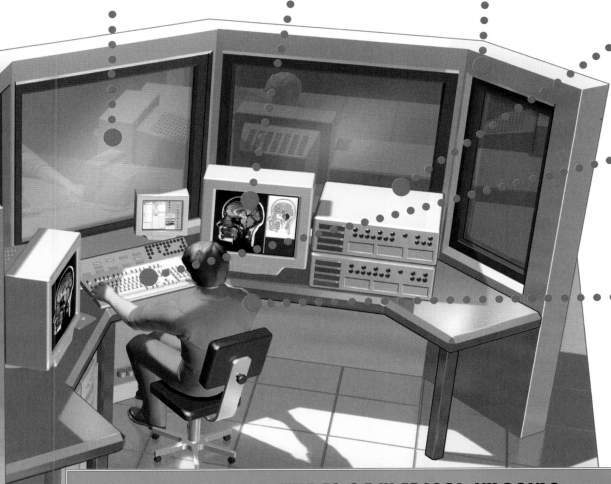

Controls
The operator controls the computer, which controls the scanner and other equipment. Most of the instructions are fed in by typing on to the keyboard as with a normal computer.

Operator
The operator is highly skilled in various areas including medicine, human anatomy (body structure), computer operations and engineering.

TYPES OF MEDICAL IMAGING

There are many ways of looking inside the body without cutting it open:

- X-rays are useful for showing bones and teeth. Modern X-rays are very safe but strong X-rays can harm the body.

- CT (computerized tomography or CAT, computerized axial tomography) uses weak X-rays that are not harmful. It scans the body slice by slice and puts the slices together for a detailed 3-D result.

- An ultrasound scan beams sound waves, too high-pitched for our hearing, into the body and analyses the echoes. It is used to examine babies in the womb.

- The MR (magnetic resonance imaging) scan gets detailed results by putting the body in a powerful magnetic field and beaming radio waves through it.

- PET (positron emission tomography) involves injecting 'tagged' substances into the body, such as hormones or blood sugar. The scanner tracks the substance and shows how it is used. PET scans are often used on the brain.

LIGHT SHOW

Wow!
Lighting displays can be so spectacular at a music show that they distract the audience from the sounds and musicians on stage.

SFX units
There are hundreds of special lighting effects (SFX). This is the stargate effect, where a pool of light seems to form a moving, rippling, glinting area like the surface of a pond.

Motorized mirrors
It takes a very powerful and expensive electric motor to tilt or swivel a whole heavy light unit so that its beam moves about. But a much smaller motor can tilt a mirror that reflects the beam to give the same effect.

Speaker banks
A massive sound system complements the lighting rig for a huge and spectacular show.

LASER LIGHT VERSUS ORDINARY LIGHT

• Laser light is the same type of energy as daylight or electric light. But it has greater intensity and power. A very strong laser beam can cut through solid metal. Almost any laser beam can harm the eyes, so it should never be shone into them.

• Laser light is one colour. The colour of light depends on its wavelength. Ordinary white light has a whole range of wavelengths that we see as all the colours of the rainbow. Light from a laser has just one wavelength so it is a single, pure colour.

• Laser light is coherent. This means its waves are arranged so that their peaks are all in line or in phase. It can travel further without fading.

• Unlike normal light rays, laser light rays don't spread out from their source. A laser beam stays the same width no matter how far it goes.

Sky pencil laser beams
Laser beams shine skywards, staying the same width and colour and brightness for as far as the eye can see. Certain types of laser light cannot be shone down towards the audience in case they harm the eyes.

Lighting gantry
Tall towers or frames on either side support a beam-like framework that runs across the top of the stage. Lights are hung from this gantry.

Spotlights
Bright, narrow beams of ordinary light illuminate small areas or spots.

Filters
White light is made up of all the colours of the rainbow. Coloured filters stop most of the colours from passing through them to leave only the required one such as red or green.

Follow spotlights
These spotlight beams move about to follow the performers as they move, keeping them brightly lit in small pools of light.

Side spotlights
More spotlight beams shine from the sides to illuminate the central area of the stage.

Wash backlights
Large areas of fainter colour are played on the surfaces at the rear of the stage by wash lights. This is much cheaper than painting the stage surfaces and the colour can be changed or turned off at the flick of a switch.

Footlights
Dimmer lights shine up from below. This helps to reduce the shadows under objects such as tables and chins caused by the bright lights from above.

Control computer
A computer system is programmed to switch the various lights on and off, make them dimmer or brighter, flash, change their colours and make the beams move around — all at precise times. This is usually faster and more reliable than having human operators for the lights, except for the follow spotlights.

175

TELECOM SYSTEM

Central exchange
The central exchange handles calls coming in and going out and routes them over a whole city. Or it may serve a wider country region where users are just as numerous but more spread out.

Exchange network
The computers and other equipment inside the exchange are all linked or networked to each other. Non-automatic calls and other information can be routed from one person to another.

Trunk cable
A trunk cable or land line is a major link carrying huge amounts of information or data. Trunk cables or landlines are usually fibre optic. They are bundles of very long but very thin rods of glass, each one thinner than a human hair. Each cable has thousands of fibres and each fibre can carry thousands of telephone calls. The information of the call passes along the fibres at the speed of light. It is not in the form of coded electrical pulses but as pulses of laser light.

SOME TELECOM DEVICES

About 30 years ago almost the only device you could attach to a telephone line was a telephone on its wire. Now the choice of devices includes:

• A cordless telephone. It has a base set attached to the phone line by a wire, and a low-power radio link to the handset so you can walk about nearby while using it.

• An answerphone that plays a pre-recorded message and then records what the caller has to say.

• A fax machine that scans writing, drawing or other marks on paper and turns them into coded signals for the telecom network.

• A computer which is linked to the network by a modem. The modem alters the digital coded signals inside the computer into analogue coded signals suitable for the general telecom system.

Microwave dish
This bowl-shaped aerial or antenna with a flat cover sends and receives narrow, focused beams of microwaves between neighbouring towers perhaps 50 kilometres (30 miles) away. The signals in the beams are coded to carry information. This saves laying a land line.

Microwave tower
Towers for microwave dishes are built on high locations such as hilltops. The higher they are, the better the line-of-sight communication – one dish needs to 'see' the dish on the next tower. Microwave dishes are also attached to tall structures such as water towers, skyscrapers and bridges.

End user
Each house or block of apartments has its own telecom line. This usually ends at wall sockets, where the user can plug in various devices.

Local exchange
Smaller than a central exchange, the local exchange deals with users in a town or group of villages. It may not be as modern as the central exchange and may have older-style equipment such as relays.

ISDN
The integrated services digital network is a telecom line system that has a much higher capacity than a normal phone line. This means that it can carry more information at any one time, for example, between videophones.

Satellite link

Local network
Telecom cables in rural areas may be the traditional metal wires. These carry less information more slowly than fibre-optic bundles.

International network
Transcontinental and undersea cables carry telecommunications between countries and continents. More and more, satellites are also part of the system.

Relays
In older equipment, banks of fast-acting switches called relays take the telephone area code and user number and route the call along the correct line.

WHAT GOES ALONG THE TELEPHONE LINE?
Information or data. This is in the form of pulses of electricity in a metal wire, flashes of laser light in an optical fibre, or patterns of waves for radio and microwaves. Each way or mode of transmission has its own coding system. The data can represent almost anything from the sound of the human voice to a full orchestra, images and pictures, lists of numbers and calculations, sentences of words and so on. Once they are put into coded form the system deals with all of them in the same way.

SATELLITE TV

Dish
The dish is an antenna or aerial that receives radio signals from the satellite broadcast. It must be pointed at exactly the right angle, both sideways and upwards, to receive the strongest signals from the satellite far above. Satellites that broadcast TV programmes are in a special geostationary orbit (GSO) above the Equator of the Earth. So in the northern parts of the world satellite dishes always point south, and in the south, they point north.

Parabolic mesh
The shape of the dish and its mesh is a parabola or similar curve. This reflects the radio signals and focuses or concentrates them on to the receiver.

TOO MANY DISHES
Some people complain that satellite dishes are unsightly. Local laws often prevent them being fixed to historic buildings.

Receiver arm
The arm holds the receiver unit at precisely the correct distance and angle from the dish to receive the focused signals.

Offset receiver
Radio signals are detected and turned into electrical signals by the receiver. This is offset, or not in line with the centre of the dish, so it does not get in the way of the incoming radio signals.

SATELLITE, TERRESTRIAL AND CABLE
Signals for television programmes can arrive at a TV set in one of three main ways.

• Satellite: This is DBS, direct broadcast by satellite. The signals are in the form of invisible radio waves that come from a satellite high in space. They are broadcast over a wide area and the individual dishes of users pick them up. As domestic dishes are quite small, the satellite must send out powerful signals. The main area where the signals can be received is called the satellite's 'footprint'.

• Terrestrial: The radio signals are beamed out by antennae on tall towers or high buildings. They can usually be received by an antenna shaped like a long bar with cross-pieces.

• Cable: The signals are sent as coded pulses of laser light flashing along a fibre-optic cable buried underground. This system is often combined with telephone and computer lines which work in the same way.

Sockets and connectors
The rear of the satellite box or unit has connections for the aerial wire, TV set, telephone line and other equipment. It may also be linked to a computer network.

Aerial wire
The aerial wire conveys the electrical signals from the receiver into the satellite 'box' or decoder. It is routed to avoid electrical equipment such as fluorescent lights that might interfere with the signals.

Remote control handset
The handset has all the buttons and controls for the decoder unit. It communicates with the decoder unit using an invisible beam, usually a low-power infra-red (weak heat) beam.

Satellite box
The 'box' is basically a decoder unit. The signals coming in are in encrypted or coded form. You must pay for a smart card so that the unit can decode them for viewing on a TV set.

Power unit shield
A metal case around the power unit prevents it from interfering with the delicate circuits in the rest of the decoder unit.

Controls
Some of the most important controls are duplicated on the unit itself in case the remote control unit is lost or broken.

TV guide
All the programmes on all the available channels allowed by the smart card are displayed on the screen. This can take time, since some satellite systems have more than 100 channels.

Card reader
The smart card slots into a card reader that detects the magnetic codes in the card's stripes.

Decryption
The signals coming in from the satellite broadcast are encrypted, or 'scrambled'. The method of encryption changes regularly. Only if the smart card is suited for the date and channel, will the decryption unit un-scramble or decode the signals so they can be fed into the TV set.

Interactive TV
Some decoder units are interactive, that is, they can send as well as receive. The user receives information via the satellite broadcast, for example, from a shopping channel. He or she then uses the handset to send information from the unit via a connection to the phone line, to order goods.

Smart card
The card has various code numbers represented by tiny patches of magnetism in its stripes. These include the dates and channels that have been paid for. They are matched to the broadcast information coming in with the pictures and sound. If the card is out of date or the channel is not on the accepted list, the unit stops its signals.

INTERNET

LOGGING ON TO THE NET

The Internet is the worldwide international network of interlinked computers and other electronic devices. It is not really one single network but complex groups of smaller networks joined together. You need a computer that plugs into the phone line or telecom system to use it. You 'log on' by sending signals to your ISP, Internet service provider. The ISP's own computer acts as a go-between or intermediate between your computer and the whole network. You 'download' by receiving along the phone line the electrical signals that represent various forms of information such as words, pictures, sounds and computer programs, and storing these in your computer.

Global telecom network
The telecommunications network involves telephone exchanges, computers of all shapes and sizes, fax machines, landlines, microwave and satellite links and many other parts.

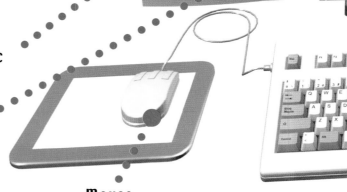

E-mail
'E' or electronic mail does not use paper. You type or make a message on your computer, address it to the recipient and send it along the telephone line to your e-mail provider. The message waits there, stored on what is effectively a huge computer disc, until the recipient uses his or her computer to call up and collect it.

Modem link
The modem is a device that changes the tiny digital electronic pulses inside the computer into electrical signals suitable for feeding into the telecom network.

Back/Forwards
Clicking on these arrows goes to the previous page you were looking at on the screen, or to the next page on the list.

Address
The address is not a physical place like a house or office. It is an electronic label for a certain website or e-mail recipient – more like the address of their computer.

Option panels or buttons
You can choose what to see next by using the mouse to position the computer's cursor or arrow on one of these panels or 'screen buttons' and then clicking the mouse.

Mouse

THE WEB

Imagine a vast library of books, pictures, movies, adverts, music, catalogues and other works and publications. The World Wide Web is like this but in electronic form. It exists as tiny electrical signals inside computers and whizzing along telephone lines. You can look up a website, which is like taking a library book or catalogue off the shelf. This is usually made by one company or organization and it is about a certain subject. You can look at the different pages on screen just as you would flick through the book. But using the Web is far quicker than visiting a library. Web sites can be continents away. They can be changed and updated at any time. Unlike a book, they are two-way – you can send information, messages, orders and money to them as well as receiving goods or information from them.

Destination computer
The message from your computer can reach another computer on the opposite side of the world in just one second. However, the various delays and changes as it passes through the system mean that the transfer time is usually slightly longer.

Search engine
You can search the Net using a search engine. This is a computer program or application that scans the network for the key words or phrases that you enter, and shows you a list of possible addresses that might be helpful. You can search in a certain country, a continent or across the whole world.

Hub
A hub is a concentrated centre where many big computers send and receive information rapidly. Gateway computers change information or data into the different forms and codes, called protocols, used in various countries.

ISP or Server

Screen and page
A page may be more than just what you can see on your screen. You may have to move or scroll the page sideways or down so you can see the rest of it as it comes on to the screen. It's like moving the large page of a newspaper or magazine around behind a smaller opening, which is the screen.

Image
Pictures tend to download (arrive in your computer) more slowly than words. They can be copied into the memory of your own computer, but they take up much more memory space than words.

Text
Words usually download, or come into your computer, very quickly. You can highlight or choose them, copy them into your own computer's memory, then store them in one of your own files or documents.

User's computer

SATELLITE NAVIGATION SYSTEM

Comsat
A communications satellite is part of the worldwide telecom network. It receives and sends on radio signals for telephone calls, TV programmes, computer messages and many other forms of long-distance communication.

Dish antenna
The large dish can send and receive faint or faraway signals. It can be moved by electric motors and pointed very precisely at a certain satellite, and moved to link with other satellites at different times.

Ground station
This is in communication with many satellites via its large dish and other aerials. It also contacts other stations on the ground by terrestrial radio and microwave links, and by the cables and landlines of the telecom network.

Ship to shore
Direct radio links between a ship and land can only be carried out over limited distances. Too far away and the curve of the Earth's surface gets in the way, since most radio signals go in straight lines and not around bends. This is why satellites are so useful. They can receive signals on the uplink and then beam them down somewhere else a continent away. They act like relay or passing-on radio sets on incredibly tall towers.

Satellite orbit
A satellite has forward motion, which means that it tries to go in a straight line. It would fly off into space, but the Earth's gravity pulls it down. However, the satellite is pulled down at a rate that matches the way the Earth's surface curves around beneath. So the satellite endlessly falls to Earth, but never gets there, because the Earth endlessly curves away from it. Round and round and ...

THE SPEED OF LIGHT

Radio and microwave signals go up and down to satellites at the fastest possible speed, the speed of light. This is about 300,000 kilometres per second (186,000 miles per second). However, some satellites are so far away that signals take more than one-tenth of a second to get there. If the signals go up and down to several satellites on their journey around the globe, the delay can add up to almost a second!

GSO

Most satellites seem to move across the sky when seen from down here on Earth. But a satellite 35,787 kilometres (about 22,000 miles) directly above the Equator has an orbit speed that means it goes once around the Earth in 24 hours. The Earth itself spins around once in the same time. So looking up from the surface of Earth, the satellite seems to hover or hang in the same place all the time. This orbit is called a geostationary or geosynchronous orbit, GSO. It means that dish aerials do not have to move or tilt to track the satellite across the sky. They can be left pointing in one direction at it. GSO is used for several types of satellite, especially those which broadcast satellite TV programmes into our homes.

SARSAT
Many ships, planes and vehicles carry a SARSAT radio beacon or transmitter. In case of trouble or emergency this sends out radio signals on an emergency channel. The signals are picked up by a world system of SARSATs, Search And Rescue SATellites. The SARSATs send alert signals down to ground stations. The time delay for the radio signals from the emergency transmitter reaching the various SARSATs in their different positions gives the location of the transmitter, and so the search and rescue can begin.

Navigation beacon
A lighthouse sends out pulses of light. The length and pattern of the pulses is a code for the identity of the lighthouse. In the same way a radio beacon sends out radio signals for its own identity or 'name', showing ships that it is nearby. The time delay between the radio signals from several beacons allows you to work out your own position in relation to them.

FUTURE GADGETS

The last few years of the twentieth century saw an astonishing increase in the numbers of gadgets. Three in particular made their mark – the mobile phone, the hand-held satellite navigation (GPS) receiver, and the MP3 solid-state digital music player. The mother of all gadgets, the computer, came into many homes. The numbers of people logging on to the Internet more than doubled each year. Never before have so many types of gadgetry taken the world by storm in this way.

BUILT TO LAST?

What will happen in this century? There are bound to be more new gadgets. We will not even know that we need some of them until they are invented. Then, like the mobile phone, they could work their way into our daily lives and become almost indispensable. Others could come and go with changing fashions.

GADGETS ON THE TABLE
This tabletop of electronic devices and equipment may look vaguely familiar. They seem like slightly more advanced versions of today's gadgets. But each item has a surprise in store...

PEN AND PAD
The electronic notepad is still around in the future but it does far more that understand your handwriting and store the addresses of friends. It is linked to the satellite navigation system and displays your exact position on a map. It shows TV channels and videos. Its diary reminds you of appointments and meetings. It has a tiny camera and microphone and works as a videophone so you can talk face-to-face with others.

3-D SCREEN
The screen is holographic. It gives a 3-D image. As you move to the side (detected by the motion sensor earpiece) you can see around and behind objects in the foreground. The screen also zooms in and out by voice control so you can see the whole scene, or look at just a small part in greatly enlarged close-up.

MUSIC AND MOOD
The speakers give out sounds and music but they are also mood generators. They produce a combination of vibrations, scents, biological chemicals called pheromones, lights, and sounds that are too high (ultrasonic) or low (infrasonic) for the ears. You cannot hear them but they affect the body in other ways. This can put you into any kind of mood or feeling you wish.

PERSONAL COMMUNICATIONS
One trend could be for the gadgets we have today to become smaller, simpler and combined together. Interactive TV and Internet computing could merge to give the full range of hundreds of channels for shopping, entertainment, business and research. In 10 or 20 years everyone might have a hand-held device that looks like a miniature TV, but is also a video recorder, a mobile phone, a voice-operated computer linked into the Internet, a radio and music player all in one small box. It's the total personal communications gadget.

NEW DIRECTIONS
Gadgets could also take us into whole new areas that we can only dream about. Our TV and monitor screens show images that are flat, in two dimensions. What about a 3-D version using hologram technology? In the corner of your room you could have a hologram TV of your favourite sports team playing for the world championship, as tiny animated models made of light.

THE WORLD ON YOUR WRIST
The wristwatch is the tiny monitor screen of a computer that is radio-linked to the Internet. It has no buttons. It is operated by your voice or by your hand and finger movements which it detects through the strap. It is also radio-linked to the earpiece so you can hear speech, music and other sounds. Oh, and it tells the time too.

THINKING AHEAD
Voice control is fine, but why not thought control? Maybe we will be able to communicate directly with our computers by holding a sensor to the head that detects our brain waves. Ideas, thoughts, memories, moods and emotions could flow between the living brain and the electronic one. In the end, where will human beings finish and electronic gadgets begin?

MONSTER MACHINES

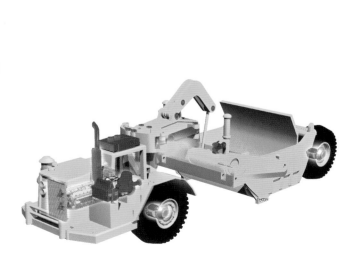

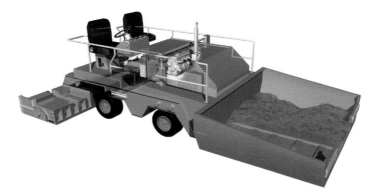

Giant Machines	188	Flight Simulator	218
Dredger	190	Roller-coaster	220
Bucketwheel Excavator	192	Church Organ	222
Concrete Mixer Truck	194	Flood Barrier	224
Earthscraper	196	Oil Platform	226
Power Shovel	198	Turbogenerator	228
Tunnel Boring Machine	200	Hydroelectric Power Station	230
Tower Crane	202	Nuclear Power Station	232
Mobile Crane	204	Wind Turbine	234
Dockside Cranes	206	Industrial Robot	236
Paper-making Machine	208	Radio Telescope	238
Printing Press	210	NASA Crawler-Transporter	240
Road-making Machines	212	Space Station	242
Glass-making Machine	214	Future Machines	244
The London Eye	216		

GIANT MACHINES

The machines in this book are monster-sized. They are the biggest machines around. The book is arranged so that you can take in these gigantic monsters at a glance. While you are looking at them, try to imagine the smell and the noise that they make and the thrill of standing next to them.

A HELPING HAND

All machines do something useful. Some machines do jobs that need enormous power. A crane lifts huge loads, multiplying the puny strength of a human being many times. A flood barrier holds back the tide. A nuclear power station splits atoms. A turbogenerator produces electricity by moving a magnet near a coil of wire. A person can make electricity in this way, but only when the process is scaled up to monster size, and a giant machine takes over, is a useful amount of electricity produced.

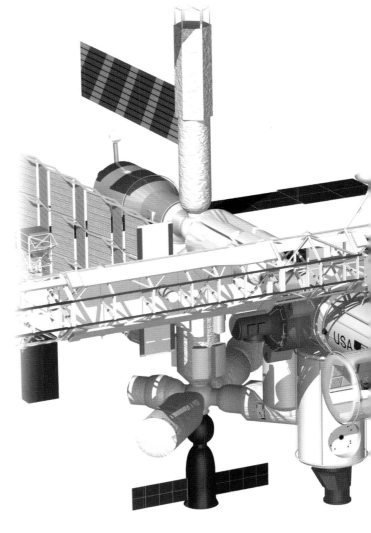

Space station
A space station (above) is a machine for astronauts to live in while in orbit above the Earth.

ROBOT WORKERS
Industrial robots help to manufacture cars. In some ways, they are ideal workers: they never get tired, sick or bored, and they don't need holidays.

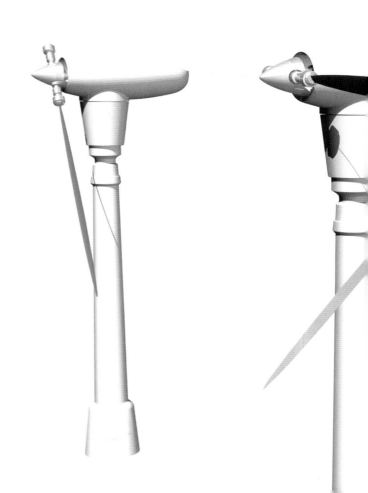

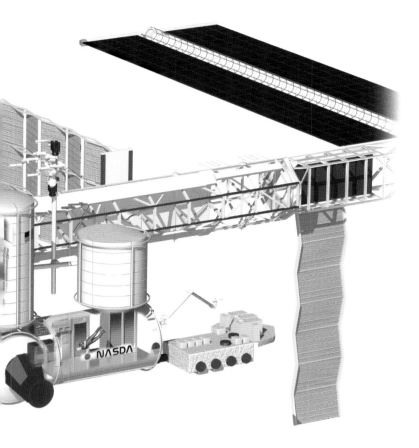

MOVABLE TYPE

Printers used to make print using individual letters, carved into small wooden blocks. The blocks were placed in a frame, wiped with ink, and pressed on to paper to produce the printed page. This process is called letterpress printing. Today, huge machines have taken over the job.

VERY ACCURATE

Monster machines may be powerful, but they are also designed for accuracy. An industrial robot can weld together the metal parts of a car body for hour after hour without getting tired, and without making any mistakes that might endanger the motorist's safety. A radio telescope looks deep into outer space and detects objects far too distant to be seen by the naked eye. A flight simulator mimics the behaviour of an aeroplane so well that a trainee pilot can't tell the difference between flying the simulator and the real thing.

JUST FOR FUN

Some monster machines have been designed just for fun. A roller-coaster makes riders sick with delight as they hurtle down stomach-churning drops. A Ferris wheel lifts its passengers high in the sky for a bird's eye view of the world.

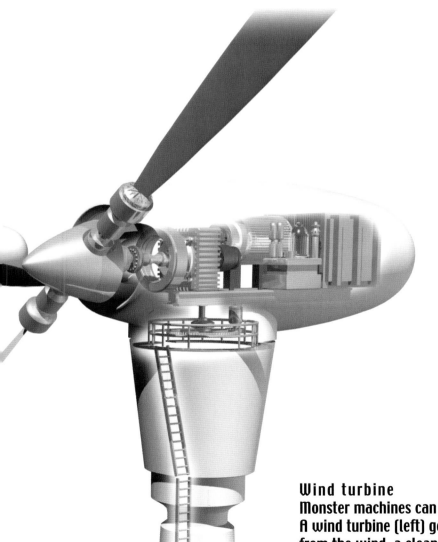

Wind turbine
Monster machines can take us into the future. A wind turbine (left) generates electrical energy from the wind, a clean and renewable source of power.

189

DREDGER

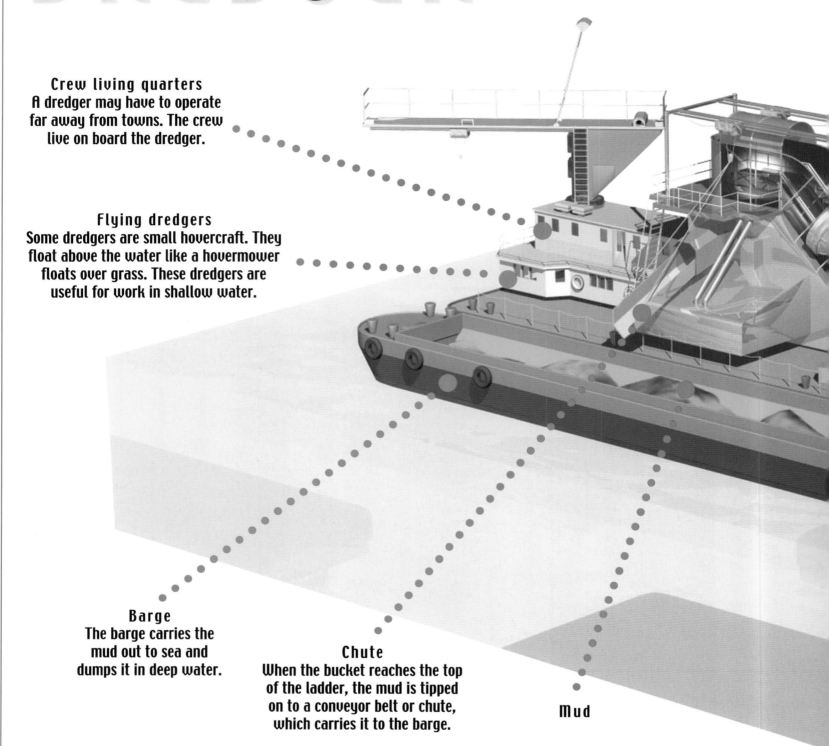

Crew living quarters
A dredger may have to operate far away from towns. The crew live on board the dredger.

Flying dredgers
Some dredgers are small hovercraft. They float above the water like a hovermower floats over grass. These dredgers are useful for work in shallow water.

Barge
The barge carries the mud out to sea and dumps it in deep water.

Chute
When the bucket reaches the top of the ladder, the mud is tipped on to a conveyor belt or chute, which carries it to the barge.

Mud

THE SHIP THAT DIGS

A dredger is a special ship that clears harbours and rivers by digging up mud or rocks from the sea- or river-bed that might get in the way of passing ships. Dredgers are used for clearing out and deepening harbours, rivers and canals. They are also used to remove the silt – soft, fine mud – that settles on harbour bottoms or river- and canal-beds. There are many different types of dredger, but they all have a mechanism that dredges unwanted material from the water-bed. The soil, silt or rock is then carried to the surface and tipped out on to a barge, which carries it away for disposal. Dredgers can work at depths of up to 50 metres (160 feet).

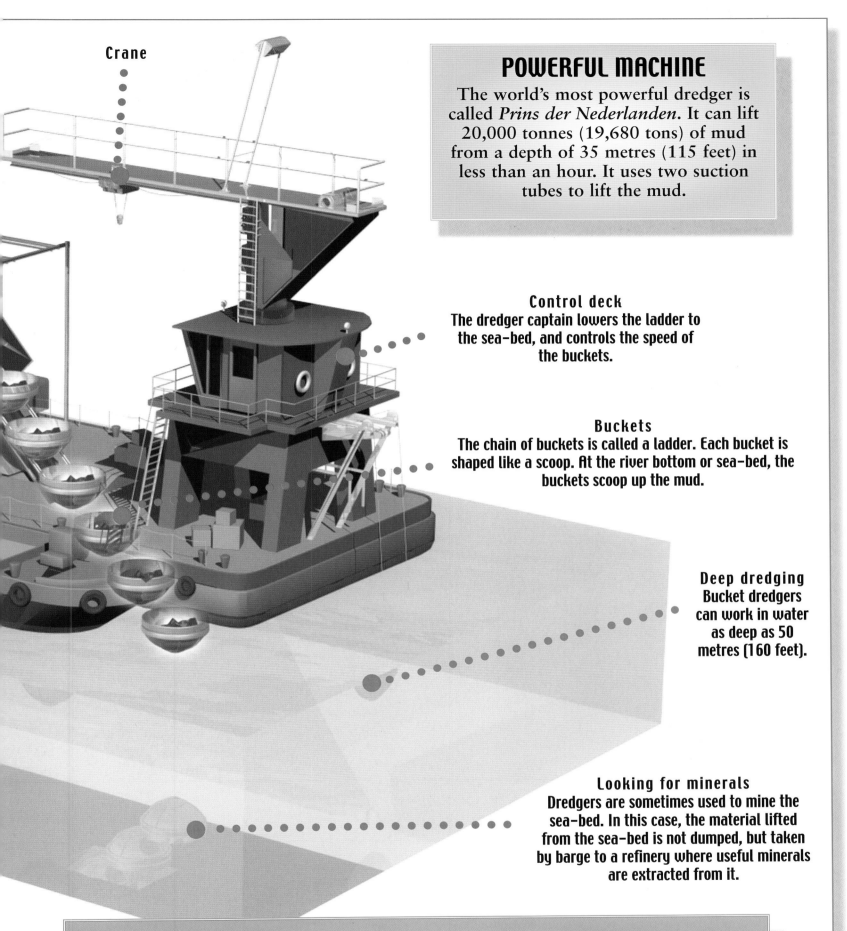

Crane

Control deck
The dredger captain lowers the ladder to the sea-bed, and controls the speed of the buckets.

Buckets
The chain of buckets is called a ladder. Each bucket is shaped like a scoop. At the river bottom or sea-bed, the buckets scoop up the mud.

Deep dredging
Bucket dredgers can work in water as deep as 50 metres (160 feet).

Looking for minerals
Dredgers are sometimes used to mine the sea-bed. In this case, the material lifted from the sea-bed is not dumped, but taken by barge to a refinery where useful minerals are extracted from it.

ALL SHAPES AND SIZES

The bucket dredger is the most common type of dredger. This has a continuous chain of buckets reaching down on a ladder to the sea-bed. The buckets go round on the chain like the stairs on an escalator. At the bottom, the buckets dig into the sea-bed. They come up to the surface carrying mud and dump it when they reach the top of the chain. A suction dredger is often used for dredging silt. It hoovers up the silt through a suction pipe. Some dredgers use a mechanical arm with a scoop that scrapes material from the water-bed. Other dredgers use an auger to lift material from the bottom. An auger is like a large corkscrew inside a cylinder. As the screw turns, it lifts material up the tube.

BUCKETWHEEL EXCAVATOR

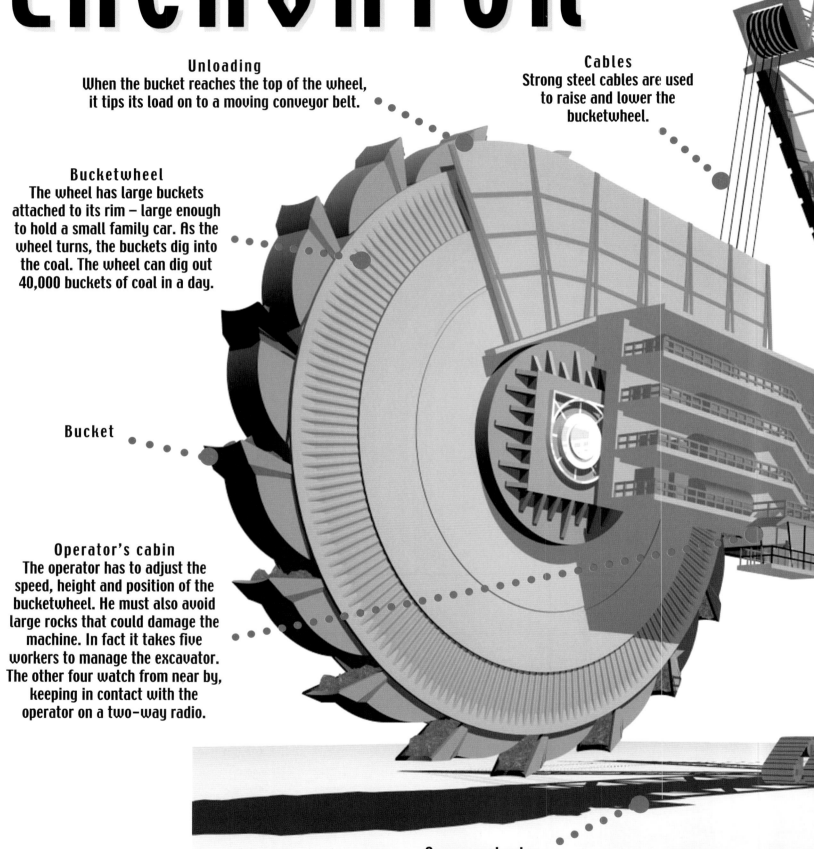

Unloading
When the bucket reaches the top of the wheel, it tips its load on to a moving conveyor belt.

Cables
Strong steel cables are used to raise and lower the bucketwheel.

Bucketwheel
The wheel has large buckets attached to its rim – large enough to hold a small family car. As the wheel turns, the buckets dig into the coal. The wheel can dig out 40,000 buckets of coal in a day.

Bucket

Operator's cabin
The operator has to adjust the speed, height and position of the bucketwheel. He must also avoid large rocks that could damage the machine. In fact it takes five workers to manage the excavator. The other four watch from near by, keeping in contact with the operator on a two-way radio.

Open-cast mine
A large mine, such as the open-cast copper mine at Bingham Canyon, near Salt Lake City, Utah, USA, can produce 270,000 tonnes (265,680 tons) of ore in a day. The deepest open-cast mine in the world is near Bergheim, Germany. It is 325 metres (1066 feet) deep.

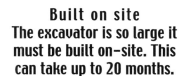

MONSTER MINING MACHINE

The gigantic bucketwheel excavator is a powerful machine used in open-cast mining, where the coal is just under the surface of the ground. First the soil on top of the coal is scraped away. Then the excavator digs the coal with its huge buckets, which turn on a revolving belt. It dumps the coal on to a conveyor belt that carries it off to be stored, or to waiting railway trucks. Bucketwheel excavators are also used in quarries to mine minerals and metal ores. For these jobs, the machine is fitted with a crusher. First the rock is blasted, then the excavator scoops it up, crushes it and feeds it on to the conveyor belts.

Built on site
The excavator is so large it must be built on-site. This can take up to 20 months.

Boom
The boom or frame supports the wheel and conveyor belt.

Engines
Powerful diesel engines are needed to turn the bucketwheel.

Crusher
The great lumps of coal or ore may pass through a crusher inside the machine. This grinds them to a size that's easier to handle.

Conveyor belt
A conveyor belt carries the coal to a railway siding where it is dumped into a railway truck. Some coal may be piled up in a storage area.

Crawler tracks
The excavator moves on huge crawler tracks. Each track is larger than a lorry. This machine has 16 tracks.

GUIDED BY LASER

It may be a monster machine, but the bucketwheel excavator is also a precision instrument that uses the very latest laser technology. A laser beam guides the excavator on its path so that its buckets cut into the coal face at exactly the right place and to the right depth. If the excavator is not in exactly the right place, it will dig out rock and soil as well as coal, making the operation less efficient and more expensive. The bucketwheel excavator was one of the first industrial machines to be fitted with a laser.

CONCRETE MIXER TRUCK

Drum
Just before the truck arrives at the building site, the driver pumps water into the drum. The drum turns about 12 times a minute to mix the concrete.

Hopper
Sand, cement dust and crushed rock are loaded into the drum through the hopper.

Mixing blades
Welded inside the drum are spiral-shaped blades called flights. These push the concrete to the front or back of the drum, depending on which way the drum is turning.

Unloading
To unload the concrete, the driver changes the direction of the drum. The concrete pours out of the drum on to the delivery chute.

Delivery chute
Concrete pours down the delivery chute to the concrete pump.

Delivery pipe
The concrete is pumped through a pipe on the outside of the boom. The pipe is made in sections that pass through the boom at the joints. This allows the pipe and boom to be folded for storage.

Swivel
This turns to point the boom in the correct direction so that the concrete goes where it is needed.

POURING CONCRETE
Concrete is pumped to the upper storeys of a tall building. The hopper delivering the concrete can move to allow the concrete to be spread wherever it is needed.

MIXING CONCRETE

Concrete is used to build tall blocks of offices and flats cheaply and quickly. It is a wet mixture of sand, cement, crushed rock and water that sets hard as it dries. When an office block is being built, wet concrete is poured into a steel framework, where it dries to form the floors and walls of the building. Concrete is made and delivered to the building site in a concrete mixer truck. The truck has a large revolving drum to hold the dry ingredients and the driver pumps in water just before the truck reaches the site. The drum turns all the time to keep the concrete well mixed and to stop it setting. The truck holds 15 tonnes (14.75 tons) of concrete. It is over 7 metres (24 feet) long and weighs 6 tonnes (just under 6 tons) when unloaded.

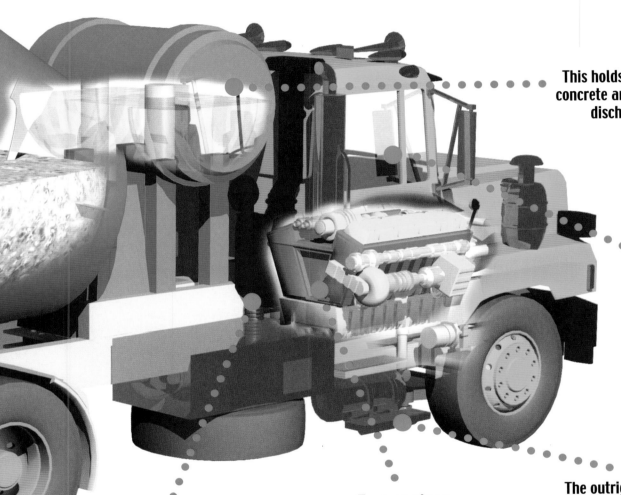

Water tank
This holds water used to make the concrete and to wash the drum after discharging the concrete.

Driver's cab
The driver operates the mixer controls from the cab.

Outrigger
The outriggers or stabilizers extend to help keep the truck steady when the boom is extended. Without outriggers, the truck could tip over.

Two engines
Some mixer trucks have two engines, one to turn the mixing drum and another to drive the truck. Other mixers have only one engine to perform both tasks.

Levers
Levers control the operation of the drum.

PUMPING CONCRETE

The mixer truck arrives at the building site and the driver unloads the concrete by reversing the direction of the mixing drum. The concrete flows down the delivery chute into a concrete pump. A piston in the pump forces the wet concrete through a long pipe and into the building. The machine has to be extremely powerful to pump concrete into the upper storeys. Workers smooth the concrete over the floor, or channel it into hollow casings to form the walls. When the concrete sets hard, the casing is removed.

EARTHSCRAPER

Quick-release mechanism
This releases the windows in an emergency.

Steering mechanism
Hydraulic rams use the pressure of oil to generate the large force needed to turn the wheels.

Scraper control
This raises and lowers the cutting edge.

Exhaust pipe
The fumes produced by the engine are carried away by the exhaust pipe.

Driver's cabin
An earthscraper is difficult to drive, as it has two separate engines to control. Also, the long body is articulated – it can bend in the middle.

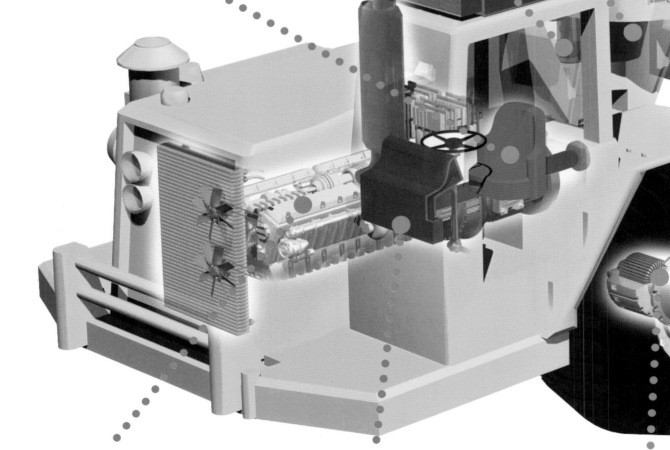

Front engine
The front engine is a powerful four-stroke diesel engine with 16 cylinders, like a large truck engine.

Automatic gearbox
The gearbox automatically adjusts the amount of power fed to the wheels from the engine. Less power is needed in loose soils than in hard, compacted soils.

Powerful brakes
The earthscraper has powerful brakes. These work by pressing a pad called a brake shoe against a drum attached to each wheel.

An earthscraper is a huge machine used to level and smooth out large areas of ground. This machine is 15 metres (49 feet) long and 3.4 metres (11 feet) wide. It weighs 87 tonnes, (86 tons) as much as 60 family cars. Road-making teams use earthscrapers to cut through low hills so that a new road can be laid. The machine stores the soil it scrapes away. It can either dump it in one place to build up an embankment, or release it gradually, spreading it over the ground to fill small hollows.

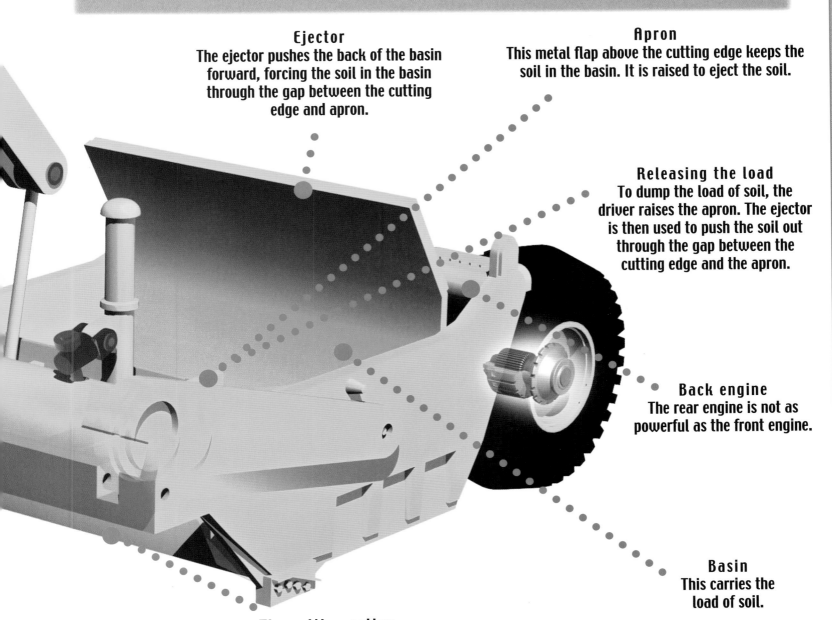

Ejector
The ejector pushes the back of the basin forward, forcing the soil in the basin through the gap between the cutting edge and apron.

Apron
This metal flap above the cutting edge keeps the soil in the basin. It is raised to eject the soil.

Releasing the load
To dump the load of soil, the driver raises the apron. The ejector is then used to push the soil out through the gap between the cutting edge and the apron.

Back engine
The rear engine is not as powerful as the front engine.

Basin
This carries the load of soil.

The cutting action
The cutting edge cuts 300 millimetres (12 inches) into the ground. It is lowered and the cutter slices easily through the ground – the soil curls up like butter on a knife. The soil moves into the basin where it is stored until dumping.

WORKING IN PAIRS

An earthscraper has two engines. One powers the front of the machine, where the driver sits, and the other powers the back, where the scraper cutting edge is. Often two earthscrapers are coupled together so a job can be done twice as fast. Double earthscrapers often bog down in soft ground. A bulldozer has to push them out. The back of the scraper is specially strengthened to cope with the force of the bulldozer.

POWER SHOVEL

Small shovel
This power shovel is a small one. It is only 13 metres (43 feet) long and weighs a mere 6 tonnes (just under 6 tons).

Boom

Open and shut
This ram uses oil pressure to transmit the force of a piston to the bucket bottom. This system, called a hydraulic ram, opens and closes the bucket.

Up and down
This hydraulic ram raises and lowers the boom.

Bucket
The bucket is hinged in the middle so it can open to drop a load. Some very big mining shovels have eight buckets fitted to a large wheel that revolves as the machine cuts into the coal-face.

Replaceable teeth
The teeth on the bucket are designed to sharpen themselves as they cut into the coal-face. They can be replaced when they eventually wear out.

Headlight
Powerful headlights shine on the coal-face for working at night.

Swing motor
The swing table is turned by an electric or hydraulic motor. This swings the boom round for unloading.

Bucket hinge
The bucket opens and shuts here.

Monster machines such as the power shovel need to be carefully controlled, or they could do a lot of damage. If they are overloaded or break down they are extremely expensive to repair. So the power shovel has built-in computer systems that automatically shut down the engine if there is a danger of overload. Sensors fitted around the shovel monitor engine performance, temperature and oil pressure. The computer gives a warning if the engine is not operating properly.

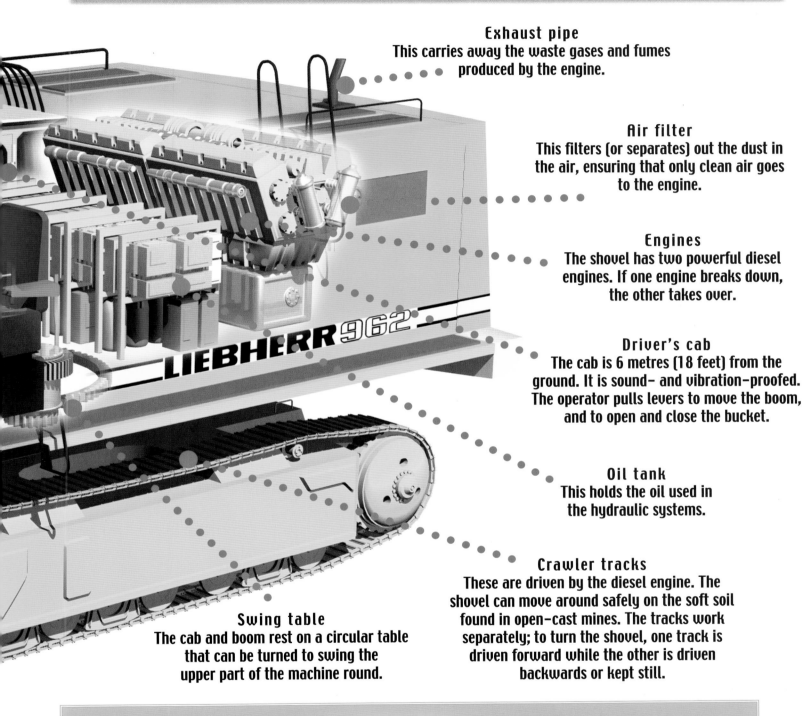

Exhaust pipe
This carries away the waste gases and fumes produced by the engine.

Air filter
This filters (or separates) out the dust in the air, ensuring that only clean air goes to the engine.

Engines
The shovel has two powerful diesel engines. If one engine breaks down, the other takes over.

Driver's cab
The cab is 6 metres (18 feet) from the ground. It is sound- and vibration-proofed. The operator pulls levers to move the boom, and to open and close the bucket.

Oil tank
This holds the oil used in the hydraulic systems.

Crawler tracks
These are driven by the diesel engine. The shovel can move around safely on the soft soil found in open-cast mines. The tracks work separately; to turn the shovel, one track is driven forward while the other is driven backwards or kept still.

Swing table
The cab and boom rest on a circular table that can be turned to swing the upper part of the machine round.

BIG DIGGER

A power shovel digs coal out of the walls of an open-cast coal mine. This monster machine has a huge bucket at the end of a long arm or boom – it carries up to 140 cubic metres (1,507 cubic feet) of coal. The boom stretches up the coal face to scrape out coal with the bucket. When the bucket is full, the driver swings the arm round and dumps the coal on to a waiting lorry. A power shovel works fast – it can fill a large lorry with 120 tonnes (118 tons) of coal in just two minutes. Power shovels are driven by petrol or diesel engines, or by electric motors.

The Marion 6360 power shovel has a boom length of 67 metres (220 feet) and a reach of 72 metres (236 feet). It weighs 1,100 tonnes (1,082 tons) and uses 20 electric motors to power the boom and bucket. It works in an open-cast coal mine near Percy in Illinois, USA.

TUNNEL BORING MACHINE

Gripper ram
The hydraulic rams in the gripper section press hard against the tunnel lining, so that the main thrusting rams have something to press against.

Main thrusting rams
These powerful hydraulic rams push the cutting head forward. They work in the same way as the hydraulic lifting arm of a digger. The force of a piston is transferred by a liquid (usually oil) to where it is needed. Hydraulic systems magnify the force of the piston and can shift heavy loads.

Cutting head
The circular cutting head turns between 2–4 times every minute. Its sharp teeth scrape away rock and soil, which is carried away on a conveyor belt.

Cutting teeth

Telescopic metal skin
This extends between the cutting head and the concrete lining. As the TBM moves forward, the skin extends to cover the gap between the TBM and the concrete tunnel lining.

Soft ground
The ground under water is usually soft and easy to cut through with a TBM. Special cutting heads are used to tunnel through hard rocks.

THE LONGEST TUNNELS

The world's longest tunnel is a water supply tunnel 169 kilometres (105 miles) long that runs from New York City, USA. The longest rail tunnel is the Seikan Tunnel between the islands of Honshu and Hokkaido in Japan. It has an overall length of 54 kilometres (33 miles), with a 23 kilometre (14 mile) underwater section. The Channel Tunnel between England and France is the longest underwater tunnel. It runs under the English Channel for 38 kilometres (23 miles).

Road and rail tunnels are cut by giant machines that burrow through the ground. The biggest of these machines are called tunnel boring machines (TBMs). The TBMs used to build the Channel Tunnel were 9 metres (28 feet) in diameter and weighed 1,575 tonnes (1,550 tons). With a service train connected behind it, the TBM was 260 metres (853 feet) long, longer than two football pitches laid end to end. These TBMs could travel through soft rock at a speed of about 1 kilometre (0.62 miles) per month.

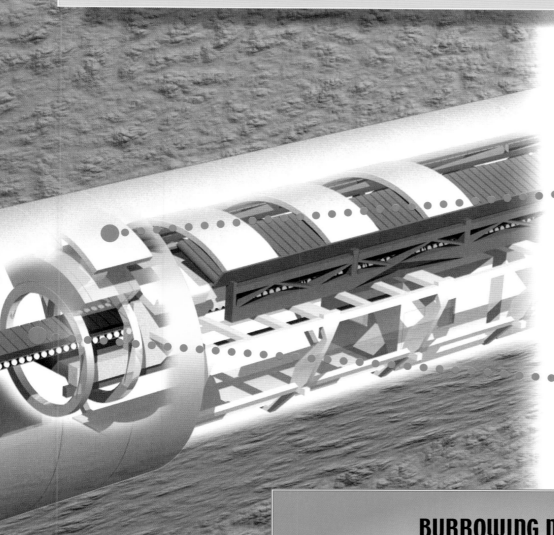

Lining segment
As the cutter moves forward, concrete lining segments are placed around the tunnel wall. These seal the tunnel and stop water getting in. As each lining segment is installed, the gripper section is moved forward to catch up with the cutting head.

Conveyor belt
This carries away the rocks.

BURROWING MACHINES

A TBM is like a long metal tube. At the front is the cutting head, which cuts through rock with huge rotating blades. Inside the tube are hydraulic rams that move the machine forward, conveyor belts to carry away the broken rock and a control cabin.

TOWER CRANE

ANCHOR
The tower is anchored to large concrete blocks or set into a concrete base. Above 60 metres (200 feet), a tower crane is often linked to the building it is working on for extra stability.

Lifting winch
This winch winds in the hoist cables to lift the load. The rope is wound round a drum. The winch is powered by an electric motor.

Trolley winch
This winch winds in the cables attached to the trolley to move it along the main jib.

Counterweight jib
This long arm or jib carries the counterweights.

Driver's cab
The driver sits in a cab and controls the winches that move the trolley along the arm and lift the load. A worker on the ground guides the driver using a walkie-talkie radio. An alarm system in the cab warns the driver if a load is too heavy to lift.

Counterweights
These heavy concrete blocks balance the crane and stop it toppling over as it lifts a load.

Tower
The tower is made up of steel sections bolted together. Each section is 6 metres (20 feet) tall.

Ladder
The driver may have to climb over 100 steps to reach the cab.

GOING UP

Tower cranes are built bit by bit on the building site. They get slowly taller as more sections are added to the tower. A small mobile crane places the first few sections of the tower in place. After that, a special section, called a climbing frame, is added. The crane lifts a new section and places it inside the climbing frame. A hydraulic ram, a lifting device at the base of the climbing frame, pushes the new section upwards. The climbing frame is then raised and the process repeated.

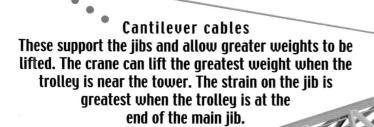

Cantilever cables
These support the jibs and allow greater weights to be lifted. The crane can lift the greatest weight when the trolley is near the tower. The strain on the jib is greatest when the trolley is at the end of the main jib.

Trolley cables
These cables control the movement of the trolley.

Trolley
The trolley moves back and forth along the jib on wheels. It is pulled along by cables attached to the trolley winch. The load hangs below the trolley.

Main jib
The jib can usually swing round in a complete circle.

Hoist or lifting cables
These cables lift the load.

Lifting hook

Turning round
The crane can swing round in a complete circle on a revolving plate. The plate is turned by an electric motor.

BUILDING SKYSCRAPERS

Tower cranes are the tallest cranes in the world. They are used to help build tall buildings such as skyscrapers. They lift things to the top of the building under construction. A tower crane has a long horizontal arm, called a jib, which turns on top of a tall tower. The jib carries a movable trolley, from which the load hangs on steel cables. Electric motors connected to winches wind in the cables attached to the load and trolley. The cables pass around pulleys, which reduce the force needed to lift the load. However, using pulleys increases the length of cable that has to be wound in.

MOBILE CRANE

Telescopic boom
The boom is made in three or four sections. They slide inside each other and are closed up like a telescope when the crane is on the road.

Hydraulic ram
This lifts the boom. It uses pressurized oil to transmit the force of a piston to the boom.

Crane engine
This diesel engine powers the hydraulic system that extends the boom. It also turns the drum to pull in or let out the lifting cables.

Main engine
This diesel engine powers the truck, moving it along at quite a fast speed. The top speed is 80 kph (50 mph)

Outrigger
The outriggers are extended outwards from the truck and lowered to lift the truck wheels off the ground to support the crane while it is working. Each has a wide foot that helps spread the weight of the vehicle and its load.

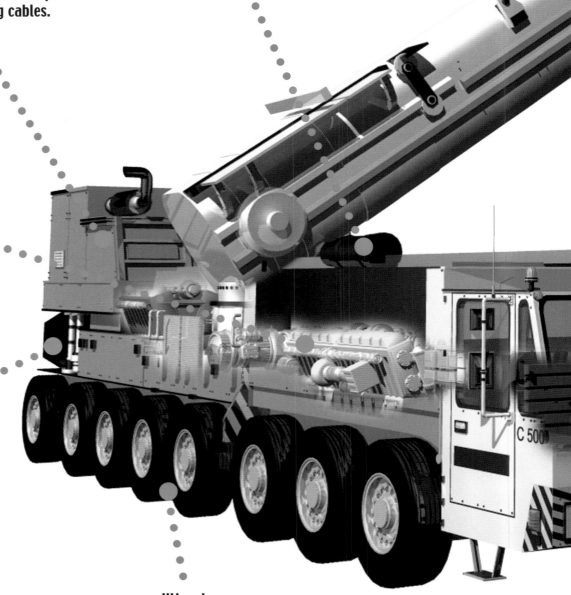

Wheels
The crane is built on the back of a large truck. The truck may have as many as 18 wheels, all of them connected to the steering. When the steering wheel is turned, the back wheels turn at a different angle to the front wheels. This system allows the huge truck to take corners smoothly.

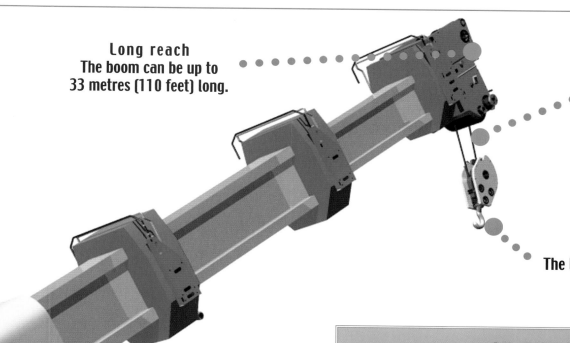

Long reach
The boom can be up to 33 metres (110 feet) long.

Lifting cables
Steel cables lift the load. They are wound in around a drum to raise the load and unwound to lower the load. The cables pass through pulleys, which increase the lifting power of the engine.

Lifting hook
The load is hooked on here for lifting.

Truck cab
The driver sits in this cab when driving the truck and crane from job to job. The crane operator uses levers to control the crane. A warning light flashes on the control panel if the load is too heavy for the crane to lift.

M399 LNG

ON THE MOVE

Mobile cranes move from job to job. Hiring a mobile crane saves building a crane at the work site, which can take seven days or more and is very expensive. A mobile crane has a long lifting arm, called the jib or boom, which is drawn in when the crane is on the road. At the work site, the jib is extended. Fully extended, it can reach the top of a six-storey building. A mobile crane can weigh 500 tonnes (492 tons) – as much as 500 family cars – and lift as much as 1,000 tonnes (984 tons).

The world's biggest mobile crane is called *Samson*. It can lift 1,000 tonnes (984 tons) on its 190 metres (625 feet) of boom. It takes 20 trucks to move *Samson*, and as many as 11 just to haul the counterweights.

KEEPING STEADY

Extending legs called outriggers hold the mobile crane steady while it is lifting. The outriggers extend from each corner of the crane and lift the truck off the ground when it is working. They slide away under the truck when the crane is not in use. To stop the crane from tipping over when the boom is extended, massive weights called counterweights are positioned at the back of the truck. The total amount of counterweight can be as heavy as the crane itself.

DOCKSIDE CRANES

Container crane
A container crane can weigh over 1,000 tonnes (984 tons) and stand more than 48 metres (150 feet) high. It can load or unload about 35 containers every hour.

Counterweight
This counterweight balances the weight of the load so that the crane does not topple over.

Trolley cables
These steel cables pull the trolley and load along the boom. The cables are wound and unwound around a drum turned by an electric motor.

Boom
The crane's boom or arm can be 60 metres (200 feet) long.

Trolley
The trolley is pulled by steel cables along the boom. The load hangs on cables underneath the trolley.

Support cables
These steel cables support the weight of the load.

Derrick crane
The cargo ship has small cranes, called derrick cranes, on its deck. These can load and unload small pieces of freight.

Working together
Several container cranes may work side by side to unload a large ship. Each ship can carry thousands of containers.

Motor
This moves the crane.

CONTAINER CRANE

At a busy port, massive ships called container ships arrive and depart carrying freight – goods for import or export. The freight is packed in gigantic containers stacked on the deck and in the ship's hold. Cranes that move on railtracks set into the dockside are used to load and unload the containers. The crane's boom or arm swings out over the ship. A trolley moves along the boom until it is above a container. Clamps are lowered on cables from the trolley. The clamps grip the container and the cable is wound in to lift the load. The trolley moves along the boom, carrying the container beneath it. When the container is correctly positioned, it is lowered on to a lorry.

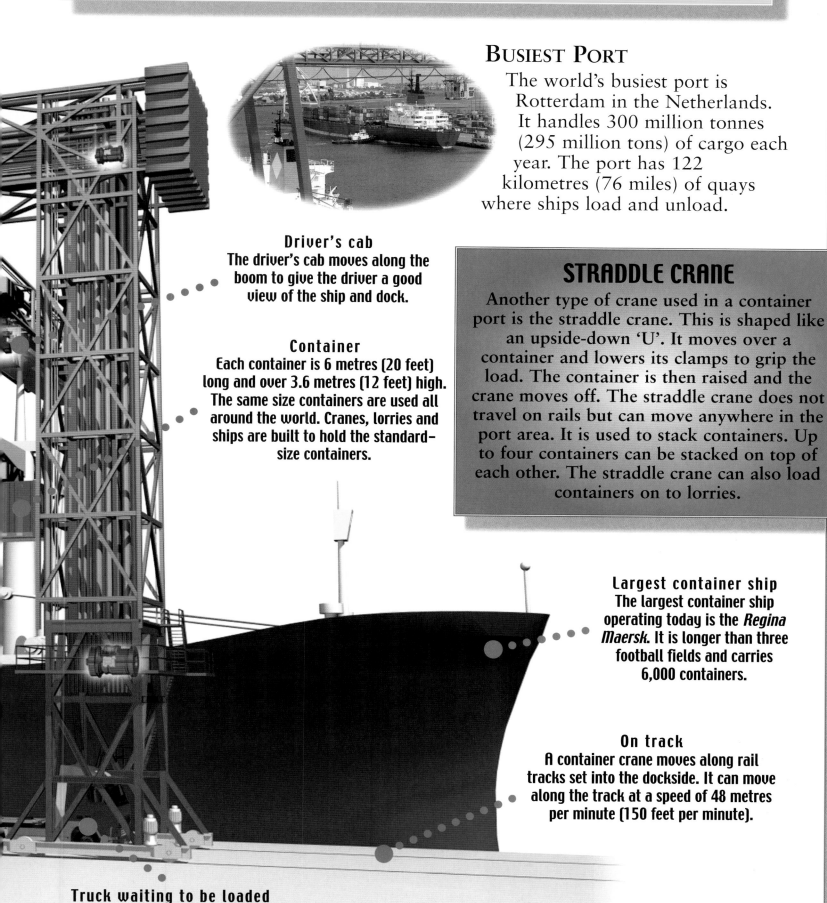

BUSIEST PORT

The world's busiest port is Rotterdam in the Netherlands. It handles 300 million tonnes (295 million tons) of cargo each year. The port has 122 kilometres (76 miles) of quays where ships load and unload.

Driver's cab
The driver's cab moves along the boom to give the driver a good view of the ship and dock.

Container
Each container is 6 metres (20 feet) long and over 3.6 metres (12 feet) high. The same size containers are used all around the world. Cranes, lorries and ships are built to hold the standard-size containers.

STRADDLE CRANE

Another type of crane used in a container port is the straddle crane. This is shaped like an upside-down 'U'. It moves over a container and lowers its clamps to grip the load. The container is then raised and the crane moves off. The straddle crane does not travel on rails but can move anywhere in the port area. It is used to stack containers. Up to four containers can be stacked on top of each other. The straddle crane can also load containers on to lorries.

Largest container ship
The largest container ship operating today is the *Regina Maersk*. It is longer than three football fields and carries 6,000 containers.

On track
A container crane moves along rail tracks set into the dockside. It can move along the track at a speed of 48 metres per minute (150 feet per minute).

Truck waiting to be loaded

PAPER-MAKING MACHINE

SPECIAL PAPER
Small paper-making machines are used to make special or high-quality paper. This is used in expensive books and presentation scrolls.

Support mesh
Wire mesh supports the wet layer of pulp while the water drains and is sucked out. The web is then strong enough to be lifted off the mesh of wire.

Keeping watch
Workers can walk around the walkway at the top of the machine to keep watch and make repairs.

Felt belt
The felt belt carries the wet web to the press rollers.

Pulp mixture
It takes 12 trees to make 1 tonne (about 1 ton) of paper.

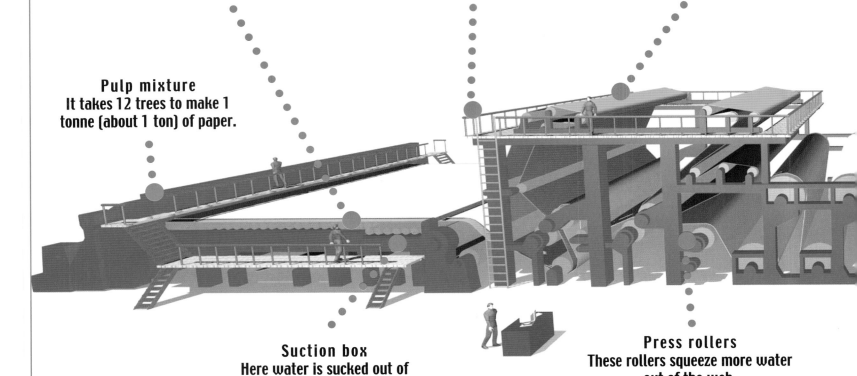

Suction box
Here water is sucked out of the wet pulp.

Press rollers
These rollers squeeze more water out of the web.

CHINESE PAPER
The Chinese discovered how to make paper about 2,000 years ago. They boiled old fish nets and rags with water, and then beat them to make a soft, wet pulp. A mesh made of fine criss-crossed wires was dipped into the pulp and then removed with a layer of pulp on it. After the water had drained away, the layer of pulp was pressed and dried to make paper.

TREES TO PULP

Today, paper-making is basically the same as it was 2,000 years ago, except that the raw material is wood from trees such as pine and spruce. They are grown in plantations specially for the paper industry. The paper-making machine was invented in 1803 by two English brothers, Henry and Sealy Fourdrinier. Paper-making machines are sometimes called Fourdrinier machines. First the wood is stripped of bark, then ground to a pulp by giant grinders. The pulp is cooked with chemicals to break it into fibres. Then it is washed, bleached and beaten to produce smaller, finer fibres. Finally, it is mixed with water and fed into the paper-making machine.

Calender rollers
The calender rollers smooth the surface of the paper.

Long machine
Paper-making machines are over 200 metres (650 feet) long and can produce more than 300 tonnes (295 tons) of paper in a day. Over 1,000 metres (3,280 feet) of paper races through the machine every minute.

Heated drying rollers
The heated drying rollers take water out of the paper in the form of steam.

Jumbo
The paper is wound on a large reel called a jumbo. It can be fitted and removed without stopping the machine.

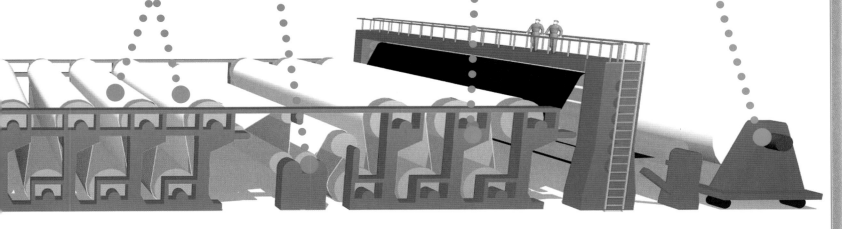

Computer control panels
A computer checks the strength, thickness and colour of the paper. Only a few people are needed to look after the huge machine.

MAKING PAPER

In a paper-making machine, the wet pulp is spread on a wire mesh that turns on rollers. The mesh vibrates and the water drains out of the pulp, leaving a smooth layer of fibres, called the web. The web passes on to a moving belt made of felt. Then it goes through a series of rollers called press rollers, which squeeze out more water. The web next passes between heated drying cylinders, which remove the remaining water. Finally, the web passes through an upright stack of rollers, called the calender, which smooth its surface.

PRINTING PRESS

Inking rollers
There are different kinds of inking roller. Some have a rubber surface, others have a metal surface. They ensure that ink is spread evenly over the plate.

Ink trough
Each of the four presses has a trough that holds the ink.

Printing press 2 prints magenta (red).

Printing press 4 prints black.

Printing press 1 prints cyan (blue).

Printing press 3 prints yellow.

Printing plate
The printing plate holds the image to be printed. Ink is spread over the image so that it transfers on to the blanket roller.

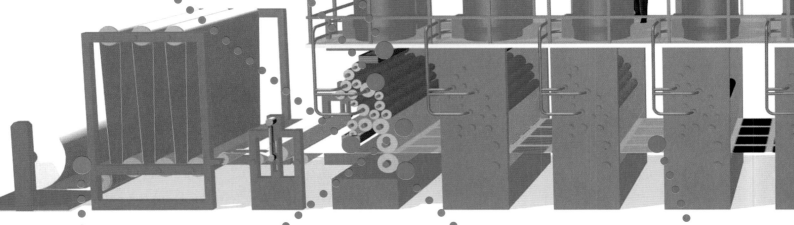

Reel of paper
In an automated press, the reel can be changed without stopping the press.

Blanket roller
The rubber-coated blanket roller transfers the image from the plate to the paper. Its rubber surface prints evenly on the bumpy paper surface.

Transfer roller
The transfer roller carries the paper to the next printing plate. Mechanical grippers on the transfer drum hold the paper accurately in place so that the four colours are printed in register (in the correct place).

Paper web
The web, a continuous strip of paper, is fed through the press.

LETTERPRESS
Johann Gutenberg, a German goldsmith, invented printing using movable type in 1439. Individual letters were carved into small wooden blocks – the type. The blocks were placed in a frame, wiped with ink, and pressed on to paper to produce the printed page. This process is called letterpress printing. It is still used today, although offset lithography, shown here, is now much more common.

PRINTING SHEETS

Small printing presses print sheets of paper. Sheet-fed machines are used for printing books which require good-quality printing, rather than many magazines and newspapers which are not intended to be kept for long.

LITHOGRAPHY

In lithography, a thin metal sheet called a plate or stereo is used to print pages. An image of the text and pictures to be printed is formed photographically on the plate. The plate is treated with chemicals to make ink stick to the dark parts of the image. The plate is often wrapped around a cylinder which rotates at high speed. As the cylinder rotates, the plate is pressed against paper coming off a large reel. The ink transfers to the paper, forming the printed image. In a similar process called offset lithography, the image is first transferred to a rubber cylinder, called the blanket roller, which then prints on to paper.

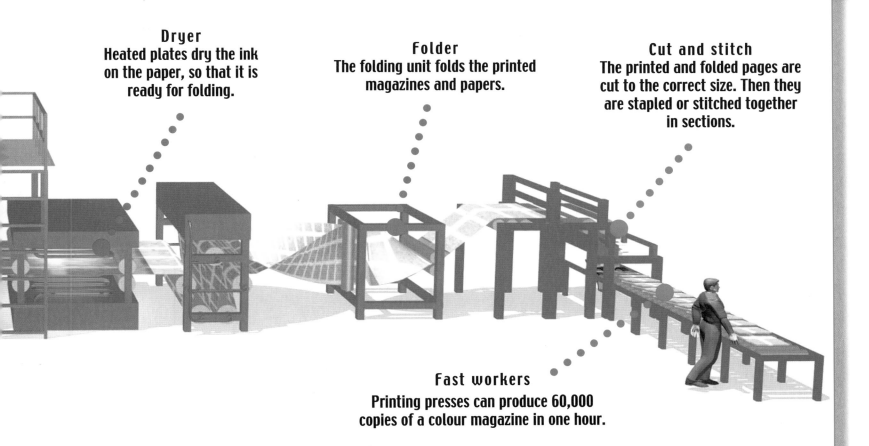

Dryer
Heated plates dry the ink on the paper, so that it is ready for folding.

Folder
The folding unit folds the printed magazines and papers.

Cut and stitch
The printed and folded pages are cut to the correct size. Then they are stapled or stitched together in sections.

Fast workers
Printing presses can produce 60,000 copies of a colour magazine in one hour.

PRINTING A PICTURE

Printed pictures are produced using a pattern of small dots of ink. There are many dots where the picture is dark and fewer where the picture is light. This allows the light and dark shades of the picture to be reproduced. To print a full-colour picture, four separate plates are made. One plate prints the cyan (blue) parts of the picture. Other plates print the magenta (red), yellow and black parts. All the colours in a picture can be reproduced using only these four colours.

ROAD-MAKING MACHINES

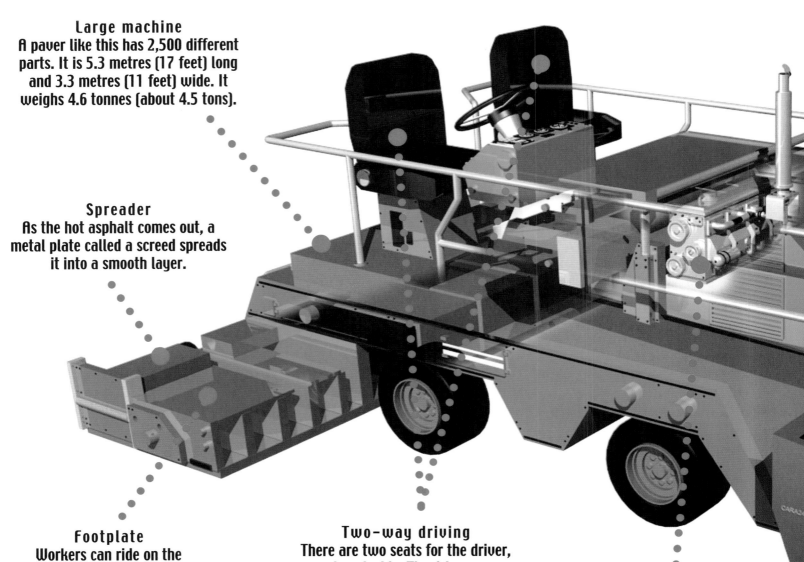

Large machine
A paver like this has 2,500 different parts. It is 5.3 metres (17 feet) long and 3.3 metres (11 feet) wide. It weighs 4.6 tonnes (about 4.5 tons).

Spreader
As the hot asphalt comes out, a metal plate called a screed spreads it into a smooth layer.

Footplate
Workers can ride on the footplate. From time to time they hop off and smooth the asphalt with their rakes before the roller moves over the surface. They use rakes and vibrating machines that jump up and down at high speed, banging the ground flat.

Two-way driving
There are two seats for the driver, one at each side. The driver swaps between seats as he checks the position of the paver. There is a brake pedal near each seat. The steering wheel and control console move from side to side as the driver changes seat.

Diesel engine
The paver has a diesel engine that burns diesel oil and air. These engines are noisy and produce smelly fumes.

SMELLY MACHINE

The road-making machine is a hot and stinking giant. It is also known as a road or track paver. Its job is to spread a layer of hot asphalt on the surface of a new or repaired road. Asphalt is a mixture of tar and crushed rock, also called tarmac. The asphalt has to be kept hot until it is spread on the road, otherwise it would set hard and clog the paver. The hot asphalt has a horrible smell.

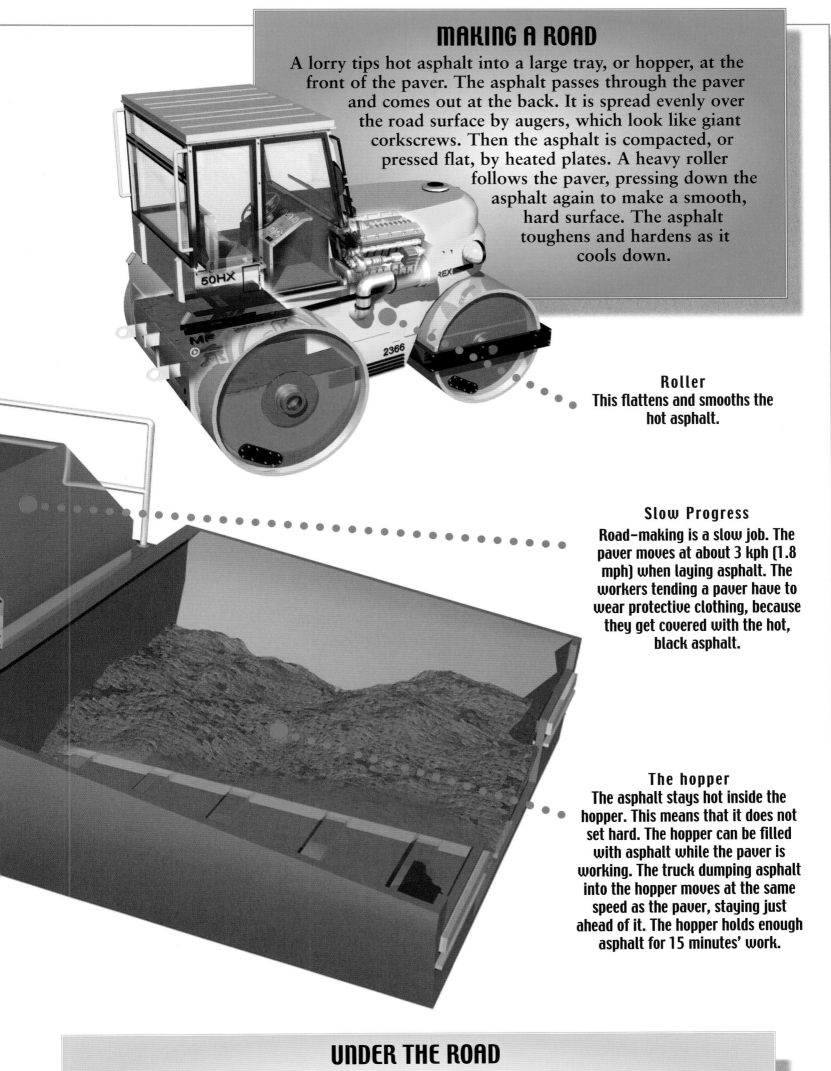

MAKING A ROAD

A lorry tips hot asphalt into a large tray, or hopper, at the front of the paver. The asphalt passes through the paver and comes out at the back. It is spread evenly over the road surface by augers, which look like giant corkscrews. Then the asphalt is compacted, or pressed flat, by heated plates. A heavy roller follows the paver, pressing down the asphalt again to make a smooth, hard surface. The asphalt toughens and hardens as it cools down.

Roller
This flattens and smooths the hot asphalt.

Slow Progress
Road-making is a slow job. The paver moves at about 3 kph (1.8 mph) when laying asphalt. The workers tending a paver have to wear protective clothing, because they get covered with the hot, black asphalt.

The hopper
The asphalt stays hot inside the hopper. This means that it does not set hard. The hopper can be filled with asphalt while the paver is working. The truck dumping asphalt into the hopper moves at the same speed as the paver, staying just ahead of it. The hopper holds enough asphalt for 15 minutes' work.

UNDER THE ROAD

The asphalt is laid on a foundation of layers of crushed stone called aggregate. There is a thick layer of large stones at the bottom. The stones are squashed down or compacted by heavy rollers. Then a thinner layer of smaller stones is placed on top and compacted.

GLASS-MAKING MACHINE

Measured amounts
The sand, soda and other ingredients have to be weighed carefully and mixed in batches. If they are mixed in the wrong proportions, the glass will be of poor quality.

Frit hopper
A mixture of sand, soda and lime (called frit) and waste glass (called cullet) is fed into the furnace. Soda is sodium carbonate. It lowers the melting point of sand. Lime is calcium carbonate. It stops the glass from dissolving in water. Sand is mainly silica or silicon dioxide; it is the material from which glass is made.

Furnace
Jets of flame stream from the sides of the furnace. The temperature in the furnace rises to 1,590 °C, and melts the ingredients.

Continuous sheet of glass
The molten glass emerges from the furnace and runs on to the molten tin, forming a thin layer or sheet.

Bath of molten tin
The molten tin is kept in an oxygen-free atmosphere. Otherwise the tin would react with oxygen, and oxidize. This would make the surface of the glass uneven.

HOW GLASS-MAKING WAS DISCOVERED

Glass was first made by the Egyptians around 5,000 years ago. They probably discovered how to make it by accident. Perhaps someone lit a fire on a sandy beach and later found shiny beads of glass in the ashes. The heat of the fire would have turned sand into glass. For this to happen, the fire must have been built on sand mixed with soda, a substance left behind when sea water evaporates in the sun. Soda helps the sand to melt and turn into glass. Today glass is made by melting soda and other sodium compounds with sand in a glass-making machine.

FLOAT GLASS PROCESS

Glass for windows and doors is produced as flat sheets. Sheet glass was once made by flattening lumps of molten glass between rollers. But this process produced sheets with an uneven surface. Today most sheet glass is made by the float glass process. Molten glass is floated on top of a huge bath of molten tin. The surface of the glass is very smooth because the surface of the molten tin is perfectly smooth. There are 170 float glass plants in the world. Each day they produce 4,800 kilometres (3,000 miles) of glass. In a year, they make a ribbon of glass over 1.6 million kilometres (1 million miles) long.

BOTTLE MAKING

Bottles are made using a mould. A lump of molten glass is put into a bottle-shaped mould and compressed air is then forced in. This pushes the glass into the shape of the mould. The bottle is then removed and left to cool.

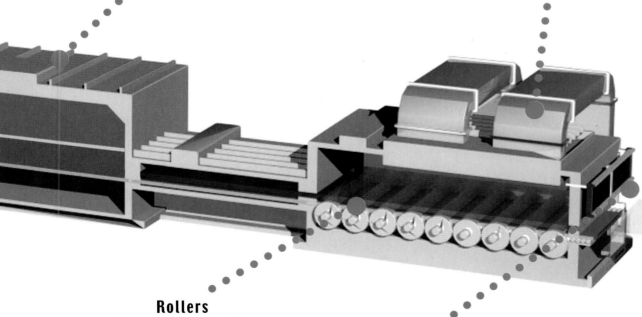

Temperature-controlled cooling section
The glass is cooled slowly, to prevent it from cracking or breaking when it is cut into sheets.

Water jets
The sheets are washed by water jets.

Big sheets
The glass sheets can be up to 6 metres (20 feet) long and 3 metres (10 feet) wide.

Rollers
These rollers carry the glass to the cutter.

Cutter
The glass is cut into lengths with a diamond-tipped cutter.

Strong stuff
Although a glass sheet is easy to break, a fine glass fibre is five times stronger than steel. Automatic stackers offload the glass sheets, then overhead cranes take the sheets to the warehouse for storage.

THE LONDON EYE

Inside an egg
The 32 fully enclosed egg-shaped passenger cars or capsules, each weighing 9 tonnes (about 9 tons), and holding 25 people. The capsules are attached to the outer rim and each has an individual motor to rotate it as the wheel goes round. They are heated in winter and air-conditioned in summer.

Round and round
One circuit of the wheel takes half an hour.

By the river
The London Eye is located on the south bank of the River Thames. Although built to last 50 years, the wheel has planning permission for only five years. After that, Londoners will have to decide whether or not they want to keep it.

MONSTER TOURIST ATTRACTION

The London Eye was built as a tourist attraction to bring people to London for the year-2000 celebrations. The 1,500-tonne (1,475-ton) structure is heavier than 250 double-decker buses.

At night, the London Eye pulses gently with soft light, at 16 pulses a minute, our natural rate of breathing.

Foundations
The London Eye is built on 45 concrete piles sunk 33 metres (108 feet) deep, containing 2,600 tonnes (2,560 tons) of concrete.

216

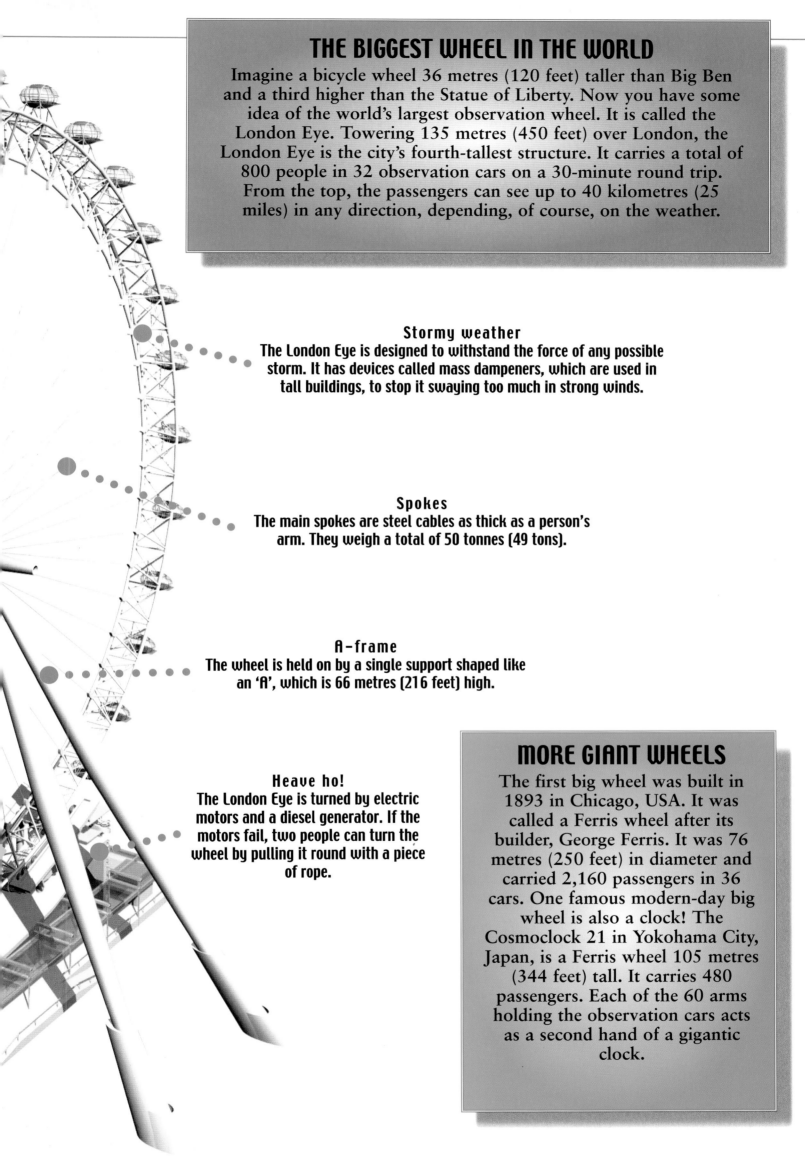

THE BIGGEST WHEEL IN THE WORLD

Imagine a bicycle wheel 36 metres (120 feet) taller than Big Ben and a third higher than the Statue of Liberty. Now you have some idea of the world's largest observation wheel. It is called the London Eye. Towering 135 metres (450 feet) over London, the London Eye is the city's fourth-tallest structure. It carries a total of 800 people in 32 observation cars on a 30-minute round trip. From the top, the passengers can see up to 40 kilometres (25 miles) in any direction, depending, of course, on the weather.

Stormy weather
The London Eye is designed to withstand the force of any possible storm. It has devices called mass dampeners, which are used in tall buildings, to stop it swaying too much in strong winds.

Spokes
The main spokes are steel cables as thick as a person's arm. They weigh a total of 50 tonnes (49 tons).

A-frame
The wheel is held on by a single support shaped like an 'A', which is 66 metres (216 feet) high.

Heave ho!
The London Eye is turned by electric motors and a diesel generator. If the motors fail, two people can turn the wheel by pulling it round with a piece of rope.

MORE GIANT WHEELS

The first big wheel was built in 1893 in Chicago, USA. It was called a Ferris wheel after its builder, George Ferris. It was 76 metres (250 feet) in diameter and carried 2,160 passengers in 36 cars. One famous modern-day big wheel is also a clock! The Cosmoclock 21 in Yokohama City, Japan, is a Ferris wheel 105 metres (344 feet) tall. It carries 480 passengers. Each of the 60 arms holding the observation cars acts as a second hand of a gigantic clock.

FLIGHT SIMULATOR

Computer
The computer ensures that the simulator moves like a real aircraft in response to the trainee pilot's actions. It also records a training session, so that the instructor and trainee pilot can learn from it afterwards.

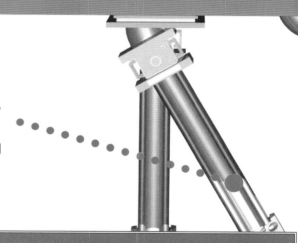

Instructor's console

The instructor sits at a console behind the trainee pilot. The console displays information about the pilot's performance. The instructor can tell the computer to simulate special conditions, such as foggy weather, or to give the trainee a difficult task, such as an emergency landing.

Pistons

The pistons tilt and roll the simulator to follow the pilot's commands. If the pilot pulls up on the joystick, the simulator tilts up to show that the aeroplane would tilt upwards. The pistons can also create the effect of air turbulence by making the simulator vibrate up and down.

LEARNING TO FLY

Trainee pilots can learn to fly an aeroplane without leaving the ground. They are trained on a computer-controlled machine called a flight simulator. This is a copy of a real cabin in which the trainee pilot sits. The simulator has all the control levers and instruments found in a real aeroplane cockpit, and the pilot 'flies' the simulator exactly as if it were the real thing. The computer makes the simulator react like an aeroplane: it tilts and rolls as the pilot moves the controls, and the instruments give realistic readings of such things as height and the amount of fuel left in the tanks. The simulator even reproduces the engine noise and the sound of air flowing past the aeroplane.

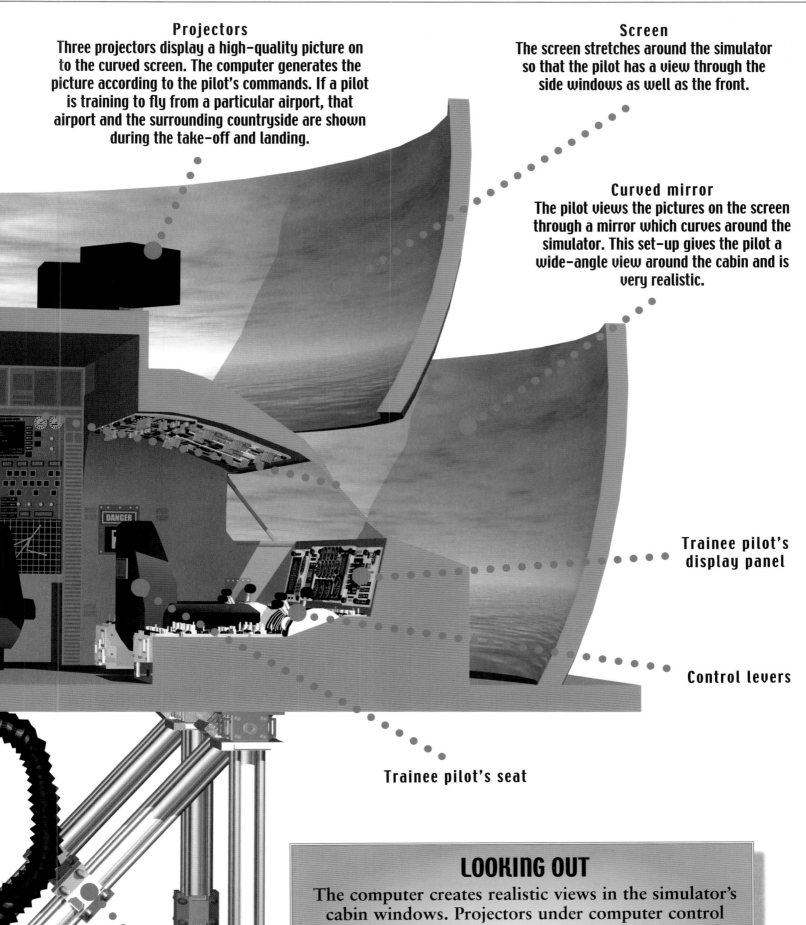

Projectors
Three projectors display a high-quality picture on to the curved screen. The computer generates the picture according to the pilot's commands. If a pilot is training to fly from a particular airport, that airport and the surrounding countryside are shown during the take-off and landing.

Screen
The screen stretches around the simulator so that the pilot has a view through the side windows as well as the front.

Curved mirror
The pilot views the pictures on the screen through a mirror which curves around the simulator. This set-up gives the pilot a wide-angle view around the cabin and is very realistic.

Trainee pilot's display panel

Control levers

Trainee pilot's seat

Fluid machines
The pistons are hydraulic machines. They are moved up and down by the pressure in a hydraulic fluid. They are controlled by the main computer and respond to the trainee pilot's actions.

LOOKING OUT
The computer creates realistic views in the simulator's cabin windows. Projectors under computer control throw pictures on to a screen. The pictures show what the pilot will see through the cabin window during a real flight. When the pilot is taking off or landing, the screen shows the airport runway just as it would be in real life. If there is a danger of colliding with another aeroplane, the screen shows the other plane approaching fast!

ROLLER-COASTER

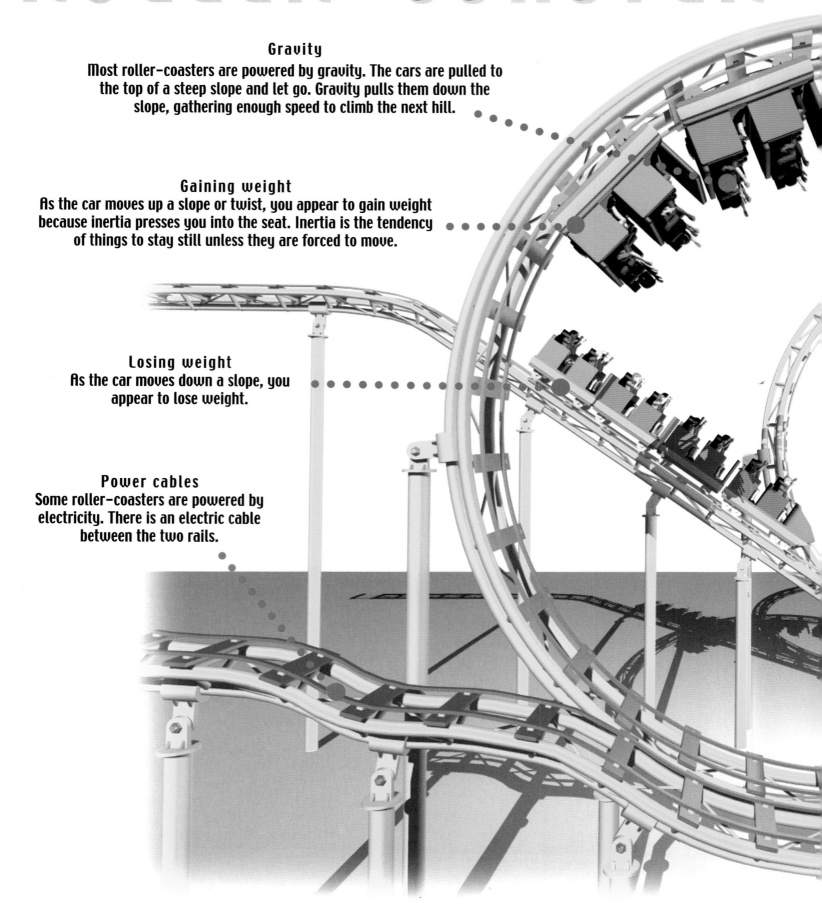

Gravity
Most roller-coasters are powered by gravity. The cars are pulled to the top of a steep slope and let go. Gravity pulls them down the slope, gathering enough speed to climb the next hill.

Gaining weight
As the car moves up a slope or twist, you appear to gain weight because inertia presses you into the seat. Inertia is the tendency of things to stay still unless they are forced to move.

Losing weight
As the car moves down a slope, you appear to lose weight.

Power cables
Some roller-coasters are powered by electricity. There is an electric cable between the two rails.

MOMENTUM
When a roller-coaster suddenly dives down, your stomach seems to get 'left behind'. This happens because anything moving tends to keep going in one direction. This tendency is called momentum. If you were not strapped into your seat, momentum would continue to carry you uphill, and you would be thrown into the air as the car hurtled down.

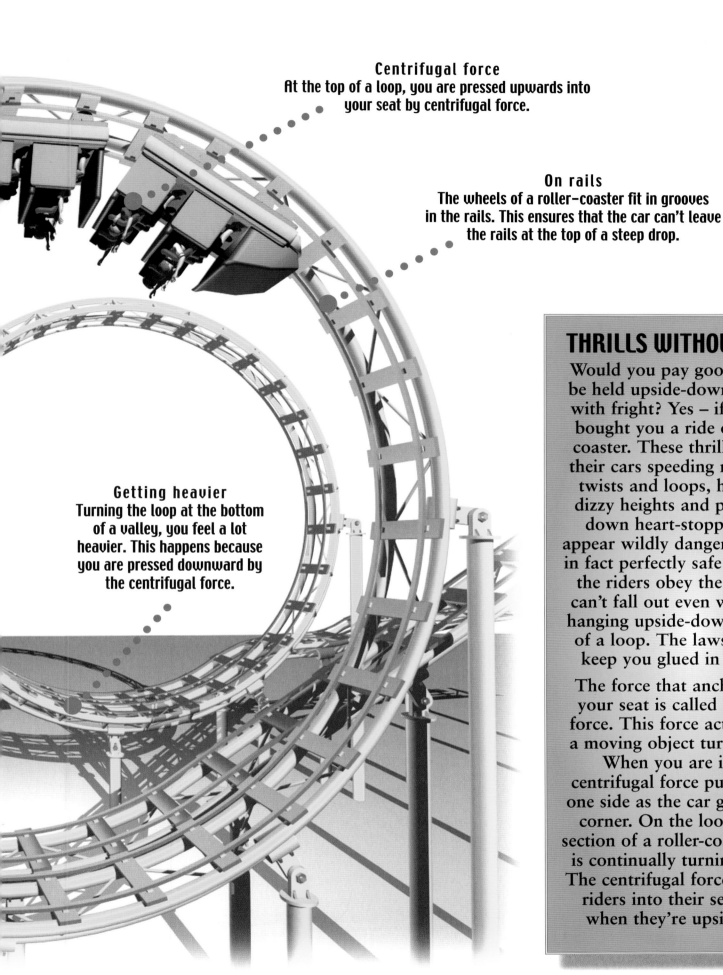

Centrifugal force
At the top of a loop, you are pressed upwards into your seat by centrifugal force.

On rails
The wheels of a roller-coaster fit in grooves in the rails. This ensures that the car can't leave the rails at the top of a steep drop.

Getting heavier
Turning the loop at the bottom of a valley, you feel a lot heavier. This happens because you are pressed downward by the centrifugal force.

THRILLS WITHOUT SPILLS

Would you pay good money to be held upside-down screaming with fright? Yes – if the money bought you a ride on a roller-coaster. These thrill rides with their cars speeding round crazy twists and loops, hurtling up dizzy heights and plummeting down heart-stopping drops appear wildly dangerous, but are in fact perfectly safe – as long as the riders obey the rules. You can't fall out even when you're hanging upside-down at the top of a loop. The laws of science keep you glued in your seat.

The force that anchors you in your seat is called centrifugal force. This force acts whenever a moving object turns a corner. When you are in a car, centrifugal force pushes you to one side as the car goes round a corner. On the loop-the-loop section of a roller-coaster, the car is continually turning a corner. The centrifugal force presses the riders into their seats – even when they're upside-down!

HIGHEST, FASTEST, LONGEST

The highest and fastest roller-coaster in the world is called *Superman – The Escape*. It is at Six Flags Magic Mountain, Valencia, California, USA. The cars reach a speed of 161 kph (100 mph). The structure is 126 metres (1,650 feet) tall. The longest roller-coaster in the world is at Lightwater Valley Theme Park in Ripon, Yorkshire, UK. Called *The Ultimate*, the ride is 2.29 kilometres (1 mile 740 yards) long.

CHURCH ORGAN

WIND INSTRUMENT

Church organs are wind instruments. Sound is produced by blowing air into pipes of different lengths and diameters. The length of the pipe determines the pitch of the note. The long pipes also have a large diameter, and so produce the loudest sounds. The organist plays a keyboard, with each key sounding a different note. An organ can also play chords, made up of several notes that harmonize, or blend smoothly together. Chords can be produced by operating the stops – the knobs at the side of the keyboards.

Pedal pipes

Stops
When a stop is pulled out, a slider blocks off the openings of some pipes. Pressing a key on the keyboard will then allow air to flow only to the unblocked pipes. This means that different combinations of notes can be sounded when the same key is pressed.

Keyboard or manual
There are usually three keyboards, called the swell, the great and the choir. Each keyboard is linked to a set of pipes with the same name. When a key is pressed, air flows through the pipe linked to that key.

Choir pipes
These pipes are connected to the choir keyboard. They produce the highest pitched notes.

Organist's seat

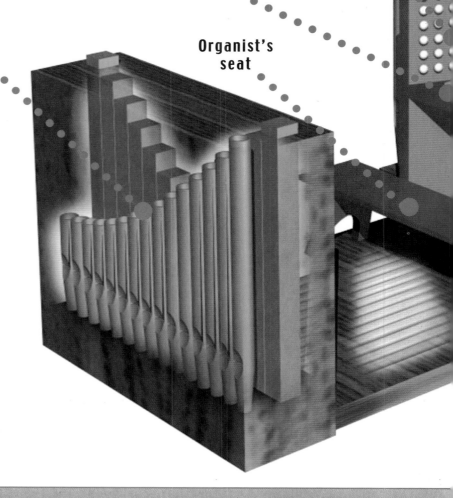

PIPES, KEYBOARDS AND PEDALS

The organ has three main parts – the wind supply, the keyboards and the pipes. The wind or air supply is blown through the pipes by fans or bellows operated by an electric motor. Most organs have two or three keyboards, but some have four or five, and one famous organ has six! Each keyboard is linked to a different set of pipes. There are three sets of pipes – swell, great and choir.

Great pipes
These pipes are connected to the great keyboard.

Pipes
There are two types of pipe in each set – the flue tone pipes and the reed tone pipes. They each produce a different musical effect, even when the same note is sounded.

Windchest
The windchest holds the pressurized air from the blower before it flows through the pipes.

Swell pipes
These pipes are connected to the swell keyboard.

BIG AND LOUD

The church or cathedral organ is the biggest musical instrument around. Some church organs are over 15 metres (50 feet) tall and have thousands of pipes. Some of these pipes are smaller than a pencil, and others are large enough for a person to fit inside.

Pedals
The pedals form a keyboard for the feet to play. They are connected to a set of pipes called the pedal pipes. There are also pedals which produce special musical effects.

FLOOD BARRIER

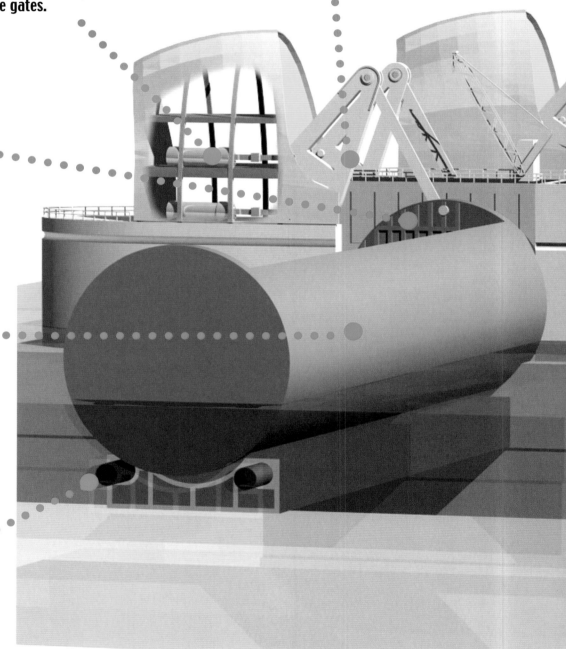

Hydraulic ram
A piston in a large cylinder applies pressure to a liquid. The liquid transmits the force to the rocker beam and lifting arm. This system, called a hydraulic ram, magnifies the force applied to the piston to lift the gates.

Lifting mechanism
This is the rocker beam and arm which raises the gate. The beam is moved by two hydraulic cylinders.

Locking the gate
A latch mechanism locks the gate in position.

Gate
The four largest gates are 66 metres (216 feet) wide and weigh 1,500 tonnes (1,480 tons) each. They are covered with steel plating 40 millimetres (1.5 inches) thick. Wooden strips protect the gates in case ships collide with them.

Power and control cables
Tunnels carry power and control cables between the piers and the control room on the river bank.

HOLDING BACK THE TIDE

For centuries, the city of London has been in danger of sudden floods. At very high tides, the River Thames can break through its banks and flood the low-lying parts of the city. Now a mighty machine, the Thames Flood Barrier, has been designed to prevent flooding. The Thames Barrier is like a great wall built across the river to hold back the tide. The Barrier is 523 metres (1,715 feet) wide. It has four main gates, each as high as a five-storey building, which are normally left open to let shipping through.

OPENING AND CLOSING THE GATES

The gates in the Thames Barrier lie on the bed of the river when they are open. This means that ships can move over the gates and through the barrier. If a very high tide is expected, the gates are raised to block the river. The gates are rotated or turned in a semi-circle to lift them from the river-bed. A large mechanical arm or beam at the end of each gate lifts it. The beams are powered hydraulically, like the arms of a mechanical excavator. At the time of manufacture, the hydraulic cylinders used in the barrier were the largest in the world.

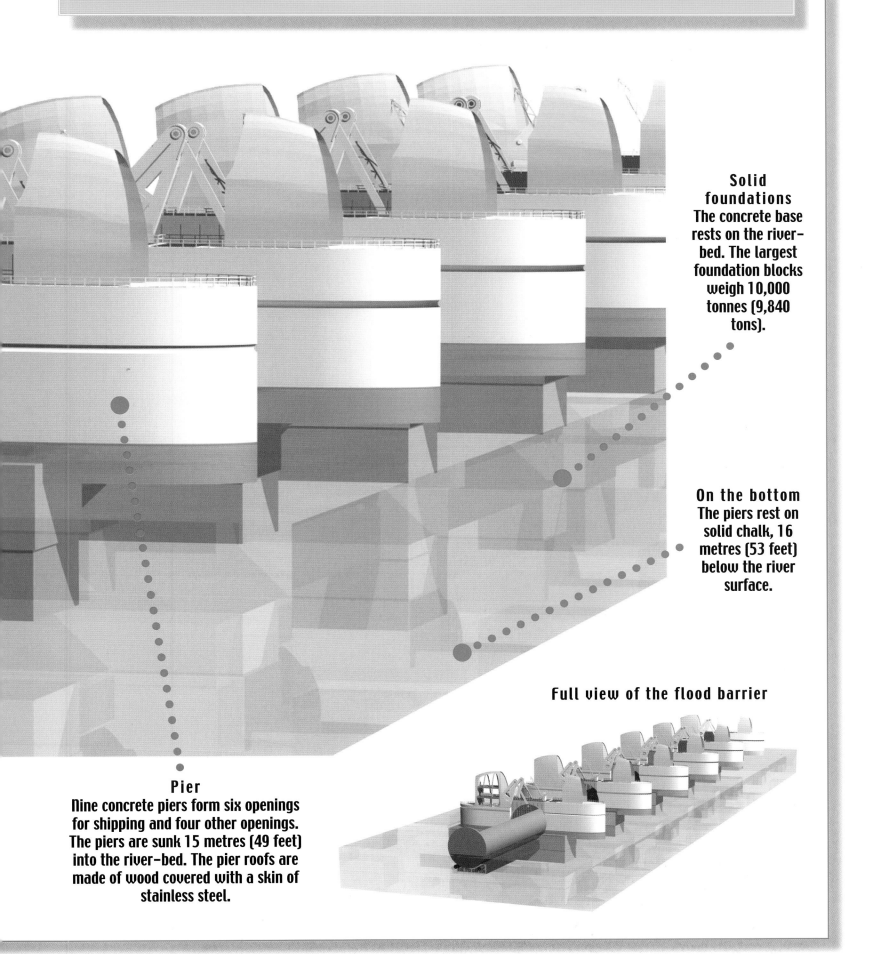

Solid foundations
The concrete base rests on the river-bed. The largest foundation blocks weigh 10,000 tonnes (9,840 tons).

On the bottom
The piers rest on solid chalk, 16 metres (53 feet) below the river surface.

Full view of the flood barrier

Pier
Nine concrete piers form six openings for shipping and four other openings. The piers are sunk 15 metres (49 feet) into the river-bed. The pier roofs are made of wood covered with a skin of stainless steel.

225

OIL PLATFORM

PLUMBING THE DEPTHS

The world consumes over 68 million barrels of oil a day. Much of it comes from large oil rigs or platforms scattered across the oceans of the world. These platforms either float on the sea or stand on the sea-bed. They drill into the sea-bed to the oil deposits beneath it. The oil is pumped to the surface and carried by tanker or pipeline to refineries on land. Natural gas is often found with the oil and can be extracted at the same time.

Gas purification system
The natural gas that comes to the surface with the crude oil is a mixture of gases. The useful part of the mixture is separated out, turned to a liquid and sent ashore.

BRANCHING OUT

A system called directional drilling allows wells to be drilled at different angles rather than straight down. This means that many oilfields can be reached from one platform. A single platform can receive oil from up to 60 wells.

Platform support legs
The legs house the drill that digs its way down to the oilfield. Once a well has been drilled, the legs contain the pipes carrying oil, gas and water. The oil and gas are separated and purified. The gas is pumped to the mainland through pipes. When the pipeline is shut down, the gas is burnt, or flared off.

TYPES OF PLATFORM

A floating platform, or semi-submersible platform, rests on huge floats called pontoons. It is held in place above the oil well by steel cables that anchor each corner of the platform to the sea-bed. Some platforms, called guyed tower platforms, stand on a steel framework that reaches down to the sea-bed. The tower is anchored to the sea-bed with steel cables. Gravity platforms are the biggest and heaviest. These huge concrete structures rest directly on the sea-bed, held in place by their sheer weight. A platform is like a small town. It has its own power supply, water supply, living quarters, helicopter pad and medical facilities. Oil workers may live and work on the platforms for weeks at a time.

The tallest oil platform is the *Mars* platform in the Gulf of Mexico. It rises 896 metres (2,940 feet) from the ocean-bed to the surface of the sea. It stands twice as high as the Empire State Building. The *Mars* platform produces 38,000 barrels of oil per day.

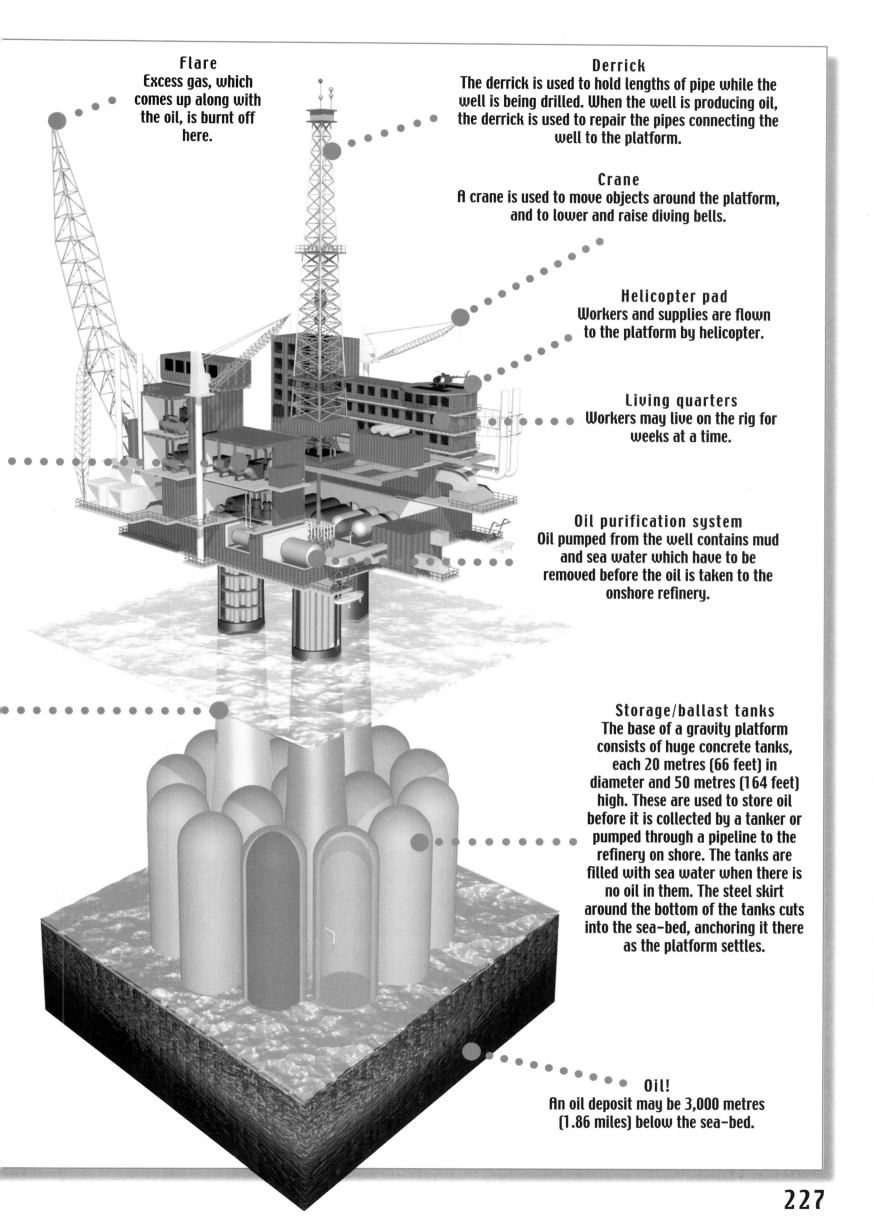

Flare
Excess gas, which comes up along with the oil, is burnt off here.

Derrick
The derrick is used to hold lengths of pipe while the well is being drilled. When the well is producing oil, the derrick is used to repair the pipes connecting the well to the platform.

Crane
A crane is used to move objects around the platform, and to lower and raise diving bells.

Helicopter pad
Workers and supplies are flown to the platform by helicopter.

Living quarters
Workers may live on the rig for weeks at a time.

Oil purification system
Oil pumped from the well contains mud and sea water which have to be removed before the oil is taken to the onshore refinery.

Storage/ballast tanks
The base of a gravity platform consists of huge concrete tanks, each 20 metres (66 feet) in diameter and 50 metres (164 feet) high. These are used to store oil before it is collected by a tanker or pumped through a pipeline to the refinery on shore. The tanks are filled with sea water when there is no oil in them. The steel skirt around the bottom of the tanks cuts into the sea-bed, anchoring it there as the platform settles.

Oil!
An oil deposit may be 3,000 metres (1.86 miles) below the sea-bed.

TURBOGENERATOR

Power take-off cables
The electricity produced flows along the take-off cables and into the transmission system to homes, factories and offices. Large turbogenerators can produce electricity with a strength of 30,000 volts. For comparison, a torch battery produces 1.5 volts.

More than one
Power stations usually have more than one turbogenerator. The steam is fed through each machine in turn until all its energy has been extracted.

Generating giants
A turbogenerator can be up to 24 metres (80 feet) long and 6 metres (20 feet) high.

Rotor
The rotating coil or rotor is made up of many coils of wire that turn between the stator (magnet) coils. Electricity is produced in the rotor coils by magnetism from the stator. In large generators, the rotor turns 3,600 times each minute.

TURBINE AND GENERATOR

A turbogenerator is a huge machine – 6 metres by 6 metres by 24 metres. It is made of two connected parts: a turbine and a generator. The turbine is like a windmill. It has many blades that turn as the high-pressure steam flows over them. The turbine turns the generator. The generator produces electricity as it turns.

The world's largest turbogenerator is at the Ignalina power station in Lithuania. It produces 1,450 million watts of power – enough for 400,000 homes.

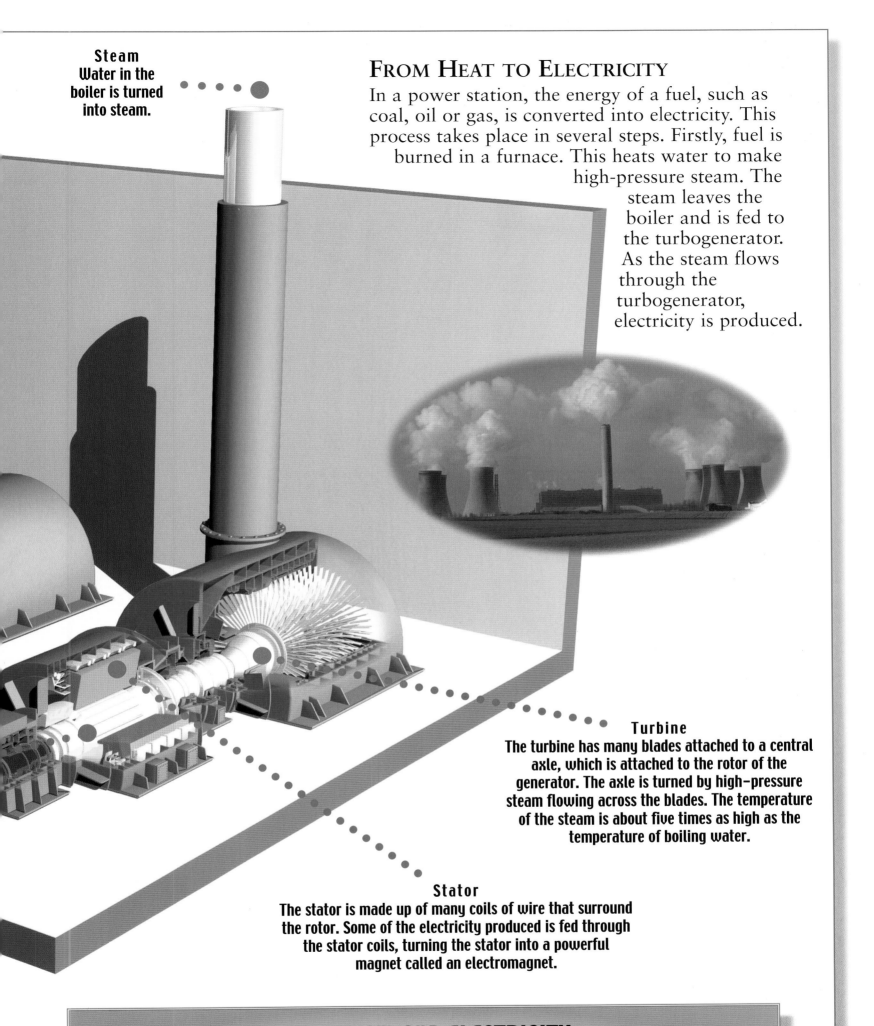

Steam
Water in the boiler is turned into steam.

FROM HEAT TO ELECTRICITY

In a power station, the energy of a fuel, such as coal, oil or gas, is converted into electricity. This process takes place in several steps. Firstly, fuel is burned in a furnace. This heats water to make high-pressure steam. The steam leaves the boiler and is fed to the turbogenerator. As the steam flows through the turbogenerator, electricity is produced.

Turbine
The turbine has many blades attached to a central axle, which is attached to the rotor of the generator. The axle is turned by high-pressure steam flowing across the blades. The temperature of the steam is about five times as high as the temperature of boiling water.

Stator
The stator is made up of many coils of wire that surround the rotor. Some of the electricity produced is fed through the stator coils, turning the stator into a powerful magnet called an electromagnet.

MAGNETISM AND ELECTRICITY

A generator uses magnetism to produce electricity. When a wire moves near a magnet, electricity flows in the wire. Inside the generator, a coil of wire is spun near a strong magnet. An electric current is produced in the coil. The coil is also called the rotor because it spins or rotates. The magnet does not move. It is called the stator because it is stationary, or still.

HYDROELECTRIC POWER STATION

SUDDEN DEMAND

Power stations have to boost power supplies when the demand for electricity suddenly increases. The hydroelectric powere station is able to do this by allowing more water to flow through the turbine.

Dam
Most dams are curved to withstand the enormous pressure of the water in the reservoir. The dam wall is thickest at the bottom. The world's highest dam is the Nurek dam on the River Vakhsh in Tajikistan. It is 300 metres (984 feet) from bottom to top.

Sluice gate
The sluice gate is opened to let water flow from the reservoir to the turbines. The water flow can be increased or reduced by adjusting the position of the sluice gate. Most power is produced when the sluice gate is wide open.

POWER FROM WATER

Water power was used thousands of years ago, and it still plays an important part in modern life. Watermills have ground grain for over 2,000 years. Around 200 years ago, water power was used in the first factories to run machines such as looms for weaving cloth. Today water power produces electricity in hydroelectric power stations. Huge dams hold back the water of a river, which builds up into a reservoir or lake behind the dam. Water from the reservoir is allowed to flow through a giant turbine – the modern equivalent of a watermill. An electricity generator is connected to the turbine. Electricity is produced when the generator is turned by the turbine.

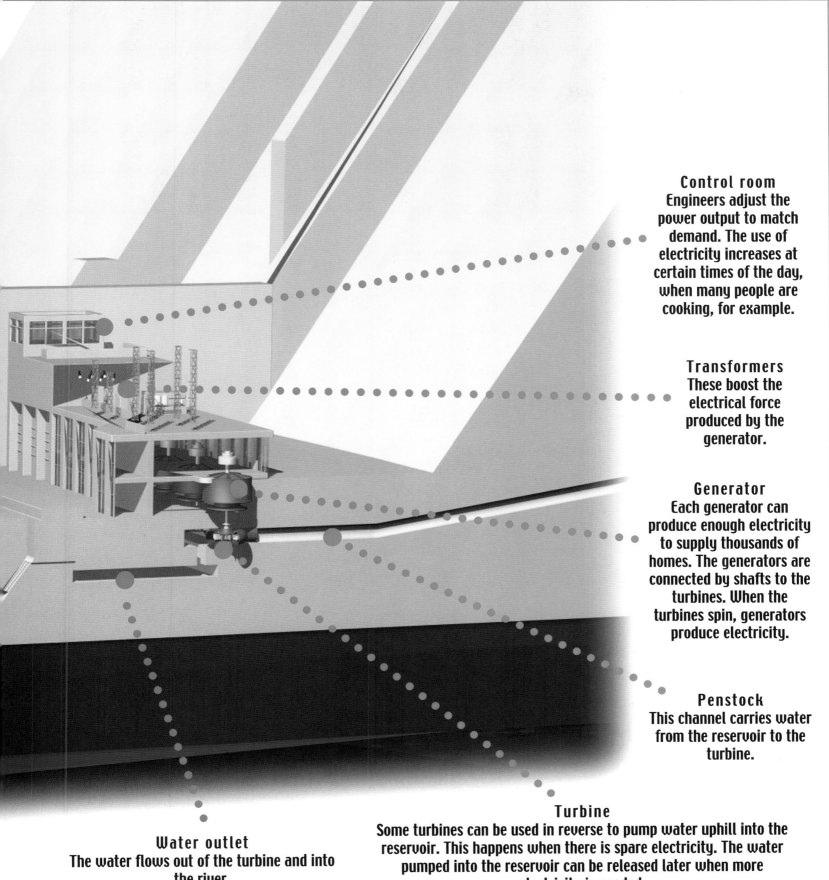

Control room
Engineers adjust the power output to match demand. The use of electricity increases at certain times of the day, when many people are cooking, for example.

Transformers
These boost the electrical force produced by the generator.

Generator
Each generator can produce enough electricity to supply thousands of homes. The generators are connected by shafts to the turbines. When the turbines spin, generators produce electricity.

Penstock
This channel carries water from the reservoir to the turbine.

Turbine
Some turbines can be used in reverse to pump water uphill into the reservoir. This happens when there is spare electricity. The water pumped into the reservoir can be released later when more electricity is needed.

Water outlet
The water flows out of the turbine and into the river.

THE TURBINE

A modern turbine is designed to be as energy-efficient as possible. Inside the turbine, the water pushes against the turbine blades, making them spin at high speed as it spirals horizontally towards the centre. When the maximum energy has been harnessed, the water flows away through an outlet in the centre of the turbine and into the river.

The world's most powerful hydroelectric station is at Itaipu on the River Paraná near the border between Brazil and Paraguay in South America. It produces 13,320 million watts of power, which is 10 times as much as an average oil- or gas-fired power station.

NUCLEAR POWER STATION

Reactor pressure vessel
The reactor pressure vessel contains the reactor. Water flows through the reactor at high pressure, absorbing heat. It then enters the boiler, turning the water inside the boiler into steam.

Boiler
The hot water from the reactor is carried to the boiler, where it turns the water inside the boiler into high-pressure steam.

Generator
The generator is turned by the rotating turbine and produces electricity. The electricity is sent to homes, factories and offices along metal cables called transmission lines.

Generator room
This room houses the turbines and generators. There are usually at least three turbines and generators.

Turbine
High-pressure steam from the boiler spins the turbine blades as it flows through the turbine. The turbine is connected to the generator.

Pump house

Control room
The power station is controlled by computers as well as by human operators. The computers control the reactor by lowering and raising the control rods.

MAKING ELECTRICITY

A nuclear power station works like a coal- or gas-fired power station. In these stations, coal or gas is burned to heat water and produce high-pressure steam. The steam turns a propeller or turbine. The turbine powers a generator, which produces electricity. But in a nuclear power station, the fuel used to heat the water is uranium. Uranium is not burned like coal or oil. Instead, its atoms are split in a process called nuclear fission. This process produces the heat energy to turn the water into steam and power the turbines.

SPLITTING ATOMS

All materials are made up of very small particles called atoms. At the centre of each atom is a dense ball of matter called the nucleus. The nucleus of a uranium atom can be split when it is hit by a small particle called a neutron. When this happens, energy is released and more neutrons are produced. These neutrons go on to split other uranium nuclei in a chain reaction, causing a continuous release of intense heat.

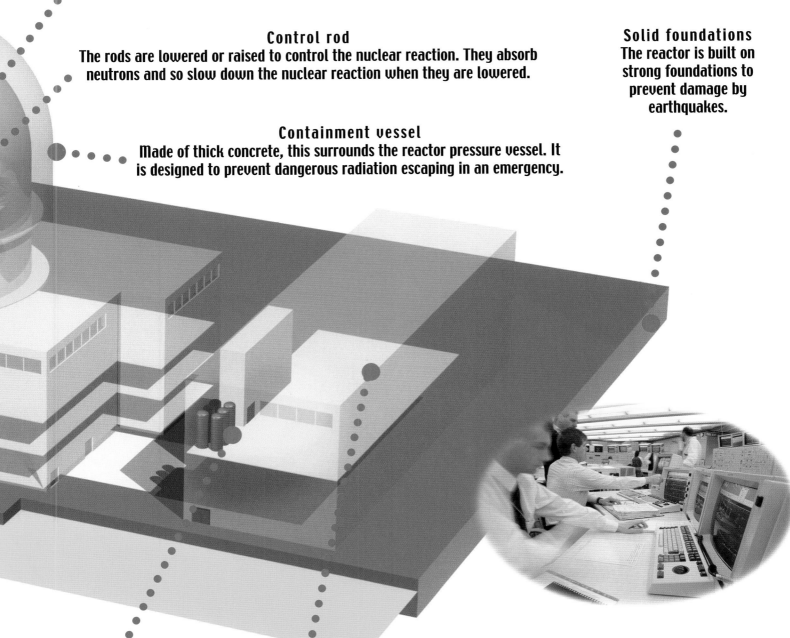

Fuel rods
The fuel rods contain the uranium fuel.

Control rod
The rods are lowered or raised to control the nuclear reaction. They absorb neutrons and so slow down the nuclear reaction when they are lowered.

Solid foundations
The reactor is built on strong foundations to prevent damage by earthquakes.

Containment vessel
Made of thick concrete, this surrounds the reactor pressure vessel. It is designed to prevent dangerous radiation escaping in an emergency.

Waste tanks
Dangerous radioactive waste materials are stored in large water tanks until they can be moved into underground storage areas.

Storage pond
Used fuel rods are kept in underwater storage units, designed to prevent dangerous radiation leaks.

CONTROLLING THE CHAIN REACTION

In a nuclear power station, the chain reaction that produces heat energy takes place in the reactor. Rods – called control rods – are lowered into the reactor to control the amount of heat it produces. The rods absorb neutrons, so less energy is produced when they are lowered, more when they are raised.

WIND TURBINE

WIND FARMS

A wind farm is a collection of wind turbines built on a high ridge, sea coast or open plain. There may be hundreds of wind turbines in a wind farm. The largest wind farms generate as much electricity as three power stations. There are around 20,000 wind turbines producing electricity in the world today.

Gearbox
A gearbox links the turbine blades to the electricity generator. The gearbox ensures that the generator turns at a high speed whatever the wind speed. When the wind is weak and turns the turbine blades slowly, the gearbox increases the speed of the generator.

Control system
The control system automatically adjusts the direction and angle of the blades. This is important as the maximum amount of power must be extracted from the wind.

Generator
The generator produces electricity. Inside the generator a coil of wire turns near a magnet. An electric current is produced in the coil.

Cables
Underground cables carry the electricity to where it is needed.

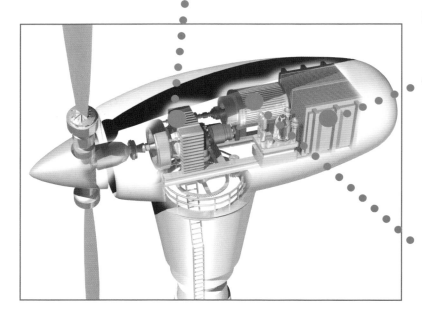

POWER FROM THE WIND

For over 5,000 years, the wind has been used as a source of power. Windmills grind corn. Modern versions of the windmill generate electricity. These wind turbines, as they are called, have huge blades to catch the slightest wind. The blades are connected to an electricity generator. When the blades are turned by the wind, this turns the generator and produces electricity.

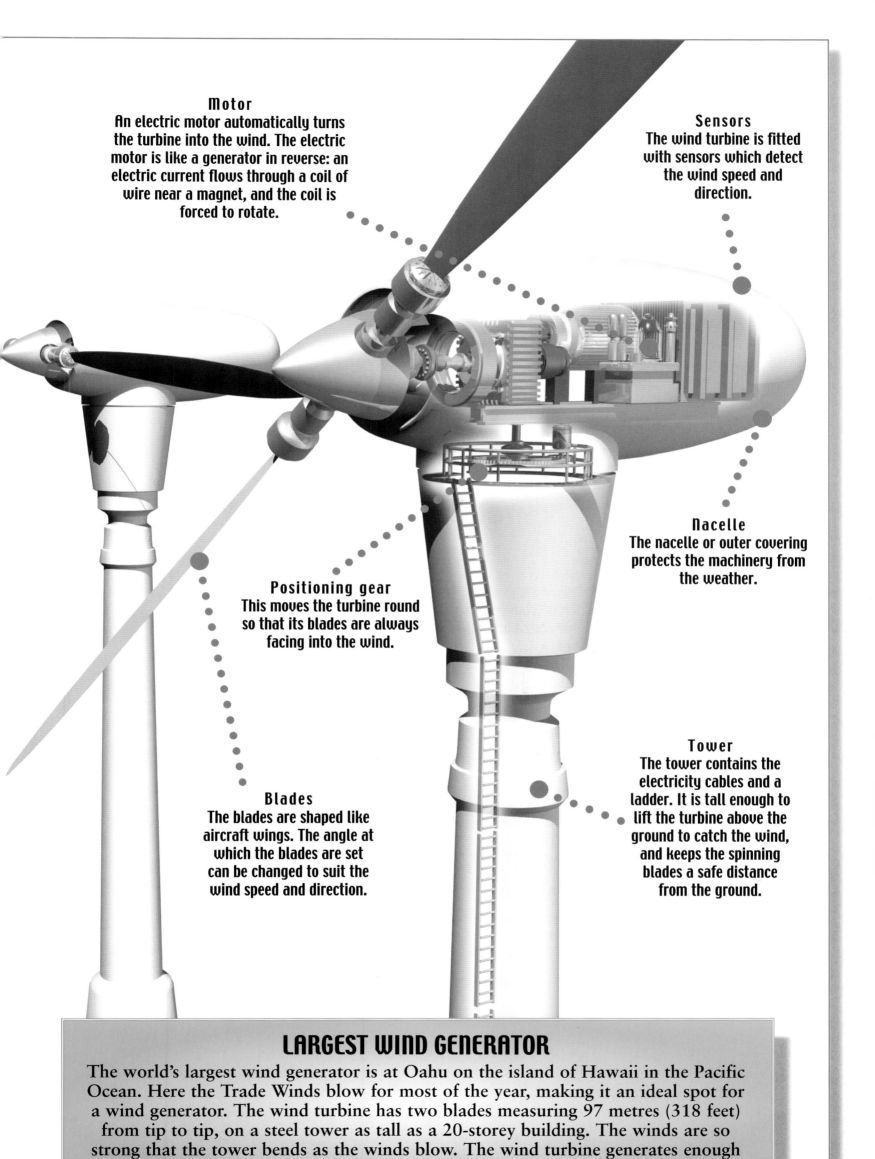

Motor
An electric motor automatically turns the turbine into the wind. The electric motor is like a generator in reverse: an electric current flows through a coil of wire near a magnet, and the coil is forced to rotate.

Sensors
The wind turbine is fitted with sensors which detect the wind speed and direction.

Nacelle
The nacelle or outer covering protects the machinery from the weather.

Positioning gear
This moves the turbine round so that its blades are always facing into the wind.

Blades
The blades are shaped like aircraft wings. The angle at which the blades are set can be changed to suit the wind speed and direction.

Tower
The tower contains the electricity cables and a ladder. It is tall enough to lift the turbine above the ground to catch the wind, and keeps the spinning blades a safe distance from the ground.

LARGEST WIND GENERATOR

The world's largest wind generator is at Oahu on the island of Hawaii in the Pacific Ocean. Here the Trade Winds blow for most of the year, making it an ideal spot for a wind generator. The wind turbine has two blades measuring 97 metres (318 feet) from tip to tip, on a steel tower as tall as a 20-storey building. The winds are so strong that the tower bends as the winds blow. The wind turbine generates enough power for 1,000 homes.

INDUSTRIAL ROBOT

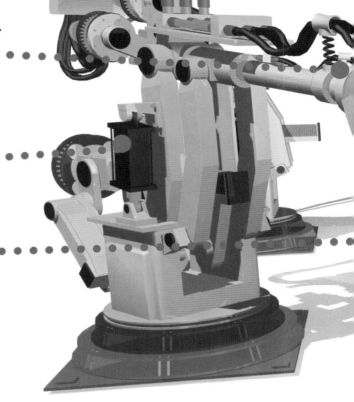

Electricity cables

Sensor
Robot arms contain sensors that detect where the arm is and feed this information to the computer control unit. The computer checks that the arm is in the correct position. If not, the computer activates the motors to move the arm.

Computer unit
The computer holds the program that guides the robot arm. It receives information from the arm sensors and controls the motors that move the arm.

Robot hand
Car assembly robots can be fitted with many different kinds of tool: welding units, nozzles for spraying paint, sanding discs for smoothing surfaces and electromagnets for lifting metal parts.

CAR-BUILDING ROBOTS
Most of the world's robots are employed in making cars. Each robot performs a single task on the car chassis as it moves along the production line.

TIRELESS WORKERS
The popular idea of a robot is a machine that looks and acts like a human. But most robots are industrial robots, and don't look like us at all. The industrial robot is a computer-controlled mechanical arm. Robot arms can bend in every direction. At the end of the arm is the robot 'hand'. This is a tool such as a welder, paint spray or gripper for grasping objects. These robots work round the clock in factories, doing jobs like welding metal parts together and painting the finished products. They live up to their name, since the word 'robot' comes from the Czech word for a slave.

ROBOT EYES

Some robots are fitted with vision units, or 'eyes', to increase their usefulness. A welding robot without vision must have the parts it is welding placed in exactly the right position. But a robot with vision can check the position of the parts and adjust its actions accordingly.

Welding metal

Welding is a process that joins pieces of metal together. The edges of the metal pieces are melted so that they flow together. Welding robots use a strong electric current to melt the metals.

Robot arm

The arm has shoulder, elbow and wrist joints that can move in any direction.

Power unit

A robot arm is moved by electric motors, or by liquid pressure (hydraulics). Electric motors are used in the joints that rotate. Hydraulic power is used in joints that move up and down.

TEACHING A ROBOT

An industrial robot has to be programmed like a computer, to tell it what to do. There are two main ways of instructing industrial robots. The first is to work out exactly what movements are needed to complete a task, and to write these movements into a program for the control computer. The second is to teach the robot a job such as painting, by guiding its arm through the movements needed to complete the task. The robot is programmed to remember what it has been taught, and will repeat the movements exactly.

RADIO TELESCOPE

RADIO WAVES FROM SPACE

Astronomers can work out how stars, galaxies and black holes behave by studying the radio waves that they produce. The radio waves coming from outer space are collected by radio telescopes. The main type of radio telescope looks like a giant dish. The dish focuses the radio waves on to a sensitive radio receiver. The radio signal is amplified (made stronger) by the telescope's electronic circuits, and displayed on a computer screen.

Radio receiver
The radio receiver can be tuned to different signals, just as a home radio can be tuned to different radio stations. Hot bright stars and hydrogen gas in space produce strong signals. The receiver contains amplifying circuits that increase the size of the signal received.

• • •

GIANT TELESCOPES

The world's largest radio telescope is at Arecibo in Peurto Rico. Its dish is built into a small circular valley and is 305 metres (1,000 feet) across, wider than three football fields. It can pick up signals 1,000,000,000,000 weaker than a small light bulb. The world's largest fully steerable radio telescope is in the Effelsberger Valley, Germany. It is a dish 100 metres (328 feet) across and weighs 3,048 tonnes (2,999 tons).

Large collecting dish
Radio telescopes need to be larger than ordinary telescopes (which collect light) because radio waves are much longer than light waves. The bigger the dish, the more detail it can detect.

• • •

WORKING TOGETHER

Several telescopes can be connected together to produce a much clearer picture of the sky. The largest of these combined instruments, known as interferometers, is the Australia Telescope. It has three dishes – one in Australia, another in Japan and a third in orbit around the Earth. This interferometer is equivalent to a radio telescope with a diameter of 27,523 kilometres (17,100 miles) – over twice the diameter of the Earth.

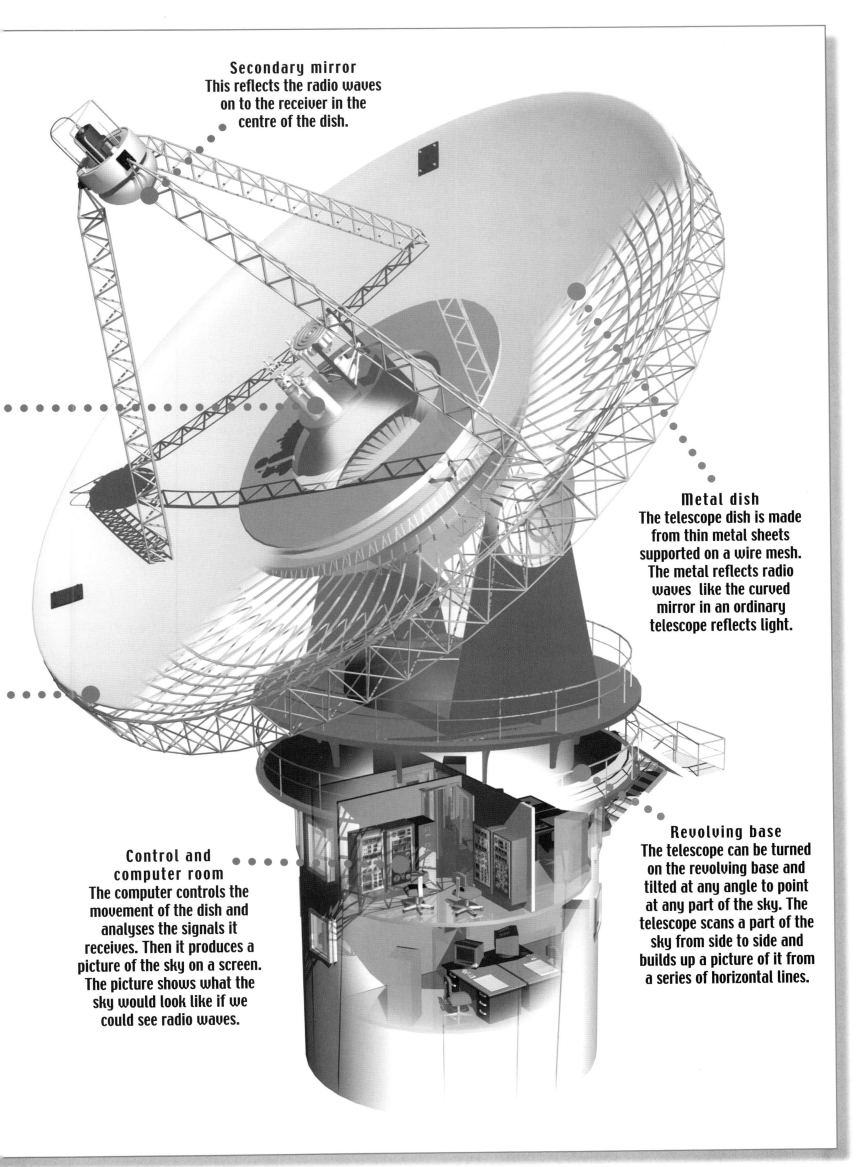

Secondary mirror
This reflects the radio waves on to the receiver in the centre of the dish.

Metal dish
The telescope dish is made from thin metal sheets supported on a wire mesh. The metal reflects radio waves like the curved mirror in an ordinary telescope reflects light.

Control and computer room
The computer controls the movement of the dish and analyses the signals it receives. Then it produces a picture of the sky on a screen. The picture shows what the sky would look like if we could see radio waves.

Revolving base
The telescope can be turned on the revolving base and tilted at any angle to point at any part of the sky. The telescope scans a part of the sky from side to side and builds up a picture of it from a series of horizontal lines.

239

NASA CRAWLER-TRANSPORTER

Operator's cabin
Two operator's cabins, one at each end of the chassis, are used to steer the crawler. The cabins have the world's largest windscreen wipers – each is 106 centimetres (3.5 feet) long.

Water cooling radiator
Water is cooled in the radiator, which is like a giant car cooling radiator. The water is then circulated around the engine to keep it cool.

Generator
There are four electricity generators. Two of these produce the power for the electric motors that drive the crawler. The other two are used for jacking, steering and ventilating the two cabins and engine control room.

LARGEST TRACKED VEHICLE

This crawler-transporter is the biggest tracked vehicle in the world. It belongs to NASA, the US National Aeronautics and Space Administration, and is used to move the Space Shuttle from its hangar to the launch site. This vehicle is a real monster – 40 metres (131 feet) wide and 35 metres (115 feet) long. Its top deck or platform is the size of a baseball field. The crawler cost US$12.3 million to build.

Tracks
The crawler runs on four double tracks like bulldozer tracks at each corner. That's 32 tracks in total. Each track is 21 metres (68 feet) long and 3 metres (10 feet) high. A track weighs over 50 tonnes (49 tons) and has 57 'shoes', each weighing 900 kilograms (2,000 pounds). Because of the important job they do, the shoes are nicknamed 'The Golden Slippers'.

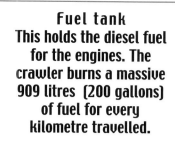

Fuel tank
This holds the diesel fuel for the engines. The crawler burns a massive 909 litres (200 gallons) of fuel for every kilometre travelled.

Platform
The Shuttle stands on the deck or platform. A levelling system in the crawler keeps the platform perfectly level at all times, otherwise the Space Shuttle would topple over.

Engine control room
An engineer in the control room keeps the two large diesel engines and 16 electric motors running smoothly.

Diesel engine
Two diesel engines drive the generators.

Electric motor
The 16 electric motors that drive the crawler are powered by four generators.

IN SLOW MOTION

The crawler's top speed when loaded is 1.6 kph (1 mph) – though it can reach twice this speed when unloaded! It takes five hours to carry the Space Shuttle to the launch pad. Even at this slow speed, the crawler has travelled a total distance of 4,000 kilometres (2,500 miles) over the years. This is about the distance from the Kennedy Space Center in Florida, where the crawler is based, to Los Angeles on the west coast of the USA.

When loaded with the Space Shuttle, the crawler is carrying the largest weight ever moved by a land vehicle. The crawler weighs 2,721 tonnes (2,677 tons) when unloaded and 8,165 tonnes (8,034 tons) when loaded. Perched on top of the crawler, the Shuttle looks like a candle on a cake.

SPACE STATION

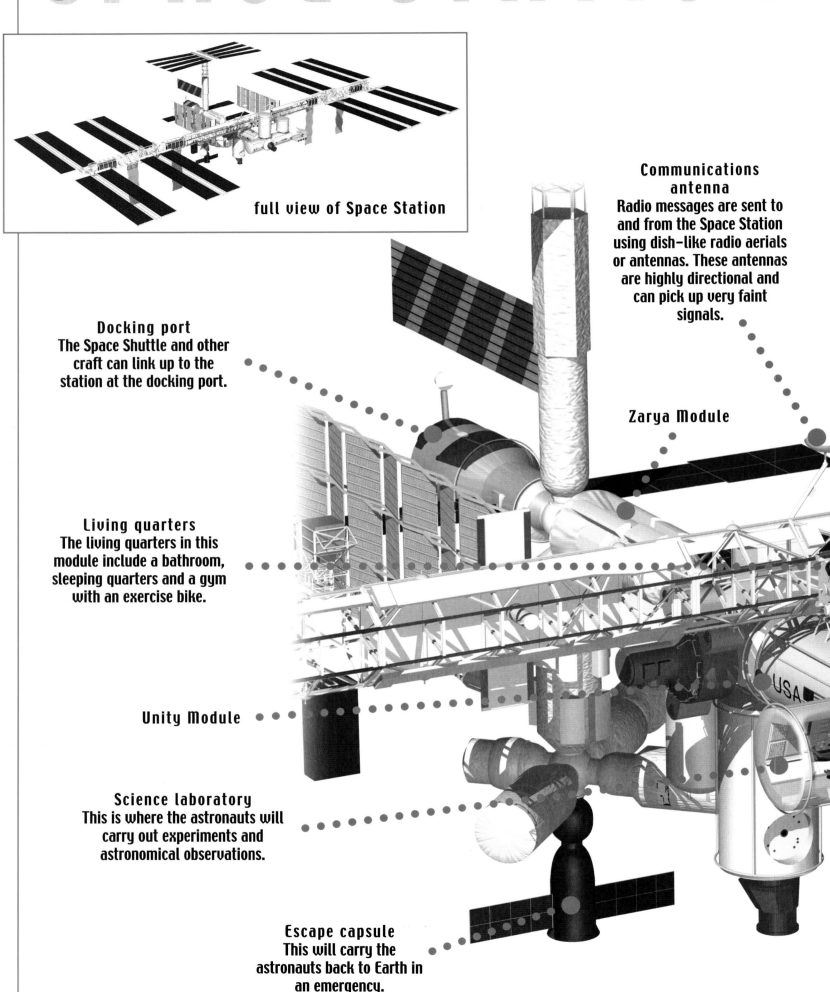

full view of Space Station

Communications antenna
Radio messages are sent to and from the Space Station using dish-like radio aerials or antennas. These antennas are highly directional and can pick up very faint signals.

Docking port
The Space Shuttle and other craft can link up to the station at the docking port.

Zarya Module

Living quarters
The living quarters in this module include a bathroom, sleeping quarters and a gym with an exercise bike.

Unity Module

Science laboratory
This is where the astronauts will carry out experiments and astronomical observations.

Escape capsule
This will carry the astronauts back to Earth in an emergency.

BUILDING THE SPACE STATION

The world's most exciting space project, the International Space Station, is currently being built 350 kilometres (217 miles) in orbit above the Earth. Assembly of the Space Station began in December 1998 and will be completed in 2004. The Space Station will be a gigantic 108 metres (354 feet) across and 88 metres (148 feet) long. It will weigh over 430 tonnes (423 tons). It will take 45 shuttle launches to carry the construction parts of the station into orbit.

NASA (National Aeronautics and Space Administration) will carry out most of the construction work and provide most of the modules that make up the station. Russia, Europe, Japan, Canada and Brazil will also take part in the building and operation of the station.

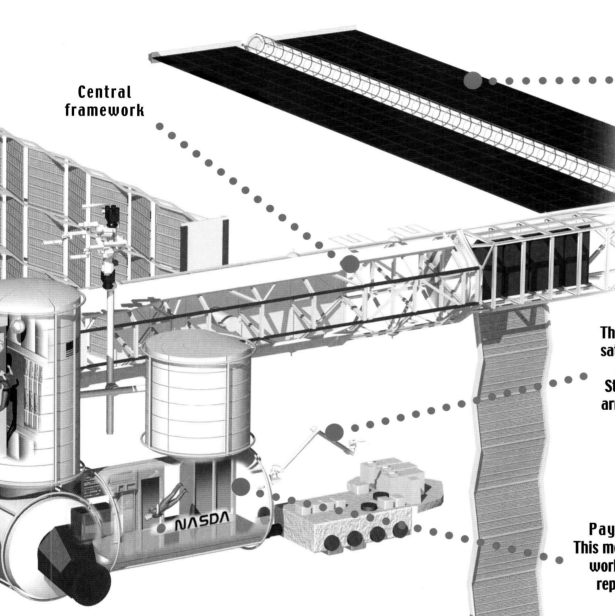

Solar panels
These provide the Space Station with power from the Sun. Two huge panels of solar cells, each the size of a football pitch, convert sunlight into electricity.

Central framework

Robot arm
This is used to grasp and repair satellites. It is controlled by an astronaut inside the Space Station. Video cameras on the arm let the astronaut see what the arm is doing.

Payload servicing module
This module will have a pressurized workshop where the crew will repair and service satellites.

LIVING AND WORKING IN SPACE

The station will have modules for astronauts to live and work in. The modules will be attached to a long spine of inter-connecting beams called a truss. Huge solar panels will supply the station with electricity.

Up to seven astronauts will spend up to three months at a time working in the station. They will carry out all kinds of experiments and observations in orbit. The almost complete absence of gravity on the Space Station will allow experiments that are impossible on Earth. The station will also be used for recovering and repairing weather and communications satellites.

FUTURE MACHINES

What sort of monster machines will be invented in the future? Today's monster machines do jobs that we can't do ourselves. Perhaps the machines of the future will help us to solve the problems that we cannot solve ourselves.

ENERGY CRISIS

One such problem concerns energy supplies. Earth's supplies of fossil fuels are being used up fast. Oil will last only another 50 years. Coal will also eventually run out. One of today's monster machines – the nuclear reactor – can make a contribution to our future energy needs. But nuclear power is expensive and creates dangerous waste products.

    A new type of nuclear power, called fusion power, is being developed, but this has the same disadvantages. Maybe the power machines of the future will harness the renewable energy of the Sun, wind and waves.

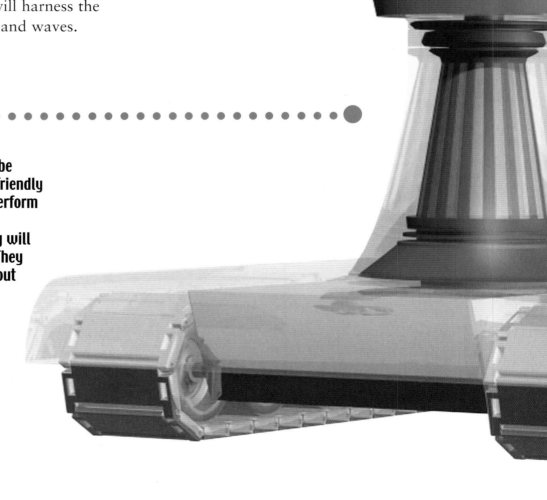

FUTURE ROBOT
A human-like appearance is thought to be suitable for household robots, but their friendly face hides a powerful machine able to perform a variety of tasks. Robots like this have already been built, but in the future they will become more useful and more reliable. They will be able to see and speak and carry out many household chores.

THINKING MACHINES

We already have monster machines that can do heavy and tedious work. In the future, we will need thinking machines that can do complicated jobs on their own. Industrial robots will obey spoken instructions, and even respond to thought control. They will be able to see and to talk. Above all, they will be intelligent.

We already have intelligent computers. They can solve problems and play complicated games such as chess. Chess machines can beat almost all human opponents. In the future, their intelligence will be much greater. Intelligent computers will be able to take over much of the brain work done by scientists and others today. Perhaps your teacher will be replaced by a computer. That would be a

monster machine indeed! Would you like an intelligent computer that could go to school for you? At school the machine would sit in the classroom and absorb knowledge from the computerized teacher. Each night, while you sleep, the knowledge could be downloaded into your brain. Each morning you would wake up brainier than you were the previous day!

KEEPING CONTROL

Science fiction stories hint that intelligent machines might eventually take control of the world from humans. However, machines have always been our helpers and under our control. Humans can control the huge forces generated by the monster machines described in this book. Hopefully, the machines of the future will also be under our control.

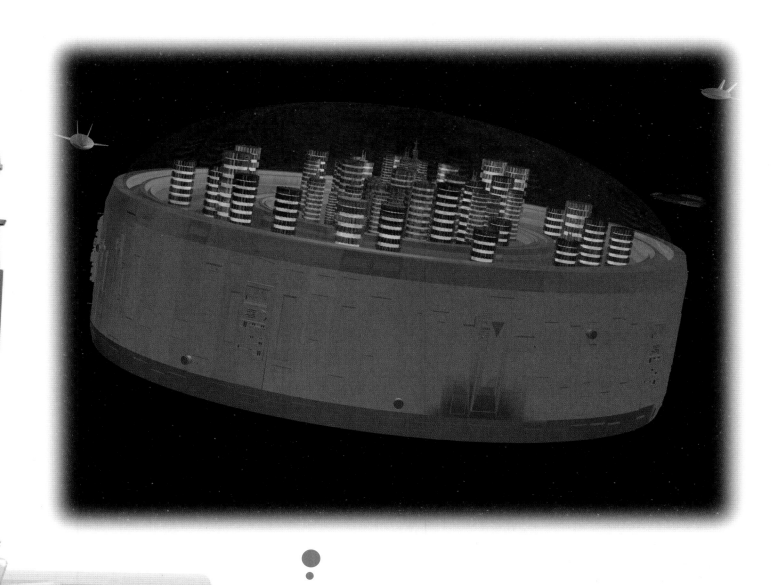

CITY IN SPACE
The ultimate space station would be a city in space, where millions of people could live under a transparent dome. The station would spin slowly to produce artificial gravity, similar to that on Earth. Residents might mainly be astronomers and other scientists working in laboratories beneath the city. The station might also accommodate tourists, but holidays in space will always be very expensive.

GLOSSARY

4WD Four wheel drive, when all four wheels of a vehicle are turned or driven around by the engine.

ABS Automatic braking system, when a vehicle's brakes slacken off slightly then come on again if the wheel is about to lose grip and skid or slide. This slows down the vehicle more safely than a skid.

aerodynamic Shaped to travel well through the air.

aerofoil The curved shape of a wing when seen from the side, with a greater curve on the upper surface compared to the lower one. Propellers and rotor blades also have an aerofoil shape.

aggregate Broken rock or stone laid as a foundation under a road or railway track, or used to make concrete.

aileron A hinged surface attached to the trailing edge of an aeroplane's wing.

airbrake A flat, oblong control surface that emerges from a wing at right angles. Airbrakes extend to disturb the flow of air over the wings, decreasing lift and increasing drag.

altitude The height of an aircraft above the ground.

analogue A device that works by electricity or another form of energy which varies in a continuous way, like waves rippling up and down, rather than in a step-wise way (see digital).

antenna An aerial, detector or sensor, usually for radio waves or microwaves.

asphalt A mixture of tar and crushed rock which is spread on the surface of a road.

ATT All terrain tyre, a tyre which has a surface or tread pattern that is suited to most types of ground – smooth roads, rough tracks and even ploughed fields.

auger A corkscrew-shaped device like a drill bit that turns around and bores a large hole, lifting the drilled material (like soil) out and away as it does so.

ballast Material loaded into the bottom of a ship or oil platform to help keep it steady in stormy weather. Also material carried in an aircraft during flight that can be thrown out to reduce the load and increase lift.

banking Turning in flight, with the aeroplane tilted so that one wing-tip is higher than the other one.

binary Counting with only two numbers, usually written as 0 (zero) and 1 (one).

biplane An aeroplane with two sets of wings, positioned one above the other.

bogie A small sub-frame or sub-chassis under a main one that carries two, four or more wheels and can swivel or pivot on its own.

bulkhead A wall or partition across a ship that can be made watertight. It stops any water that gets into the ship from flooding along the whole length. Also a solid partition that separates one part of an aeroplane from another.

calender The set of rollers which press a sheet of paper to smooth its surface.

caliper A device with two rigid arms pivoted at one end, usually in a V or C shape, so the open ends can close together.

canopy The transparent covering to a cockpit, made of either toughened glass or plastic.

capstan A rod, pole, drum or similar shape that turns around to wind in a cable or move something along.

CAT Also known as a catalytic converter. This piece of equipment absorbs some of the more dangerous exhaust fumes. Most family cars have CATs these days.

catenary The curved shape made by a flexible hanging cable, wire or rope held up only at each end, as in a suspension bridge.

cathode In electrical equipment, a disc or rod or plate which is connected to the negative (rather than positive) of the electricity supply.

cathode ray tube (CRT) A shaped glass tube with no air inside, along which beams and particles pass, driven by high-power electricity. The main 'rays' come from the negative end or cathode. They were once called cathode rays but they are really beams of particles called electrons. Certain types of CRTs were developed into televisions. The main part of a television or monitor is still called a 'tube'.

CB radio Citizen's band radio, a two-way radio system that can be used by the public rather than being reserved for special use, such as by the emergency services or professional broadcasters.

CCD Charge-coupled device. An electronic 'chip', which detects patterns of light rays that shine on it and produces a corresponding pattern of tiny electrical signals.

centrifugal force The force which throws occupants of a car, for example, to one side when the car turns a corner.

chassis The main framework or 'skeleton' of a vehicle or structure, which provides it with strength and support.

cockpit The compartment where a pilot or aircrew sits during a flight.

control surface A movable surface on the tail or wing that changes the airflow over an aeroplane.

conveyor belt A continuous belt on which goods or materials are moved.

counterweight A heavy weight attached to a crane or other lifting machine to balance the weight of the object being lifted.

CPU Central processing unit. The 'brain' of a computer where all the vital altering, changing, processing and manipulating of the tiny electrical pulses take place.

cylinder An object shaped like a hollow rod or tube, usually with a piston moving to and fro inside it.

damper A device that damps down or lessens vibrations and shaking.

DBS Direct broadcast by satellite. When a satellite beams out radio waves for radio and TV programmes over a wide area, which can be received by individual users in their homes, offices and factories.

digital A device that works by electricity or another form of energy which varies in a step-wise way, with the steps representing numbers (digits). This differs from analogue where it varies in a continuous way, like waves rippling up and down.

dorsal On the back of an aircraft.

drag A force acting on an aircraft that resists its forward movement through the air.

duralumin A strong lightweight metal made of aluminium mixed with copper, magnesium and sometimes silicon.

elevator A hinged control surface on an aeroplane's horizontal tail-plane.

elevon A combined elevator and aileron. Delta-winged aeroplanes such as Concorde have no tail-planes, so they have elevons on the rear edges of the wings.

fairings Outer body parts that are shaped and smoothed for streamlining, to cover sticking-out parts and sharp corners and edges, and so cut down on wind resistance or drag.

fibre optic Very thin and flexible strands or fibres of special glass or plastic that work optically – by light. They carry pulses of light inside.

filter A device that removes impurities, such as dust, from liquid or gas that passes through it.

fin The vertical part of an aeroplane's tail assembly. The fin gives stability and stops the rear of the plane swinging left or right.

flak Anti-aircraft fire.

flap A hinged surface attached to the trailing edge of the wing. Flaps slide back and down to increase lift at slow speeds, especially when taking off and landing.

flaperon A combined flap and aileron, consisting of a very long control surface along a plane's trailing wing edge.

former A vertical supporting frame inside an aircraft's fuselage that helps to give it shape.

freight Goods or materials carried by road, rail or air transport.

FST Flatter squarer tube. A television or monitor screen which has a flatter (less domed) surface and squarer (less rounded) sides and corners. This reduces the distortion or bending of the picture.

fuselage The tubular body of an aircraft, to which the engines, rotors and wings are attached.

FWD Front wheel drive, when only the front wheels of a vehicle are driven or turned by the engine.

GPS Global positioning system for what is called 'satellite navigation'. A network of satellites going around the Earth (the globe) enables people on the ground to pinpoint their position.

GSO Geostationary orbit. When a satellite goes around or orbits the Earth exactly once each day. The Earth spins around exactly once each day, too.

gravity The force which pulls objects towards the Earth and makes them fall.

hawser A large, strong rope or cable, as used for tying up big ships.

helical A line or shape that goes around in a circle and also along, like a corkscrew or the thread (raised ridge) of a bolt.

hopper A funnel-shaped opening or container used to load material into a machine.

horsepower A measure of power produced by an engine, motor or similar device. A typical small family car engine is about 80-100 horsepower.

hydraulic Powered by a pressurized liquid pumped through cables. A hydraulic device can exert great pressure or force, such as a car's brakes or a car-crusher.

hydraulic machine A machine worked by water, oil or some other liquid.

jetfoil A hydrofoil (boat on 'skis') powered by a waterjet rather than the usual revolving propeller or water screw.

inertia The tendency that all objects have to remain motionless or moving at a constant speed unless acted upon by a force.

interferometer A type of telescope that combines two small telescopes to produce the effect of a large telescope.

ISDN Integrated services digital network. A method of connecting computers, scanners, printers, cameras, telephones and other equipment so they all work digitally.

jet engine An engine that draws air in, burns fuel inside a combustion chamber, and then expels a jet of hot exhaust gases to provide thrust.

jettison To cast off or discard in flight.

jib The arm of a crane that reaches over the load.

jinking Moving with a rapidly changing left-to-right motion.

jumbo Very large.

LCD Liquid crystal display. A screen or similar kind of display or readout that uses crystals which can change the way light passes through them.

letterpress A type of printing process that uses raised metal letters to print the words on to a page.

lift The upwards force that raises an aircraft off the ground. Lift is generated by wings, rotor blades or lighter-than-air gases.

limiter A device that limits the movement or action of another, usually for control purposes and to stop the machine 'running away' too fast and damaging itself.

lithography A type of printing process that uses a flat printing plate. The letters to be printed are formed on the plate in ink and transferred to paper during printing.

longeron The main horizontal strips in the frame of an aircraft's fuselage.

maglev Magnetic levitation, when an object is raised or held up without physical contact, by magnetic forces.

magnetron A device that uses an electric current which changes direction to and fro very fast (oscillates) to produce microwaves.

mass dampener A heavy weight sometimes built into a tall building to stop it swaying in strong winds.

metal ore A rock or mineral from which metal can be extracted.

megabyte (MB) One million bytes, that is, one million pieces of computer data.

megaHertz (mHz) One million Hertz. A Hertz is a measure of frequency, which is the number of vibrations, to-and-fro movements or up-and-down waves each second.

microchip A very thin slice or 'chip' of the substance silicon with thousands or millions of microscopic electronic components on it. Each chip does a certain job like hold memory for a computer or carry out the computer's main processing.

monohull A ship or boat with the usual single hull, as opposed to multihulls like the catamaran.

monoplane An aeroplane with one set of wings.

MP3 A music gadget that records, stores and plays back music or other sounds in digital form. It can be connected directly to a computer and the Internet.

MRI Magnetic resonance imaging, a way of making pictures of the inside of the body using very strong magnetism and weak radio waves.

neutron A small particle found inside atoms.

open-cast mining A method of mining in which the soil overlying a coal or mineral deposit is removed to get at the deposit.

outrigger Legs or stabilizers that keep a crane or concrete-mixer truck steady when the boom or jib is extended.

oxidize A chemical process in which a material combines with oxygen.

pantograph An extending system of levers, used for many purposes such as copying drawings at different sizes, collecting electrical current from the overhead wires in an electric train or reaching an object to pick it up with a 'lazy hands' device.

parabola A certain shape of curve often used for a dish or bowl antenna which picks up radio waves.

PCB Printed circuit board, a flat board made with metal tracks or 'wires' already built into it for connecting up electrical components.

pillion A second or passenger seat behind the main rider's seat, as on a motorcycle.

piston The part of an engine that moves inside the cylinder.

pitch The up-and-down movement of an airplane's nose, when the aircraft climbs or dives.

pixel A single group of glowing dots on the screen of a television or monitor, which can be controlled in brightness and colour.

platen A flat plate or platform, especially in printing and photocopying machines.

press roller A cylinder in a paper-making machine that squeezes water out of the newly made paper.

pneumatic A device worked by air or a similar gas under pressure, from a road jackhammer or 'pneumatic' road drill to the huge brakes on high-speed trains.

power assistance When a person controls a machine, such as turning on a car's brakes, but an engine or motor is also switched on to give extra power since the human body's physical strength alone may not be enough.

preamp A pre-amplifier, an electrical device that changes or alters electrical signals before they are made stronger in the main amplifier.

pressurized Kept at normal atmospheric pressure. Aircraft cabins are pressurized for high altitude flight so that crew and passengers can breathe normally, without the aid of oxygen masks.

PPT Personal powered transport. A small craft or vehicle with a motor or engine designed mainly for one person.

PSV Public service vehicle, a vehicle approved for carrying members of the public such as a bus, ferry or train.

pulp A soft, wet mass of material; for example, a pulp of wet newspaper.

PWC Personal water craft, a small water craft such as a jetski or waterbike designed to carry and be operated by one person.

pylon A projecting part of a wing or fuselage to which weapons or extra fuel tanks can be attached.

radar (Radio Detection And Ranging) A navigation and tracking system that sends out radio waves and detects the 'echoes' that bounce back off clouds, landscape features, aircraft and ships.

radome Radar or radio dome, a dome or ball shape covering a radar or radio dish, scanner, antenna or aerial.

RAM Random access memory. The temporary working memory of a computer which stores the information for a particular task. When the computer is switched off the contents of the RAM are usually lost.

retractable Able to be withdrawn into the body of an aircraft.

rheostatic braking Slowing down an electric motor by feeding electricity through it in a certain way, usually in the opposite way to the electricity used to make it go faster.

RMT Rapid mass transit, a transport system for carrying lots of people (or goods) quickly but usually over short distances.

roll The side-to-side movement of an aeroplane, in which the plane tilts so that one wing rises and the other falls.

rudder A hinged control surface attached to the tail fin. The rudder controls yaw, making the plane turn left or right.

RWD Rear wheel drive, when only the rear wheels of a vehicle are driven or turned by the engine.

SFX A short way of writing 'special effects'. These are sounds, lights or pictures that are unreal tricks – they cannot be made by real, everyday processes.

silt The mud and small rocks found at the bottom of rivers, canals and the ocean.

skid A ski-like runner under an aircraft to support the craft on the ground or prevent damage when landing.

slat A control surface on the leading edge of the wing.

soda A chemical used in glass-making. Its chemical name is sodium carbonate.

spar A main load-carrying support in the framework of a wing. Spars run along the length of the wing.

spoiler A panel built into the wing that can be raised to spoil or disrupt the flow of air over the wing, reducing lift and slowing the plane down.

sponson A float projecting from the side of an aircraft that gives it buoyancy and keeps it balanced in water.

stroke The one-way movement, from one end to the other, of a piston inside a cylinder.

suspension Machinery involving springs, dampers and similar equipment that reduces vibrations and irons out bumps for a smoother ride.

subsound Sounds which are so deep or low that they are not so much heard by the ears as felt by the body as it shakes, such as the rumble of thunder.

suction pipe A pipe that sucks up liquid or other materials.

SWL Safe working load. For example, the weight of soil, bricks or other load that can be lifted by a crane or carried in a truck within approved safety limits.

tacho Tachometer, a gadget that measures the speed of a vehicle or craft, usually by measuring the speed or revolution of the road wheels, or the speed of spinning of the engine shaft.

tailgate A rear fold-down door or similar hinged rear part of a vehicle or craft.

tail-plane A horizontal, wing-like surface attached to the rear of an aircraft that stops the tail bobbing up and down.

terrestrial In television, programmes which are broadcast as radio waves from towers or antennae on the ground, rather than from satellites in space or along cables under the ground.

throttle A control device that changes the amount of fuel and air going into a petrol or diesel engine, and in this way control's the engine's speed.

thrust The force that pushes an aircraft forwards through the air.

thruster A machine or engine that makes a thrust or pushing force, to propel a craft along, control its sideways movement (steering) or help it slow down.

torque Turning or twisting force.

transformer An electrical device that changes the voltage (pushing strength) of electricity.

triplane An aeroplane with three sets of wings, positioned one above the other.

turbine A set of angled, rotating blades that produces power from the energy of a stream of fluid, such as fast-moving air or engine exhaust gases. Also a kind of engine that is powered by a jet of gas, such as steam, or liquid such as water.

turbofan A jet engine with a huge fan in front to suck more air into the engine and give extra power. Most of the air bypasses the combustion chamber and is expelled as a cold jet.

turbogenerator A machine used to produce electricity in which a turbine operates a electrical generator.

turbojet A jet engine that channels all of the air-intake through its combustion chamber, expelling it as a hot jet.

turboprop An engine in which compressed air and fuel are burnt and the hot waste gases used to turn a set of turbine blades. The turbine then drives a propeller.

turbulence The rough flow of air. Turbulence gives aircraft a bumpy flight.

tweeter A small type of loudspeaker designed to give out mainly high or shrill sounds.

undercarriage An aircraft's wheels and the struts that link them to the aircraft. The undercarriage supports the aircraft on the ground and during take-off.

ventral On the 'belly' or underside of an aircraft.

voltage The force or pushing strength of electricity.

wavelength The length of one wave, for example, from one peak to the next. All kinds of waves can be measured in this way.

web In printing or paper-making, the long strip of paper being printed or made.

winch A device for lifting things using a rope wound round a cylinder.

woofer A large type of loudspeaker designed to give out mainly low or deep sounds.

yaw The left-to-right movement of an aeroplane's nose, when the plane turns left or right.

Index

add-ons 163
aggregate 213
Airbus Beluga 96-7
air-cushioned vehicles (ACVs), 60
airliners 93, 94-5, 124
airships 80-81, 124
amplitude modulation (AM) 133, 153
analogue 159, 176
Antonov 97
Apollo 11 Saturn V rocket 118-9
asphalt 212-3
automatic braking systems (ABS), 19

B-52 Stratofortress 117
balloons 68, 78
Bell
    Osprey 104-5
    X-1 116
bicycles, 10-13
binary code 159
biplanes 83, 86

body-bags 75
Boeing
    Clipper 88-9
    Flying Fortress 90-1
    Harrier 108-9
    Jumbo Jet 92-3, 120
    Osprey 104-5
    Vertol Chinook 100-1
bottle making 215
Breitling *Orbiter* 78
British Aerospace Harrier 108-9
bucket dredger 191
bucketwheel excavator 192-3
bulldozers, 32-3

cable cars, 42, 43
cable TV 178
camcorder 149, 150-1
camera 148-9, 160
Canadair CL-215 106-7
cargo carriers 96

cars, 18-25, 64, 65
cassette tape 132, 153
Cassini/Huygens space probe 122-3
CD-ROM 155, 158, 162
cells 131
centrifugal force 221
Cessna 70-1
chain reaction 233
charge coupled devices (CCDs) 150-1
church organ 222-3
coaches, 38-9, 64
coal-fired power station 232
combine harvesters, 28-9, 64
compact disc (CD) 129, 152, 153, 158-9
computers, 29, 59, 64, 163
Concorde 94-5
concrete mixer truck 194-5
cranes 202–7

crawler-transporter 240-1
crude oil, 63, 64
cruise liners, 56-7
cubic centimetres (CCs), 17
cylinders, 15

Daedalus 112-3
De Haviland Comet 92
differential, 19, 25
diggers, 30-31
digital 159, 164, 168, 176, 184
directional drilling 226
dockside crane 206-7
downloading 180, 181
drag, 58
dredger 190-1

early warning planes 103, 114
earpieces 132, 133
earthscraper 196-7
electricity 229-34
electromagnetic (EM) energy 136

excavator 192-3

family cars, 18-19
fax 166-7, 171, 176
ferries, 58, 61, 64
Ferris wheel 217
fibre optics 177-8
fighters 82-3, 90-1, 110-11
fire-fighters 106-7
fission 232
flight simulator 218-9
float glass process 215
floating platform 226
flood barrier 224-5
Flyer 68, 72-3
flying boats 88-9
Fokker triplane 82-3
Formula One (F1), 20-21, 53
Fourdrinier machine 209
four-wheel drive (4WD), 24-5
frequency modulation (FM) 133, 153

front-wheel drive (FWD), 25
future gadgets 184-5
future vehicles, 64-5

games console 154-5
gas-fired power station 232
gearing 139
gears, 10-11, 13
Gee Bee Super Sportsters 86-7
glass-making machine 214-5
gliders 68, 74-5, 76-7
global positioning system (GPS), 18
go-ped 140-1
Granville Brothers 86-7
gravity platform 226
Grumman Hawkeye 114-5
guyed tower platform 226

hang-gliders 74-5
headphones 133, 135
helicopters 68, 98-103, 105
hi-fi system 152-3, 163
Hindenburg 80-1
hi-tech office 170-1
hologram 144-5, 185
hovercars, 64
hovercraft, 60-61
hydraulic cylinders 225
hydraulic systems, 31
hydroelectric power station 230-1
hydrofoils, 58-9

image scanner 164-5, 171
industrial robot 236-7
information 158, 177, 180-1
interferogram 145
interferometer 238
Internet 128, 130, 180-1, 184, 185

jets 92-3, 108-9, 120
jetskis, 50-51, 65
jib 203, 205
jumbo jets 120
jump jets 108

kick start, 15

laser 174-5, 177-8
letterpress 210
light aircraft 71
light show 174-5
lithography 210-11
Lockheed
    Blackbird 117
    Constellation 93
locomotives, 9, 40-41, 47
London Eye 216-7
London Underground, 44
loudspeakers 133, 134, 135, 152, 153, 162, 168
luxury coaches, 38-9

McDonnell Douglas
Apache 98-9
Mach numbers 94
magnetic levitation
(Maglev) trains, 48
magnetic resonance
(MR) imaging 173
magnetism 239
maximum gross weight
(MGW), 34
medical scanner 172-3
micro air vehicles
(MAVs) 125
microlights 75
microwave oven 136-7
mini-bubble car 141
mobile crane 204-5
mobile phone 128, 129,
130-1, 184
modem 176
momentum 220
monoplanes 83
monorails, 48-9
monster trucks, 36-7
motorbikes, 14-17
motorized gliders 76-7

mountain bikes, 10-11,
65
mountain railways, 42-3
movie camera 149, 151
MP3 player 184
Mustang 91

NASA 240-1, 243
North American X-15
116-7
Northrop Grumman
Tomcat 115
nuclear power station
232-3

offset lithography 211
oil platform 226-7
oil tankers, 62-3
open-cast mining 193,
198-9
organ 222-3
outrigger 205

paper-making machine
208-9
pedal-powered planes

112-3
personal computer (PC)
162-3
personal powered
transport (PPT)
141
personal stereo 128,
132-3
personal water craft
(PWC), 51
petrol engines 68
pick-up trucks, 26-7
Pitts Special 87
Planet Explorer (PlanEx),
65
powerboats, 52-3
power drill 138-9
power shovel 198-9
power stations 230-1
press roller 219
printer 163, 170, 171
printing press 210-11
public service vehicles
(PSVs), 39

radio telescope 238-9
radio waves 136, 177,

183
railways, 40-49
rapid mass transits
(RMTs), 48-9
rear-wheel drive (RWD),
25
resolution 165
road-making machine
212-3
robot planes 124
robots 236-7, 244
rocket-powered planes
116-7
rockets 118-9
roller-coaster 220-1
Rockwell B-1 Lancer 91

sampling 134
satellite navigation
system 182-3, 184
satellites, 29, 52, 64
satellite TV 177, 178-9,
183
Saturn V rocket 118-9
scanner 164-5, 170,
171, 172-3

scuba 142-3
semi-submersible
    platform 226
Sikorsky Sea King 68,
    102-3
single lens reflex (SLR)
    149
sound-radar (sonar), 59
space probes 122-3, 125
Space Shuttle 117, 120-1,
    240-1
Space Station 242-3,
    245
speed bikes, 12-13
Spirit of St Louis 84-5
steam locomotives, 9, 40-
    41, 47
straddle crane 207
stretch limos, 22-3
strokes, 15
subway trains, 44-5, 48
suction dredger 191
supersonic flight 94-5
supertankers, 62-3
synthesizer 134-5

tachometers, 39
telecoms system 128,
    129, 171, 176-7,
    180, 185
telemetry, 20
telephone 168-9, 176,
    178
teleporters, 28
telescope 238-9
terrestrial TV 178
Thames Barrier 224-5
thermals 75, 77
thought control 185
Thunderbolt 110-11
tilt-rotor aircraft 105
tomography 173
torque 139
touring bikes, 14-15
tower crane 202-3
track paver 212
trains, 40-49, 64
trains à grande vitesse
    (TGV), 46-7
transporters, 34-5
triplanes 82-3
trucks, 26-7, 36-7, 64
tug boats, 62

tugs 77
tunnel boring machine
    (TBM) 200-1
turbines 228, 231-2,
    234-5
turbogenerator 228-9
two-wheel drive (2WD),
    25

ultra large crude carriers
    (ULCCs), 63
ultralights 75
ultrasound scan 173
underground railway
    systems, 44-5, 48

video cassette recorder
    (VCR) 146-7, 150,
    152, 185
videophone 168-9, 170
virtual reality (VR)
    headset 129, 156-7
voice control 185

warp drive 125
water bombers 106
water craft, 50-63

water power 230-1
website 181
widescreen TV 130-1
wind instruments 222
wind turbine 234-5
wing-warping 73
World Wide Web 181

X-planes 116
X-rays 136, 153

yachts, 54-5

Picture
Acknowledgements

The photographs in this book were supplied by: Roger
Buckingham (69, 87, 91, 93, 97, 128); Tony Stone
Images 135 (Bruce Ayres), 148 (Stephen Johnson), 155
(Arthur Tilley), 166 (Jon Riley); The remaining photos
are from MPM Images.